Ireland Beyond Boundaries

Contemporary Irish Studies
Series Editor Peter Shirlow (School of Environmental Studies,
University of Ulster, Coleraine)

Also available

Ireland Beyond Boundaries

Mapping Irish Studies in the Twenty-first Century

Edited by
LIAM HARTE
and
YVONNE WHELAN

Pluto Press
LONDON • DUBLIN • ANN ARBOR, MI

First published 2007 by Pluto Press
345 Archway Road, London N6 5AA
and 839 Greene Street, Ann Arbor, MI 48106

Distributed in the Republic of Ireland and Northern Ireland by
Gill & Macmillan Distribution, Hume Avenue, Park West, Dublin 12, Ireland.
Phone +353 1 500 9500. Fax +353 1 500 9599. E-Mail: sales@gillmacmillan.ie

www.plutobooks.com

British Library Cataloguing in Publication Data
A catalogue record for this book is available from the British Library

Hardback
ISBN-13   978 0 7453 2186 8
ISBN-10   0 7453 2186 0

Paperback
ISBN-13   978 0 7453 2185 1
ISBN-10   0 7453 2185 2

Library of Congress Cataloging in Publication Data applied for

10   9   8   7   6   5   4   3   2   1

Designed and produced for Pluto Press by
Chase Publishing Services Ltd, Fortescue, Sidmouth, EX10 9QG, England
Typeset from disk by Stanford DTP Services, Northampton
Printed and bound in the European Union by
Antony Rowe Ltd, Chippenham and Eastbourne, England

Contents

Figures and Tables

Acknowledgements

The idea for this book emerged when we were both members of the Academy for Irish Cultural Heritages at the University of Ulster. We are grateful to the Academy for its financial support and would like to thank former Academy director, Brian Graham, for the assistance he gave us. The fact that we both changed jobs and countries during the course of the book's production delayed its publication, thereby inconveniencing contributors and publishers alike. We would therefore like to express our appreciation to all twelve contributors for their patience, and thank Roger van Zwanenberg and the editorial staff at the Pluto Press for their forbearance and efficiency. Thanks are also due to Patrick Crotty, Murray Pittock and the anonymous readers at the Pluto Press for their helpful comments and suggestions. Grateful acknowledgement is made to Martyn Turner for granting us permission to use the cartoon in chapter 9, and to the Battery Park City Authority in New York for allowing us to reproduce photographs of the Irish Hunger Memorial in chapter 11.

Liam Harte
Yvonne Whelan

Introduction:
Where Irish Studies is Bound

Liam Harte

Reviewing Colin Graham's *Deconstructing Ireland* (2001) in 2003, Eugene O'Brien declared:

That Irish Studies is a significant discipline within the academy is without question, as attendance at IASIL, ACIS, or EFACIS conferences will indicate. However, what is needed at a meta-level, it seems to me, is a range of enquiry into the grounds of this discipline in terms of its epistemological and ethical status. (O'Brien, 2003: 223)

The present volume can be read, at least in part, as a response to this call for meta-discursive reflection, one which also subjects O'Brien's presupposition about Irish Studies' institutional embeddedness to critical scrutiny. It is not, of course, the first or only such response. Even in the short time since O'Brien's review, reflexive commentary has flourished, fuelled by Irish Studies' ongoing reconfiguration in the light of cultural theory. Indeed, his comments coincided with the publication of the first Irish cultural criticism reader, *Theorizing Ireland*, which, in seeking 'to show how theory has helped mark out a space between scepticism and reverence' in Irish culture (Connolly, 2003: 10), offers a varied and challenging set of answers to the key question around which the discipline currently constitutes itself: is Ireland postcolonial? The most explicitly affirmative of these answers comes from Joe Cleary, who champions the postcolonial analytic as 'by far the most outward looking of the modes of socio-cultural analysis currently shaping Irish Studies' (Cleary, 2003: 93–4). Within months, sociologist Linda Connolly issued a forceful rebuttal of this viewpoint, protesting that the postcolonial paradigm is not only 'totalising and contextually insensitive' but also largely uninformed by Irish feminist scholarship (Connolly, 2004: 150). Since then, Eóin Flannery has restated the case for the defence, characterising Irish postcolonial studies as heterogeneous and internally differentiated, capable of 'wresting the past from the petrification of linear narrative' and 'liberat[ing] subsumed, fragmentary histories' (Flannery, 2005: 453).

On the evidence of these three recent critical interventions alone, twenty-first-century Irish Studies discourse continues to be 'combative but above all dynamic, engaged in a relentless reappraisal of its own fundamental principles and, moreover, that of the culture of which it is both product and analysis' (Richards, 1999: xiv). Self-reflexivity is indeed one of its distinguishing characteristics. Contemporary Irish Studies is perhaps best understood as a discipline – however contested its constitution as such – in a continual state of deconstruction, perpetually preoccupied by 'questions of beginnings, intention and method' (Cleary, 2003: 94), forever anticipating 'the next act of definition and criticism', rather like one influential view of Ireland itself (Graham, 2001: x). As an academic field, it is contested and multifaceted, yet whereas some regard this as cause for subdivision, others – myself included – wish to retain the Irish Studies rubric for a more inclusive cultural, historical and sociological praxis. In doing so, one must acknowledge the difficulty of defining a subject area, whose boundaries are permeable, according to a homogeneous set of methodological precepts or discrete theoretical principles. In practice, Irish Studies is 'used and conceptualised in a variety of ways internationally' (Connolly, 2004: 141), as the contributors to this volume amply testify. The view that 'there is neither a global concept nor a single canon available to us' (Sharkey, 1997a: 113) is as valid today as it was a decade ago, not only because Ireland is a complex material and discursive zone, but also because of the highly contingent nature of the relationship between subject and object of study. Yet while its methods of enquiry and analytical procedures resist easy codification, a critically and historically nuanced Irish Studies mode of analysis can have a transformative impact on received views and prevailing orthodoxies.

My emphasis here on Irish Studies as a mode of analysis is deliberate, since one can realise the critical potential of this heuristic without necessarily being affiliated to a formal Irish Studies department. I speak from a double perspective, having taught from within and without institutionalised Irish Studies programmes at different locations in Britain and Ireland over the past 14 years. My first post was as an Irish Studies lecturer at St Mary's College, Twickenham, where I taught on an undergraduate degree programme whose chief constituency was second-generation Irish students, many of whom harboured an engrained nostalgic essentialism towards their parental heritage. When in 2002 I joined the newly formed Academy for Irish Cultural Heritages at the University of Ulster, I found myself teaching a very different cohort: Northern Irish students taking a degree in English literature. Whereas many of those from a nationalist background read Irish texts and authors out of a sense of cultural affinity, some unionist students were disposed to view Irish literature as a foreign, even a 'Fenian', phenomenon that held little relevance for them. Two years later, I took up my present post at the University of Manchester, where I offer a specialist final-year option on twentieth-century Irish literature and culture to English and American Studies students. To date, the majority of those who have elected to take my course have surprisingly little knowledge of Irish literature beyond Yeats, Joyce and Heaney, whom they have typically encountered previously as part of a British literary canon.

Students in each of these constituencies have admitted to having had perspectives that were formerly closed or obscured to them opened up by an Irish Studies model of enquiry. Sometimes this amounts to 'the revelation of a suppressed dimension of a larger complex story', leading to an elevation or reversal of perspective (Chandler, 2006: 24); on other occasions it can lead to the detection of hidden codes of Irishness. More often, it is a matter of teasing out the complexities at work in Irish–English and Irish–Scottish literary relations and exploring their modifying impact on stereotypical thinking and dominant conceptual frameworks. I have found it repeatedly instructive to observe how often students are prone to interpret Ireland in relation to a putative British 'norm'; how reluctant some are to have their uncritical equation of Irishness with a dissident exotic otherness interrogated; how others struggle with the notion that 'Ireland has more than one story' and is constituted as much in difference as in commonality (Hamilton, 2003: 283). And while I have frequently seen attitudes polarise around explicitly political issues such as the history of Irish republicanism or the Northern Troubles, I have also been intrigued by how less obviously ideological themes can divide a class. Take the concept of diaspora, for example. The very qualities that make it an attractive and useful analytical category to some students – its destabilising dynamic, its potential to accentuate the multiple and dialogical aspects of Irish cultural identities and the ambiguity of transnational interactions – can arouse suspicion and even hostility in others.

My experience of teaching across national and disciplinary boundaries has therefore made me realise how the intellectual and ideological potential of an Irish Studies approach can be tapped in different pedagogical contexts. It seems to me that to have effective force, an Irish Studies heuristic *should* upset the order of things, should destabilise canons and disturb established categories of knowledge. But it is not only a matter of alerting students of English literature to the riches of the Gaelic literary tradition, for example, or of presenting them with the 'Irish' as well as the 'English' Swift, or reading Joyce in relation to Irish revivalism as well as European modernism. The deeper challenge lies in directing students' attention to the historical specificities that make Ireland an instructive model for the formation and reconfiguration of cultural identities within the overlapping forcefields of empire and emigration, decolonisation and globalisation, modernity and tradition. This does not mean that Irish culture need be seen as an exceptional anomaly, or become so flexibly exemplary and so thoroughly globalised that it is emptied of all meaning, or that the ideological category of Irishness be magically transformed into 'a terrain on which some of the most typical, world-historical issues of our day can be seen to congregate' (Eagleton, 1997a: 12). On the contrary, the task is to elucidate the local specificities that actuate and qualify global generalisations, and brush national and regional interrelationships against the grain of hierarchical power relations.

It was in considering the conditions of possibility of Irish Studies that the germ of the idea for this collection first took shape. The project itself was set in motion by the perceived need for a volume that would assess the current state of Irish Studies in its various institutional settings internationally and represent some of the many directions in which the discipline is developing. The fact that the only comparable critical guide[1] appeared in the late 1980s, at a time when Irish Studies was still in its institutional infancy in Ireland and Britain, was a further spur, as was my sense that discussions of Irish Studies' institutional embodiment have too often been overshadowed by debates about its intellectual agendas and possible futures. Certainly, a systematic exploration of the question of 'whether "doing Irish studies" in Australia, the UK or the US is the same as "doing Irish studies" in Ireland' has been long overdue (Mathews, 2000: xvii). Hence the decision of my co-editor and I to devote Part One of this volume to a brief survey of Irish Studies programmes in university curricula in the United States, Canada, Australia, Britain and Ireland, drawing on the views of new and established practitioners. Each was given scope to consider the factors that have shaped the discipline's evolution in his or her constituency and asked to analyse the kinds of local and global challenges the subject now faces. The contributors to Part Two were given a slightly different brief, being invited to offer an assessment of significant recent critical trends within some of the key areas that constitute the field. Decisions about which strands of Irish Studies scholarship should be included were arrived at after much deliberation, and the final selection is shadowed by our acute awareness of the many regrettable omissions. Thus, in seeking to offer readers an informed overview of contemporary Irish Studies, both as an institutionalised programme of study and as an intellectual enterprise, *Ireland Beyond Boundaries* makes no claims to exhaustive, or even coherent, coverage, but rather hopes that its critical reflections will initiate further debate.

Part One begins with Christina Hunt Mahony's account of the changing fortunes of Irish Studies in American universities, where the discipline first established an institutional presence in the postwar decades. Her synoptic opening survey reminds us of the valuable pioneering work of scholars such as John V. Kelleher, the first holder of the Shattuck Chair of Irish Studies at Harvard in 1945, Richard Ellmann, who wrote his great biography of Joyce while a professor at Northwestern University in the 1950s, and Thomas Flanagan, author of *The Irish Novelists, 1800–1850* (1959), a work which Seamus Heaney has credited with creating 'a country of the mind as well as a field of study. Fifty years ago, after all, what are now called "Irish Studies" did not have any institutional existence in American (or Irish) universities, but once the Flanagan book appeared, it showed what was needed and how it should be done' (Heaney, 2004: x). Mahony's observation that 'The centre of gravity in Irish Studies is no longer somewhere south of Boston, but somewhere west of Tara' succinctly summarises today's changed landscape and frames her analysis of the factors that differentiate contemporary Irish Studies programmes in the US, where it is 'an almost entirely entrepreneurial undertaking', from their state-subsidised Irish counterparts. This lack of public funding, coupled with the fact that many programmes are sustained by a small number of dedicated scholars, are key factors in the discipline's precarious position within the American academy. One notable by-product of these constraints has been the emergence of hyphenated programmes in Irish-American Studies, which stand a greater chance of attracting funding. Mahony's reservations about this trend leads her to propose that Irish government agencies and universities should provide greater financial support to enable overseas-based scholars to carry out research in Ireland. Such provision, she argues, would not only be a practical means of honouring the contribution of the diaspora to the discipline, but would also help ameliorate the 'nostalgia gap' that hinders much Irish Studies pedagogy in the US.[2]

That the challenges of institutionalising Irish Studies in the US are replicated in other national contexts is confirmed by Elizabeth Malcolm and Michael Kenneally, both of whom share Mahony's concerns about Irish Studies programmes' vulnerability to the vagaries of university funding and echo her misgivings about the '"one-man band" syndrome'. Instructive contrasts emerge, however, in their respective accounts of the development of the discipline in Australia and Canada. Malcolm's sober assessment of the state of Irish Studies Down Under tempers Mahony's sanguine view of the discipline as 'thriving'. Further, Malcolm laments the lack of intellectual breadth and theoretical sophistication of Irish Studies scholarship in Australia and bemoans the fact that the subject remains 'ethnically ghettoised', appealing primarily to those of Irish birth or descent. Kenneally has a much more positive tale to tell about the Canadian experience, largely because Irish Studies programmes there have managed to engage students from diverse ethnic backgrounds by accentuating those aspects of the Irish immigrant experience that are instructive for other immigrant groups. 'In the context of a society that is multi-ethnic and multi-racial', he observes, 'Irish Studies is perceived as exploring issues relating to the challenges of preserving cultural identity, whether within colonised Ireland or as part of the multicultural fabric of Canada itself.' The moral seems clear: where Irish Studies shows itself to be an adaptive and purposeful discipline, ready to respond reflexively and imaginatively to changing local circumstances, it can attain an exemplary status within the twenty-first-century university curriculum.

If Kenneally's account of Irish Studies' evolution in Canada constitutes an oblique rebuttal of the thesis that it is an inherently 'crisis-driven discipline' (Kiberd, 2000: 620), the last two chapters in Part One return us to the site on which this thesis was originally forged: the Anglo-Irish axis. Shaun Richards's analysis of the current state of Irish Studies in Britain begins with an examination of the political subtexts that shaped the discipline's formal emergence in the mid-1980s. He traces its origins to the confluence of two crises, the Northern Ireland Troubles and the theory-inspired revolution within 'English', which together fuelled demands for a politically engagé critical praxis. While this originary moment generated much productive intellectual and institutional ferment, two decades on, the diminution of political conflict in the North has meant that 'the frisson of violence and transgression surrounding the discipline are correspondingly diminished'. Yet Richards rejects the suggestion that Irish Studies is necessarily 'parasitic on catastrophe' and emphasises instead the need for a committed intellectual and political praxis that possesses 'a strong and immediate sense of purpose in order to engage both students and scholars in advancing its claims to relevance'.

The historian Michael Brown recapitulates this theme in his chapter, situating it in the context of an increasingly internationalised Irish university classroom that is also undergoing corporatist restructuring. Writing in the immediate aftermath of the IRA's decommissioning statement of July 2005, he foregrounds the need for Irish Studies to reinvent itself if it is to engage the current generation of university students in the Republic, most of whom have little personal experience or even memory of the Troubles. In answer to the question: 'How now do we begin again, after the end as it were, to refashion our past, our literature, our culture, our country?', Brown proposes a new Irish Studies meta-narrative, one that seeks to transcend national and imperial contexts by bringing the local and the global into critical propinquity. He finds a serviceable prototype in the Enlightenment conception of civil society, a form of democratic community capable of accommodating difference and dissent. If, as Kiberd suggests, the time has come 'to imagine just how the son of a Brazilian worker in a midlands meat factory might read *Gulliver's Travels* or how the daughter of Nigerian immigrants might respond to *Dancing at Lughnasa*' (Kiberd, 2005: 20), then Brown's intriguing suggestion offers one practical means of reorienting today's students towards the plural, polyphonic voices of the past, the better to understand a present that is becoming more and more multicultural.

Because the boundary between the two sections of this volume is as porous as that which demarcates the field of Irish Studies itself, several of the themes and issues raised in Part One are recapitulated in Part Two. Conor McCarthy's chapter is a case in point, in that he expansively surveys ground earlier reviewed synoptically by Shaun Richards and reconfigures questions posed by Michael Brown within a different analytical frame. McCarthy's theme is the changing location and function of literary and cultural criticism in contemporary Irish society. He begins by examining the nature and ramifications of the crisis in political and critical authority affecting both parts of Ireland since the 1970s, the origins of which he traces to the differentiation of the material and cultural spheres in the earlier post-independence period. By inhibiting the emergence of an indigenous Marxist praxis, this separation of the spheres facilitated the development of an idealist cultural criticism stretching from the oppositional discourse of *The Bell* in the 1940s through to the *Crane Bag* and Field Day polemicists of the 1980s. McCarthy's critique centres on what he regards as the most regrettable consequence of this culturalist tendency: Irish postcolonial theorists' preoccupation with national discourses rather than state structures. He interprets this failure as a symptom of Irish criticism's pervasive depoliticisation, which is exacerbated by its blindness to the institutional and material grounds of its own possibility. McCarthy's unease with this textualist trend leads him to elaborate an alternative agenda made up of seven key questions that Irish criticism needs to address if the reification of the public sphere is to be redressed.

McCarthy's thesis that current discursive trends are determined by intellectual debates of a much earlier period chimes with the central premise of Mary E. Daly's chapter on Irish historiography. According to her analysis, history writing in contemporary Ireland remains broadly indebted to principles laid down in the 1930s by T. W. Moody and R. D. Edwards, whose foundational frameworks form the backdrop to her overview of recent historiographical trends and practices. She begins with a cogent critique of the damaging effects of the revisionist controversy, in which she indicts Irish historians for their resolute empiricism and their privileging of Irish political history over other varieties. She also criticises a pervasive isolationist tendency within Irish historiography, but is careful to balance this against recent efforts to locate the Irish past within transnational contexts, as evidenced by research on early modern Ireland. Daly's desire to dispel further the myth of Irish exceptionalism prompts her to emphasise the continuities of political life since the Famine, and to argue for a reading of twentieth-century Irish history in Eurocentric rather than postcolonial terms. It is on this issue that her disciplinary allegiances are most visible; historians' attention to contingency and complexity is prized over postcolonialists' attachment to totalising grand narratives. Hence her preference for 'forty shades of grey, rather than black and white or orange and green'.

The next two chapters, by Tom Inglis and Louise Ryan respectively, represent a strand that Irish Studies practitioners have recently been criticised for ignoring: sociology (Connolly, 2004: 155–6). Inglis, indeed, prefaces his exploration of the significance of religious affiliation in contemporary Ireland with a brief but incisive critique of the material consequences of Irish Studies' 'symbolic domination' by history and literature. 'One of the characteristics of Irish Studies', he avers, 'is the almost automatic, intuitive way in which the key players constituted the field of investigation, and instituted policies and practices of exclusion based on this configuration.' His own chapter shows how the deployment of a different critical vocabulary and analytical approach can reframe what he terms 'the existing *habitus*' of the subject. His historicised elucidation of the social, political and economic significance of religious identity in both parts of Ireland is predicated on a conceptualisation of religion as a field of power, 'a social arena of relational differences, opposition and competition'. In exploring the constitution and dynamics of this field, Inglis contends that whereas religious identification was once centrally linked to social advancement and the attainment of political power, creeping secularisation and individualism have precipitated a progressive devaluation of religious capital, the effects of which are more manifest in the South than in the North.

Whereas Inglis opens his chapter by questioning the narrowness of the existing boundaries of Irish Studies, Louise Ryan begins hers by admitting to a certain frustration with the discipline's capaciousness. Her subsequent self-positioning serves as a further reminder of the determining role of national and institutional contexts in both the constitution of Irish Studies and the categorisation of Irish Studies scholars. Ryan explains how her own migrant academic status led her to consider how a focus on the sociology of migration, grounded in an interdisciplinary Irish Studies approach, might illuminate aspects of Ireland's 'hidden diaspora', specifically, pregnant Irish women's covert journeys to Britain. In an analysis that is closely attuned to the link between the actual and the metaphorical excision of unwanted babies and their mothers from Irish social and discursive space, she argues that far from being nation-bounded, Ireland's reproductive policies and practices have long been defined in relation to sites beyond the national boundary, especially Britain. Combining the insights of her own research with the findings of earlier studies, she traces the origins of Irish women's secret migrations back to the 1930s, the very decade in which mothers were valorised as the symbolic guarantors of national continuity in de Valera's new Constitution. The stigmatised fate of those who failed to live up to this ideal was astutely summarised by an anonymous English social worker, whom Ryan quotes: 'These girls are the scapegoats of a tradition of puritanism that will not admit that things are as they are.'

The last four chapters in the book address areas of study that are often marginalised within Irish Studies curricula: the media, geography, music and sport. Lance Pettitt considers the challenges of writing a cultural history of Irish media institutions, texts and audiences. His review of the dominant critical trends that have emerged in the past two decades attends to the ways in which the contours of a changing Irish mediascape have been conditioned by the country's ambivalent relationship to modernity and the dislocating effects of global capitalism. The accent throughout is on the non-linearity of Irish media history, which he characterises as 'a complex dynamic composed of successive conformities and countervailing forms of dissent'. Yvonne Whelan and I, meanwhile, explore the productive interface between Irish Studies and cultural geography by tracing some of the lines of enquiry that have been opened up by scholars' converging interests in the power-laden relations between culture, space and narratives of belonging. Using a spatial rather than a temporal paradigm, we examine the role of material and symbolic landscapes in the mediation and contestation of power, history and memory in Ireland and its diaspora. Our close analysis of three case-study examples of such landscapes seeks to highlight the ways in which the ideologies inscribed by spaces of public spectacle and commemoration shape the nature as well as the subject of remembrance.

The contributions by Gerry Smyth and Mike Cronin are both animated by a desire to reinvigorate existing critical paradigms and methodologies. Smyth addresses the dearth of musical analysis within Irish Studies scholarship, which persists in spite of the longstanding association between Irishness and musicality. He first addresses the failure of Ireland's principal music traditions to develop an integrated discourse of music criticism and critiques the pervasive critical deafness to the function of music in Irish literary texts. He then outlines the enabling potential of an aural approach to contemporary Irish culture, specifically one that is informed by Jacques Attali's theorisation of music's predictive power. 'By *listening* to contemporary Irish society', Smyth contends, 'we shall come not only to a stronger sense of where we have come from and where we are, but also, in the political struggles that are conducted over the relations between music, noise and silence, of where we might be going.' Meanwhile, Mike Cronin's desire to open up new ways of understanding the significance of sport in Irish culture leads him to consider its representational and ideological dimensions rather than rehearse its historical and political functions. In an analysis that rejects the theorisation of sport as 'serious leisure' in favour of a view of sport as an essentially evanescent pleasure, Cronin shows how certain literary and musical representations of major sporting occasions can yield important insights into changing social attitudes to masculinity, class, emigration and national identity.

A volume whose remit includes the examination of the processes of Irish Studies' institutionalisation in different national contexts cannot ignore the extent to which its constitution as a 'new' discipline is inextricably bound up with the fractious issue of interdisciplinarity. In soliciting these essays, therefore, my co-editor and I invited contributors to consider the claims made for interdisciplinarity's progressive potential and weigh them against its practical applications. Despite being repeatedly invoked as a key organising principle of Irish Studies teaching and research, interdisciplinarity has not always been persuasively practised or indeed clearly understood. Part of the problem lies in the slipperiness of the term itself, which can refer to the forging of connections across different disciplines and to attempts to transcend disciplinary divisions altogether. This semantic indeterminacy means that what is referred to as interdisciplinarity is often in fact multidisciplinarity, where disciplines are brought into proximity without any real interaction taking place. This is certainly the view of Mary Daly who, in noting the burgeoning of multidisciplinary approaches to particular historical periods, questions 'whether such initiatives and dialogues extend beyond polite conversation'. Elsewhere, Conor McCarthy's sceptical observation that 'the old disciplinary boundaries die hard' resonates with Shaun Richards's contention that interdisciplinary cooperation will remain unrealised while disciplinary wars still rage. Michael Brown, on the other hand, offers a more upbeat assessment of the capacity of interdisciplinary methodologies to yield holistic understandings of Irish culture and society, while Louise Ryan and Lance Pettitt emphatically endorse their enabling heuristic potential. Implicit throughout is a sense that interdisciplinarity is central to Irish Studies pedagogy, and that while specialisation in one form or another is here to stay, it is important that cross-disciplinary conversations continue, and that we strive to make connections across generic boundaries, without necessarily dissolving them.

It would clearly be unwise to base too many generalisations about Irish Studies on this selection of short essays, which constitutes little more than a snapshot of current conditions, trends and debates. The picture that emerges is of a subject in process, its boundaries and topography being reshaped by a plethora of competing forces, its future within the academy by no means assured. Although many undergraduate programmes offer innovative and varied curricula, their continuing existence – let alone expansion – is heavily conditional upon the operation of market forces within the university sector and institutional constraints on interdisciplinarity. Institutionally, therefore, Irish Studies' survival depends on its ability to adapt to shifting priorities and changing local circumstances. This will call for more creative curricular thinking, especially at graduate level, where there is much scope for the development of relational programmes such those in Irish and Scottish Studies, which have the added advantage of encouraging comparativist perspectives, of which there is still a marked dearth. Such programmes can also boost the discipline's global reach and enhance its capacity to unsettle naturalised assumptions and articulate alternative conceptual and ideological perspectives, which is the hallmark of the best Irish Studies scholarship and research. But perhaps the most crucial factor bearing on the future prospects for Irish Studies consists in the degree to which scholars can continue to evolve flexible reading practices and reflexive methodologies that will help us think through the problematics of Irish experience in order to deepen our intellectual and affective understandings of it. My co-editor and I hope that the range of critical perspectives proffered by this volume will help to advance this process of mapping the new and demanding directions in which Irish Studies is bound.

NOTES

1. *Irish Studies: A General Introduction*, edited by Thomas Bartlett, Chris Curtin, Riana O'Dwyer and Gearóid Ó Tuathaigh (Dublin: Gill and Macmillan, 1988) had its genesis in an annual Irish Studies summer school hosted by University College Galway (as it then was), and its structure and content were largely determined by that forum. As such, it paid little attention to the wider institutional forces that were then shaping Irish Studies teaching and research.

2. Mahony's concerns about the ever-widening 'nostalgia gap' echo those of Desmond Fennell, whose analysis of the subject matter of four major Irish Studies conferences held in America in the early 1990s led him to conclude that there existed 'a considerable out-of-touchness' among US-based scholars, which he attributed to 'certain essentialist conceptions of Ireland and things Irish which got embedded many years ago in Irish Studies circles' during its foundational 1960s phase (Fennell, 2003: 22–3).

Part One
Irish Studies in Practice

1

Changing Transatlantic Contexts and Contours: Irish Studies in the United States

Christina Hunt Mahony

The special relationship that exists between Ireland and the United States has been the subject of much rhetoric, especially since the founding of the Irish state. This link is rehearsed at appropriate intervals, usually at times of political or emotional significance, such as President John F. Kennedy's 1963 visit to Ireland or the signing of the Good Friday Agreement in 1998. The perception in Ireland of Irish political clout in America has always been somewhat distorted, however, and cannot compare with the special relationship between the US and Britain. Irish clout is also asserted in the social and cultural realm, where perhaps it is on firmer ground. It is not unusual, then, that Irish Studies as a composite sub-discipline in the university curriculum should have moved first from the foundation site at the Institute for Irish Studies at Queen's University, Belfast, begun in 1965 (but which remained a research venue until teaching began there in the late 1980s), and such early programmes as University College Dublin's Master of Arts degree and Trinity College Dublin's Higher Diploma in Anglo-Irish Literature (begun in the late 1960s), to certain east coast American universities, most of them private and Catholic. It was here, and in some Canadian cities, that there was a ready-made constituency for such degrees, comprising a critical mass of students from well-established emigrant families largely of Irish descent.

These US programmes, then, pre-dated most of the Irish degree courses in what is now called Irish Studies, and were also well established long before any such curricula appeared in Britain or in Australia. Indeed, the emergence of scholars and critics whose reputations were made in Irish literature was at first an American phenomenon, and began with the post-World War II generation that included Hugh Kenner, Richard Ellmann, Tom Flanagan and

Harry Levin. The field was not exclusively American, but those who were not were mostly Oxbridge scholars and few were Irish – John V. Kelleher at Harvard being an important exception, along with A. Norman Jeffares and T. R. Henn in Britain. In history the case was clearer cut; the leading figures – T. W. Moody, R. Dudley Edwards and F. X. Martin – were all Irish. The critical terrain, however, has shifted drastically in recent decades and it is now indisputable that the most trenchant and exhilarating writing in all areas of Irish history, literature and the newer interfacing disciplines of cultural studies is largely being written by Irish scholars.

American universities should be credited with nurturing this phenomenon, as they made Irish Studies *qua* Irish Studies canonical in the first instance. They may currently be lagging behind in terms of cutting-edge scholarship and research, and in course content, but without the groundwork laid by American pioneers, universities in Britain and elsewhere would not necessarily have adopted the Irish Studies concept. The Irish university system doesn't – or didn't – lend itself at all readily to interdisciplinarity, or more accurately, to multidisciplinarity, and there was little entrepreneurial spirit or incentive in the system. For years, Irish universities played host to large numbers of US students who came to Ireland on potentially lucrative American-run junior year abroad programmes. They allowed them into their classrooms, or set up 'apartheid' classes for them on campus or off, receiving a per capita fee from the host American institution. The apartheid factor, which was an irritant as many US students wanted to study alongside their Irish counterparts, was one of the first of many continuing expressions of the Irish conviction of the inferiority of American standards and student preparedness. This has always been a complex and arguable point. American higher education is more egalitarian and has no national standard; the best US students are equal to and often better than their Irish counterparts, whereas the worst would not be permitted to enter university in Ireland. Irish universities during this period gained little financially from this arrangement, except for tuition fees from visiting 'occasional' students, as they were then called. Now they benefit much more from running the programmes themselves, drawing students from Ireland, America and elsewhere.

So there is now a shift of focus. The centre of gravity in Irish Studies is no longer somewhere south of Boston, but somewhere west of Tara, with spokes radiating outward to Galway, Cork, Belfast and Dublin. Meanwhile, the American commitment to Irish Studies continues, and continues to expand. It is perhaps the divergence that has occurred between these two centres of expansion that is of most interest in our assessment of the possible future directions of Irish Studies in the United States – a blueprint for those who labour in the field, and for current and prospective students. The subject itself has already been the focus of several recent conferences and has attracted some press scrutiny in Ireland.[1] That the future of the discipline is being discussed in this way has both positive and negative implications – the discipline is established; it has been around long enough to consider renovation; the conditions under which it emerged no longer prevail; outside forces could threaten its survival; or perhaps ossification has made it take itself too seriously.

Irish Studies in the US seems now an almost entirely entrepreneurial undertaking, thriving not because of universities' commitment but because of large donations earmarked for things Irish. The three best-known Irish Studies centres in the country are those at Notre Dame in Indiana, Boston College and New York University (NYU). All three colleges are private institutions; the first two are Catholic. Notre Dame was founded by the Holy Ghost Fathers – although it is now administered by lay Catholics – and Boston College is Jesuit. New York University is often mistaken, especially by those from outside the US, as the name of a state university, but it is in fact an elite and expensive private institution with a huge endowment. Large infusions of cash from individual wealthy benefactors are responsible for funded chairs and other positions, public lecture series, scholarships and general running costs. At Boston College, tuition and university sponsorship accounts for a higher percentage of these costs. Smaller, older programmes, such as those at the Catholic University of America (CUA) in Washington DC, at Fordham in New York, and at Northeastern University in Boston, have remained small precisely because they have been unable to attract large donations or wealthy benefactors. Universities' unwillingness to put money into such programmes is not unusual, even while they attract students and tuition dollars.

There are significant differences between these programmes. Most of the impressive names on Notre Dame's Irish Studies programme letterhead are those of scholars who are, by and large, based in Dublin. These include the Director of the Dublin programme, Kevin Whelan, and Seamus Deane and Luke Gibbons, both of whom also lecture at Notre Dame. The South Bend campus seems to have suffered somewhat in that connection, although faculty members from many departments work there to form a large Irish Studies faculty, which includes the valuable recent appointment of Breandán Ó Buachalla. This is standard procedure on most American campuses, making these offerings more cost-effective than they might seem at first to administrators. Boston College, on the other hand, seems to favour importing stellar Irish scholars, rather than having students go to Dublin to encounter them. The Burns Library attracts a major scholar annually, and there have been visiting positions in both the English and the History departments on a regular basis. The position left vacant by the untimely death of the founder of the Irish Studies programme, Adele Dalsimer, has been filled by Yeats scholar, Marjorie Howes. NYU has a similar approach, and has had a revolving chair in History, which is currently occupied by J. J. Lee, who resumed that post on his retirement from University College Cork. Additional chairs in different disciplines seem not to have materialised at NYU, although the programme can boast the distinguished presence of literary critic Denis Donoghue in a peripheral and consultative position within the English department.

What the three largest American programmes now share, though, is their major presence in Dublin. Among them, only NYU continues to use Trinity College's facilities, an unusual arrangement for an institution that owns or leases property in an array of foreign cities for its other overseas initiatives. Boston College and Notre Dame have their own Dublin bases, which have become more highly developed in terms of real estate, course offerings and faculty in the last few years. This development is an outcome of, and also a good working solution to, a problem that arose earlier in the evolution of Irish Studies in the US, when substantial amounts of private funding first became available. At first there were numerous searches for major Irish writers and academicians to fill prominent positions. Seamus Heaney, after all, held a chair at Harvard for many years, commuting between Cambridge, Massachusetts and Dublin, so there was a precedent. It was hoped to replicate this envious arrangement elsewhere, but the searches were not entirely successful. An unacknowledged reason for the difficulties that ensued, despite the offer of lucrative salaries, is that Irish writers, historians and critics must remain in Ireland or be there frequently enough to remain *au courant* with matters Irish. Indeed, many Irish writers are on record as saying that their inspiration is in the first instance Irish, and writing under different cultural conditions can produce different writing. Some have universal muses, of course, or portable ones. For academics, the problem is that primary research materials are often found only at home, despite the growing availability of fine internet resources. Arrangements of the kind Notre Dame has successfully negotiated, with Irish academics living in Ireland on the payroll of American universities, cater superbly to those scholars' needs, but do not always fulfil the requirements of potential donors or university administrators who prefer their stellar faculty *in situ*.

The Catholic University of America's Irish Studies Masters degree course centres on contemporary political and cultural issues in Ireland, thereby taking advantage of its position in Washington, and offering a 'study in two capitals' approach. It maintains its Irish connection through a long-standing administrative arrangement with the Institute for Public Administration in Dublin, which acts as agent with Dáil Éireann and assigns legislative internships to CUA students and others who attend the programme. The contemporary political emphasis has a benefit in that it helps to dispel romantic or outdated views of Ireland, and involves students in research, elections and personal interaction in areas of learning such as the Irish voting system, health care service, Ireland's position in the EU, neutrality, current tribunals, and evaluations of Irish journalism and media. On its Washington campus, the Mullen Library boasts an impressive Irish-American and Fenian archive, and the programme relies on being at the political centre of American activities to attract prominent Irish public figures at regular intervals.

There are many more Irish Studies programmes in the US than a chapter of this type can discuss in any appreciable depth. Villanova University in suburban Philadelphia has a longstanding commitment to the subject, as evidenced by a chair (not solely intended for Irish Studies scholars), which has been held in recent years by poet Nuala Ní Dhomhnaill and publisher-poet Peter Fallon, among others. In a similar fashion, the University of Missouri at St Louis has hired poet Eamonn Wall to occupy its new Irish Studies chair, and Howard Keeley was appointed Director of Irish Studies at Georgia Southern University in 2004. Emory University, also in Georgia, hosts the distinguished Ellmann lectures, has acquired some of Seamus Heaney's manuscripts, and boasts Yeats scholar Ronald Schuchard. At the University of Wisconsin, historian James Donnelly has trained many scholars in the field, as has Kerby Miller at the University of Missouri at Columbia. Loyola University, Chicago is now reviving interest in Irish Studies since the retirement of historian Lawrence McCaffrey, while Emmet Larkin remains at the University of Chicago across town, though Perry Curtis has retired from Yale. Columbia University sponsors the Irish Studies Forum, a prestigious speaking venue for visiting and American scholars. The wide-ranging and valuable work of the American Conference for Irish Studies, one of the oldest and largest scholarly organisations in the discipline, is inestimable and has involved practically every American scholar in its activities. The newest area of interest in the field on both sides of the Atlantic, and one with the greatest possibilities for expansion, is that of online Irish Studies. At present, degree programmes exist in Northern Ireland, the Republic and in Colorado, and more are in the planning stages.

Irish-interest publishing in the US academy continues at Syracuse University, the Catholic University of America and the University of Wisconsin, while Wake Forest University Press publishes a stellar line of Irish poets. Long under the direction of Dillon Johnston, it is now run by Jefferson Holdridge who moved there from UCD. The University of Kentucky Press also publishes an Irish line, and its faculty includes Jonathan Allison, recent director of the Yeats Summer School. In addition, there are the journal and review venues, most prominently the *Irish Literary Supplement*, now sponsored by Boston College, and long under the editorship of Robert Lowery. *Éire-Ireland* is now based in New Jersey and is the publishing arm of the Irish American Cultural Institute, while *New Hibernia Review* is located at the University of St Thomas in St Paul, Minnesota, where Irish Studies was begun by Eoin McKiernan many years ago.

However, the breadth and variety of Irish Studies programmes on offer, and the number of major scholars involved in the subject in the US, should not shield us from recognising just how precarious most of these programmes are. Irish Studies in many places remains what I have elsewhere called '"a one-man band" syndrome', with dedicated people forwarding curricular ideas to university deans, often raising their own funds, recruiting students, editing journals and putting in a lot of unpaid hours (Mahony, 2003: 9). Often, when these individuals retire or move, Irish Studies – whether in the community or on campus – withers and eventually dies. Usually the reasons are financial and occur because such programmes are viewed as bijou luxuries, whereas in fact Irish Studies professionals often have begun their careers teaching in other fields and continue to teach broader-based courses. It is therefore incumbent upon retiring academics in prominent positions to insist as part of their retirement packages that their successors will be specialists in their fields and that the programmes they have devised will remain securely in place.

The situation described above differentiates greatly the relative positions of Irish Studies in the US and in Ireland, where programmes are state-subsidised and attract foreign tuition fees. Irish Studies in Ireland, both north and south, is becoming highly institutionalised and integrated into government paradigms for universities. Witness the many Government of Ireland scholars who are now funded in the Republic to undertake Irish Studies research, and the Arts and Humanities Research Council-funded Irish Studies centres and publishing projects in Northern Ireland. These developments represent a major point of divergence between the current US and Irish models, and suggest that Irish Studies as a discipline in Ireland is secure, whereas Irish Studies in the US, where government monies are no longer earmarked for Eurocentric projects, remains vulnerable. The institutionalisation of Irish Studies programmes in Ireland has also had hidden consequences for history and literature departments there, because of the strong incentive to research, teach and publish in Irish-related fields. Moreover, Irish Studies specialists in Ireland, because they are in their own country, are more likely to gain media prestige or to attract grants than colleagues teaching, say, Spanish literature or the history of sub-Saharan Africa. The American equivalent of this phenomenon has resulted in another major divergence between Irish Studies in the US and in Ireland, and one that may be an important part of the future of the discipline there: the emergence of Irish-American Studies as a subsidiary research area that is gaining in scope and prestige. This development is again fuelled by the availability of grants, many of which, especially in times of shrinking university and foundation budgets and growing patriotic fervour, are directed toward issues and initiatives with an American focus.

Irish Studies in the US also deviates from the experience in Ireland in that Irish students generally come to the subject with a solid background in literature and history, and with a knowledge of the Irish language, having been required to study these in school. American students, by contrast, enter Irish Studies graduate programmes with a scanty grounding in the subject. The best will have taken a couple of courses in literature and history, while only a few will have had any Irish-language instruction. This marked difference between programmes at home and abroad (those taught in Britain, Canada and Australia have a similar dynamic in this regard) makes the decision to teach theory or literature, history or historiography – especially on entry graduate level – a pressing concern. The dilemma thus posed is certainly one that has implications for the future of the subject in the US, and begs a number of key questions. Is it appropriate or advisable to teach postcolonial or feminist reassessments of the canon to a student body with insufficient reading of canonical materials to make informed critical use of such approaches? If not, does this condemn graduate programmes in the US to teaching primary materials? Where then should theory enter the classroom and when? Are we condemned to a two-pronged system in which diasporic students study a different curriculum from those 'at home'? Does this not perpetuate the problem?

One recent positive development in the US and elsewhere is the broadening of the Irish Studies curriculum beyond the traditional concentration on history and literature into new areas such as film and media, politics, peace studies, women's studies, cultural anthropology and music. Again, however, American students do not begin with the same knowledge base and general level of awareness that Irish students bring to the study of their own culture, thereby prompting further questions. Should knowledge of musical technique and repertoire be a prerequisite for studying theoretical applications designed to re-position traditional music in a broader musical context for contemporary listeners? Should US graduate students be writing theses on heritage centres as cultural signification projects, or the commemorative politics of parades and memorials, when the significance of the sites and historical events that occasion them are only marginally understood, and often figure insignificantly in the writing of such theses? Students in the US will sign up readily for courses focused on contemporary Northern Ireland, but courses on earlier periods go undersubscribed through lack of interest.

There has also been a time warp, a nostalgia gap, in the teaching of Irish Studies in the US and elsewhere in the diaspora. Outworn templates have been handed down, and because many Irish Studies practitioners are or have been unable to visit Ireland regularly, interact with Irish scholars, and keep abreast of developments in Irish popular, political and intellectual culture, some of the resultant teaching has lagged behind the critical curve. Consequently, outdated approaches to subjects like nationalism, cultural identities and the reassessment of key historical and cultural figures in Ireland's recent past still prevail in the course materials, reading lists and curricula of some programmes. It seems that the nostalgia gap is narrowing of late, but it still exists and remains an issue that affects the quality of Irish Studies degrees in the US.

Despite these problems, a case can be made for US and diasporic Irish Studies programmes not to go down the hyphenated route of Irish-American Studies, Irish-Canadian Studies or Irish-Australian Studies. Those avenues do open up broad and interesting areas of scholarly research, and one would hope in the future that a truly diasporic approach to Irish Studies would emerge. Currently, diasporic research tends to take place within self-enclosed enclaves, constituted largely as described above. However, I believe that genuinely comparative studies are the way forward, as we learn that Irish diasporic communities in Manchester, Montana and Melbourne share experiences that are germane. Furthermore, scholars studying the Boston Irish need to talk more and write more with those studying the Birmingham Irish, as do those in San Francisco with those in Sydney.[2] The most convincing reasons for truly diasporic research are to avoid reinventing wheels, to make the most of financial and research resources, and, most importantly, to present a unified force that enhances Irish identity. These are the proper concerns of scholars, and of course scholarship does and should have a direct trickle-down effect on teaching and curriculum revision. But twenty years' teaching experience in the field in the US confirms one trait, if it confirms nothing else: students are primarily interested in Ireland. They are interested in going there, and in learning more about its history, literature, culture and language. For this reason, I believe that Irish Studies programmes in the US will make a mistake if they turn over their offerings, particularly at the undergraduate level, to diasporic studies entirely – and the trend just now is strong. The reasons are compelling and are often, again, a matter of funding: using available faculty from other departments, being able to coordinate teaching efforts and research, and submitting grant proposals in collaboration with faculty researching other American ethnicities and religious identities makes funding more likely and more generous.

To suggest a course that is somewhat radical, it might be time for the Irish government, and Irish universities, to recognise officially the shift in Irish Studies that has occurred in recent years. Offering American and other diasporic scholars greater opportunity to avail of fellowships and grants that would enable them to spend more time in the country, and conduct more research there, might help to close the ever-widening transatlantic gap that, this chapter has argued, will continue to exist in the future. At present such scholarly opportunities are limited, and Ireland remains an expensive destination for anyone contemplating a long stay to avail of primary research materials. It is also not well known that many US, Canadian, Australian and British academics do not earn as much as their Irish counterparts who, at least in the Republic, are among the best paid in the world.

Irish Studies is now canonical. It is part of an international curriculum, and not merely confined to the Anglophone world. It is a thriving discipline, continually growing and changing, so we should welcome innovation and do what is required to ensure its continuing health. Diasporic Irish scholars are, moreover, continuing to shape its development, as they have shaped it in the past, and their efforts should be recognised and rewarded in Ireland as much as elsewhere. The time has come for Irish government agencies, universities and scholars to acknowledge both the intellectual and financial contribution of the diaspora to Irish Studies, past and present, and to make genuine efforts to sustain ongoing research and interactive institutional links with those who toil on the shop floor abroad. For many years US institutions have provided excellent opportunities for visiting Irish scholars, writers and artists, and subsidised Irish universities, and they will continue to do so in the future. The time has come for the Irish to return the favour.

NOTES

1. The Irish Department of Education, in the sort of governmental support of diasporic projects this chapter advocates, sponsored an academic conference organised by Boston College as part of a week of cultural programmes entitled *Island: Arts from Ireland* at the Kennedy Center in Washington, DC in May 2000. The academic portion of the week's programme was entitled 'Ireland: Politics, Culture and Identity.' In November 2003 the British Association for Irish Studies and the Institute for English Studies hosted 'Irish Studies in the Curriculum' at the University of London. Some of the topics addressed were 'Irish Studies and (Non-British) European Syllabuses', 'Troubled Relations: Irish Texts and English Students' and 'Lessons from an Irish Studies Programme'. Publications on the subject are varied; for a sense of the issues at stake, see Bartlett *et al.* (1988), Sharkey (1997a, 1997b) and Mahony (2003). The latter paper was first delivered as a keynote address on Irish Studies in North America at the Princess Grace Irish Library in Monaco in October 2002. When subsequently published in the *Irish Times*, it occasioned letters to the editor and follow-up articles during the summer of 2003 on threats to the funding of Irish-language degrees in the Republic, and the rationalisation and closure of small university departments and academic units in both parts of Ireland.

2. The American Conference for Irish Studies (ACIS) has made institutional strides in this area by beginning a practice of combining its annual conferences at times with those of the Canadian Association, and also with a pattern of holding regular conferences in Ireland. Summer 2004 featured the most comprehensive of these initiatives to date, as the ACIS went to the University of Liverpool, where the Institute for Irish Studies hosted the joint conference of ACIS, the British Association for Irish Studies (BAIS) and the European Federation of Associations and Centres of Irish Studies (EFACIS).

2

Reconfiguring Irish Studies in Canada: Writing Back to the Centre

Michael Kenneally

Since its emergence as an academic subject in the 1960s, Irish Studies in Canada has evinced some of the tendencies characteristic of the discipline in general, while also moving in directions that can offer instructive critical models for further development both at home and abroad. Despite Canada's relatively small academic population, the accomplishments of the founding generation of Irish Studies scholars over the past four decades constitute an impressive body of work. However specific their original areas of research, many of these scholars embraced and contributed to the international trend to expand both the objects of their scrutiny and the critical principles of their fields of investigation. This bidirectional extension of boundaries stemmed from a confluence of circumstances that began to emerge in the early 1970s and influenced the international evolution of Irish Studies. These included the growing cross-disciplinary validity of the critical perspectives offered by poststructuralism, postmodernism and, in particular, postcolonialism; the escalating violence in Northern Ireland that invited some form of contextualisation, if not outright explanation, from academics studying the subject of Ireland; and the sheer imaginative vitality and range of Irish cultural production in the period, from film, music and literature to theatre, visual arts and popular culture.

The widening domain of Irish Studies, therefore, and the expansion of critical theory were central to the transformation of the discipline in the last decades of the twentieth century. It is a paradigm shift readily apparent in Canada from the changing contents of the *Canadian Journal of Irish Studies*, and in the papers presented at the annual conferences of the Canadian Association for Irish Studies (Ronsley, 1999). Whereas these trends mirrored the dynamic evolution of Irish Studies internationally in this period, the pronounced impetus in Canada towards the appropriation of a wider critical scope is evident in the research by historians and geographers, specifically on aspects of the Irish experience in Canada. This research may be seen as a reflection of the country's expansive geography and its social and cultural diversity along regional lines. Given that other chapters in this volume address the paradigm shifts that have occurred in recent years in Irish Studies, my main focus will be on the implications of the developing nature of research by Canadian scholars on specific aspects of the Irish experience in Canada. As I hope to demonstrate, themes and issues relating to Irish emigration and settlement in Canada are not only inherently valuable in themselves but can be instructive in identifying neglected aspects of Irish-Canadian history and suggestive of research options in other national contexts.

Beginning in 1984 with *The Irish in Ontario*, Donald Akenson rapidly established an international reputation as a pre-eminent historian, not only of the Irish in Canada but throughout the diaspora (Akenson, 1999). Using extensive statistical evidence and comparative data on the migration and settlement patterns within the total population, Akenson argued that the Irish in Ontario became successful and affluent by transforming the forested hinterlands into productive farms and small towns into active centres of commerce. It was also his contention that the differences in the acculturation process for Irish Protestants and Catholics were less significant than popular conceptions would suggest, and that such differences were consistent with Irish immigrants in other areas of Canada and the US. Cecil J. Houston and William J. Smyth's *Irish Emigration and Canadian Settlement* continued the work of Akenson, but widened the focus to give some attention to areas outside Ontario (Houston and Smyth, 1990). Their argument is that contrary to popular belief, the Irish arrived earlier in Canada, formed a larger proportion of the founding communities, and were largely rural-based. Moreover, more than half the Irish emigrants were Protestant. Houston and Smyth focus on the phenomenon of chain migration and settlement patterns, and devote a significant proportion of their book to biographies of several representative individuals, supplemented by analysis of selected emigrant letters.[1]

Bruce Elliott explores the phenomenon of chain migration (usually involving kin) in greater detail in *Irish Migrants in the Canadas*, by tracking 775 Protestant settler families from Tipperary and environs, both before and after their arrival in Ontario (Elliott, 1988). In *A New Lease on Life* Catherine Wilson compares the changing nature of the landlord–tenant relationship in Ireland and Canada by reconstructing the family circumstances and estate management of two landlords who each owned extensive lands in Ireland, and consecutively owned the estate of Amherst Island in Ontario (Wilson, 1994). By following more than 100 tenant families who migrated from County Down during the mid-nineteenth century, Wilson demonstrates the importance of studying social and economic history topics in their international contexts. Inherent in the methodologies of all these works is close scrutiny of the social, religious, economic and geographical origins of Irish emigrants, examination of statistical evidence (especially compared with the population at large), consideration of the settlement sponsors and chain emigration, and analysis of a wide range of primary documents such as diaries, letters, estate papers, account books and ledgers.

This body of historical work served to transform stereotypical images of the Irish in Canada, a narrative shaped in popular memory by the huge influx of Famine immigrants and the tragic events associated with the island of Grosse Île in the middle of the St Lawrence river. The association of this isolated quarantine station with coffin ships, typhoid fever, burial at sea and mass graves had tended to overdetermine the larger narrative of Irish emigration and settlement in Canada. The general profile of the Grosse Île narrative has been established by the exceptional work of Marianna O'Gallagher, along with that of André Charbonneau, André Sévigny and others who drew attention to its value as a site warranting further investigation through the application of new theoretical and methodological principles (Charbonneau and Sévigny, 1997; O'Gallagher, 1984; O'Gallagher and Masson Dompierre, 1995).[2] Taken in conjunction with the specifically local focus of the research on the Irish in Ontario, the need to conceptualise Grosse Île from multiple perspectives that accommodate interdisciplinary investigations of its regional, national and international implications, underlines geographic differentiation as a shaping factor in the experience of Irish immigrants to Canada. New arrivals encountered realities determined not only by the historical moment but also by the physical and cultural environment of their chosen destination. These modalities, along with the follow-on research suggested by the impressive foundational work on the Irish in Ontario, combine to point to a wide array of additional topics and disciplines awaiting exploration. For example, in both their regional and national contexts, issues relating to the role of the Irish in labour, education, politics, sports, business, journalism and culture constitute some of the broad categories that deserve greater attention.

In Quebec, critical investigation requires different inflections to accommodate the distinct features of its dominant ideologies – the most obvious being language, religion and culture. The complex nature of the Irish experience in the province, as well as potential areas awaiting critical attention, are readily apparent from Robert J. Grace's study (Grace, 1993). In the ever-volatile linguistic environment of Quebec, a crucial question to be examined is the degree to which the Irish became French-speaking and embraced Francophone culture. What factors fed into this process: location, address, religion, education, employment, marriage? Did the Irish mediate between the French and the English, in Quebec and on the national stage? If so, what roles did language, religion and culture play in this process? Grace has pointed to the large number of single Irish female emigrants who arrived in the province in the mid-nineteenth century. What became of these women? Historically, how was an Irish dimension factored into the construction of Quebec identity? How might postcolonial theory be used as the basis for a comparison of the development of a national literature in Ireland (W. B. Yeats *et al.*) and in Quebec (Abbé Casgrain *et al.*)? How might the Irish-language writings of Patrick Pearse and Douglas Hyde (who, incidentally, visited Montreal in 1890 on his way to spend a year as Professor of Modern Languages at the University of New Brunswick in Fredericton) form a further basis for comparison? And what role did public policy play in regard to economics, culture, sport, education and especially language, in both Ireland and Quebec, in the formation and buttressing of national identity?

Other comparative studies of Ireland and Quebec might profitably examine the careers, policies and achievements of various sets of influential political and cultural figures: Henry Grattan and John Neilson, Daniel O'Connell and Louis-Joseph Papineau, Douglas Hyde and Henri Bourassa, Eamon de Valera and Maurice Duplessis. In more recent times, comparative lessons might be drawn from looking at how a transition from an ethnic to a civic nationalism begins to influence new conceptions of identity in both societies.[3] While some of these issues are unique to the Ireland–Quebec nexus, others might serve as a template for new directions in Irish Studies elsewhere, not just in the obvious areas of the United States, Britain, Australia and New Zealand, but also in France, South Africa, Latin America, and indeed in Ireland itself.

Moving further eastward, scholarship undertaken by researchers in Newfoundland is all the more commendable because of its application of diverse theoretical perspectives to specific regions of the country. John Mannion's *Irish Settlements in Eastern Canada* remains the seminal text dealing with the relationship of Irish emigrants to the physical landscape of their new home (Mannion, 1974). Strongly influenced by E. Estyn Evans and Henry Glassie, Mannion's book focuses on three Irish-Canadian rural communities, in Newfoundland, New Brunswick and Ontario, in order to examine the processes of immigrant adaptation to new physical habitats. Through assiduous fieldwork and close examination of the artefacts of the material culture of a given community, this study in cultural geography provides a nuanced understanding of the daily practices of Irish immigrants in distinct regions of Canada. Ranging across several disciplinary and cultural forms – sociology, anthropology, folklore, linguistics, historical and literary narratives, oral and folk memory, vernacular architecture, even ballads – Mannion demonstrates how traditional farming methods, building styles, migration patterns, settlement morphology and other aspects of culture were maintained, altered or adapted by these communities. Equally innovative is Mannion's decision to construct a study of the pre-emigration practices of Irish settlers, a task not always undertaken by historians or sociologists, before going on to analyse the processes of transfer and adaptation in the New World. Thus, social history, agricultural practices, community activities and cultural traditions are examined in the context of both the physical landscape and the built environment. The result is a model of how such a nuanced methodology can offer concrete, distinctly palpable evidence of the lived reality of Irish settlers in Canada.

Mannion's influence, along with that of Evans and Glassie, has led to further field studies of predominantly Irish settlements in Newfoundland, the best of which demonstrate how an examination of emigrants' negotiated adjustment to landscape, engagement with the material artefacts of everyday life, and adaptation of cultural traditions can offer a multivalent perspective on the past, and reveal the manner in which heritage manifests itself in the present. Gerald Pocius's *A Place to Belong* is an exemplary prototype for the study of close-knit communities, whether in Ireland or elsewhere in the diaspora, because of its adept interdisciplinary negotiation of disciplines such as history, geography, sociology, architecture and folklore (Pocius, 1991). At the heart of the book are the principles of material culture studies, the examination of objects that have been shaped by human contact, be it the physical landscape, a piece of furniture, a fishing net, a photograph, a painting or a garden fence. Living ordinary lives marked by frequent hardships, generations of people in Calvert may have left little in the way of textual, documentary records of their history, culture, ethos or even their memories of an Irish ancestry. Yet under the scrutinising gaze of Pocius, who was trained as a folklorist and practises the tenets of material culture pioneered by Glassie in such works as *Passing the Time in Ballymenone* (1982) – a classic text that should be required reading for all Irish Studies scholars – the story of this Irish settlement is brought vividly to life. In the process, this community's history, its methods of cultural transfer and adaptation from Ireland to Newfoundland, and the whole matrix of factors through which identity is shaped and expressed are established in convincing relief.

More recently, architect Robert Mellin's *Tilting* focuses on the unique features of the artefacts of an isolated village inhabited by the descendants of eighteenth- and early nineteenth-century Irish emigrants (Mellin, 2003). Objects examined include houses, outbuildings, furniture, tools, fences and docks; and this reading of the past as palimpsest is given added depth through interspersed oral narratives, as well as through Mellin's exquisite pencil drawings and evocative photographs. Employing methodologies derived from material culture, anthropology, geography, architecture, storytelling, even linguistics, this work opens multiple doors into the history of the settlement patterns and acculturation practices of subjects who have evolved through several generations, with little influence from other immigrant groups. It reveals how their sense of identity in this isolated outpost has been constructed by specific traditions of remembrance and storytelling, and by continual adaptation to an inhospitable natural environment – the unforgiving landscape, implacable sea and fickle weather conditions. If Irish Studies is to move in a genuinely interdisciplinary direction, works such as those by Mannion, Pocius and Mellin need to be more widely known and their methodologies more broadly utilised within the mainstream of the discipline.

The forms of cultural geography and material culture practised by these Canadian scholars echo the work of Kevin Whelan and other Irish scholars, which shows convincingly how one of the purviews of material culture – the landscape – can be read as the embodiment of material, visual and topographical culture, with a richness of implication and a depth of resonance that rivals, and thus should certainly complement, traditional textual or archival sources

(Aalen, Whelan and Stout, 1997; Stout, 2002; Whelan, 1998). In a similar vein, Yvonne Whelan's *Reinventing Modern Dublin* shows how aspects of Dublin's built environment were used in the formation of nationhood in the early years of the Irish Free State as it attempted to eradicate the physical colonial legacy in the capital (Whelan, 2003). Awareness of the focus and techniques of such studies can greatly enhance our response to the work of many Irish cultural figures – writers, filmmakers, visual artists, local historians, musicians and a whole spectrum of practitioners in arts and crafts. They can also enrich and broaden the discipline of Irish Studies by further erasing the perceived segregation of disciplines.

Current Canadian scholars of Irish Studies have followed international practice in embracing theories that now constitute a floodtide of critical discourse in the field, including postmodernism, postcolonialism, revisionism and the new historicism. However, the ubiquitous application of such perspectives, especially the pervasive debates emanating from postcolonial discourse, has tended to occlude theories that would open up other vistas on established subjects, whether within history, cultural studies, geography, literature or film. This is not to argue for an abandonment of discourses that have so energised and valorised Irish Studies in recent years. Indeed, an Ireland–Canada political comparison awaits examination in postcolonial terms, since both countries have wrestled with the issue of constructing and buttressing national identity – each in two official languages – in an era when colonial influences have abated, yet still retain elements of formal control and presence. While Canada does not have a counterpart to the Northern Ireland issue, it retains, as part of the Commonwealth, the iconography and public signage of the Queen as head of state, a literal and symbolic presence viewed by many, especially French-Canadians and new Canadians who have emigrated from colonised jurisdictions, as anachronistic holdovers from the past.

Terry Eagleton, himself no stranger to the postmodern agenda, has commented that an outsider to Irish Studies 'might be forgiven for concluding that the Irish literary pantheon was populated more or less exclusively by Yeats, Synge, Joyce, Beckett, Flann O'Brien and Northern Irish poetry', and goes on to complain:

Much in Irish cultural studies is shaped nowadays by what one might loosely call a postmodern agenda, which brings into play some vital topics but in doing so tends to sideline other questions of equal importance. It is ironic that a discourse of marginality should have shoved so many other matters brusquely off stage.

Religion and education, for example, are at least as weighty matters in Irish cultural history as gender or racial stereotyping, but they happen not to be such favoured items on the postmodern menu, or in North America academia. (Eagleton, 1998: ix)

Inevitably, the question arises as to how graduate students and scholars new to Irish Studies – in Canada or elsewhere – might, at the minimum, be made aware of the broadest spectrum of topics and approaches available within the discipline. Perhaps this prescriptive overview can best move toward a conclusion by referring to two personal projects that suggest the beginnings of a reconfiguration of Irish Studies in Canada. As editor of four recent issues of the *Canadian Journal of Irish Studies*, my primary intention was to seek essays that explored fresh topics from new critical perspectives. A second goal was the active encouragement of research on Irish-Canadian issues. While initially uncertain about the existence of sufficient numbers of scholars whose work would reflect these priorities, I was gratified by the volume and variety of submissions, particularly on Irish-Canadian subjects as diverse as the public iconography of the Irish in nineteenth-century Montreal, the material culture of Newfoundland and the 'Irish police' in Canada and the US. Others factors have obviously induced scholars to research these topics, but the presence of a receptive scholarly publication did play a nurturing role. That some eventual contributors availed of the invitation to develop embryonic ideas for submission confirms the validity of this proactive editorial position.

Multidisciplinarity has also been the hallmark of *Éire-Ireland* under the stewardship of Vera Kreilkamp and her co-editors, and the degree to which a given discipline can be broadened to include new approaches is evident, too, from the various publications Kevin Kenny has recently edited on Irish-American history. Aside from encouraging young scholars in new areas of research, such publications also impress upon university administrators the legitimacy and complexity of the discipline itself, and increase the likelihood of attracting financial support from informed members of the Irish community, as is the case with *Éire-Ireland, New Hibernia Review* and the *Canadian Journal of Irish Studies*.

A second sustaining catalyst for Irish Studies is related to the courses offered in university undergraduate and graduate programmes. My own experience has confirmed the potential student interest in areas beyond a strict focus on Irish literature and history. The shift in curriculum options was predicated to some degree on the profile of the average student attracted to the subject. It is no longer necessary – if it ever had been – to conceptualise Irish Studies from perspectives of cultural nostalgia or genealogical curiosity, of interest only to the children of Irish emigrants seeking some understanding of a hybridised identity. Irish Studies exclusively or primarily for the Irish contributes to the marginalisation and ghettoisation of the discipline, and ensures its precarious position in any curriculum.

In Montreal, students on Irish Studies courses are drawn from diverse cultural backgrounds and academic interests, and are by no means restricted to those of Irish ancestry. Granted, most have an initial interest in the 'big-ticket' courses – those on the Literary Revival, James Joyce, the Famine – which fill on a regular basis. But courses that address aspects of a student's own interests or incorporate comparative perspectives are also well subscribed. For example, a course on cinema in Ireland and Quebec explores similarities and differences in the representation of issues dealing with religion, British colonialism, language, nationalism and state formation. Similarly, a course on Irish women encourages students to investigate how such women's experiences of nationalism, feminism, religion, education, sexuality and cultural production compare with those of women in Canada, or more specifically in Quebec. A cultural geography course examines the varying manifestations of Irishness in Newfoundland, with an emphasis on how class traditions, political agendas and educational experiences have shaped the perception of this particular ethnicity in that province. For students, an important element of the course is their calibration of similar influences on identity formation in either their own or another ethnic group. Finally, a course on the Irish economy in the context of the European Union has found broad appeal among students with no ostensible interest in Irish Studies, presumably because Ireland's policy with regard to capital mobility, migration, currency transfer and taxation can be read as an instructive model for economic and public policy in other jurisdictions.

In the multicultural reality that prevails in Canada's large urban centres, students of diverse ethnic backgrounds constitute a large proportion, if not the majority, of those enrolled in any given class. Since the Trudeau era of the 1970s and 1980s, public policy has actively promoted multiculturalism as being central to Canadian heritage, within the framework of the linguistic and cultural traditions of the English and French founding groups. In the context of a society that is multi-ethnic and multiracial, Irish Studies is perceived as exploring issues relating to the challenges of preserving cultural identity, whether within colonised Ireland or as part of the multi-cultural fabric of Canada itself. Indeed, a recent trend has seen some scholars develop an interest in Irish Studies because the discipline encourages them to reframe questions and apply methodologies originally honed in unrelated areas (Retallack, 1999, 2002/03; Rudin, 1994, 1997; White, 2001). The historical narrative of the Irish in Canada can be seen, then, not so much as having been swallowed by a multicultural society but as offering to other ethnic groups strategic examples of adapting to a changing environment. Central to an appreciation of such manoeuvres is knowledge of the challenging historical continuum in which Irish culture survived and evolved, both in Ireland and in Canada. Given the obstacles to social integration sometimes faced by Irish immigrants, whether because of religion, language, class or education, their experiences can serve as instructive models for subsequent immigrant groups seeking accommodation within Canadian society. Irish Studies courses that address the story of Ireland and of the Irish in Canada within such broad parameters can therefore strike a responsive chord with students from many backgrounds whose primary academic interest may lie elsewhere.

An important subtext here is the perennial challenge of institutionalising Irish Studies within the university curriculum, and of providing continuity beyond the appointment of a given individual. Because of the denotative and therefore ostensibly restricted focus suggested by the Irish Studies rubric, it is not a discipline likely to attract students en masse, who might create a sustained demand for university courses and programmes, as has been the case with women's studies, peace studies and environmental studies, among others. Yet given the broad constituency to which Irish Studies can be made relevant – created by such factors as the popularity of contemporary Irish culture, the international appeal of Ireland's national narrative of political emancipation, the size and range of the Irish diaspora, the inadvertent role of the British Empire in projecting aspects of Irishness around the world, and the accessibility of Irish culture through the English language – the discipline can legitimately claim a broadly based academic authority. The challenge of finding a way forward between the presence of this potential interest and the absence of bottom-up student pressure will usually devolve on individual academics who ultimately must assess how best to proceed within their own institutional and community environment. At Concordia University in Montreal, for example, financial support from both the university and the community at large was channelled into the creation of a Centre for Canadian Irish Studies and a chair in Canadian Irish Studies. These were intended to ensure a continuity for the subject that would supersede the vagaries of individual appointments and fluctuating administrative priorities. By loosely modelling the chair on a series of federally funded academic 'Canada Research Chairs' – intended to support a cohort of scholars who would combine research, teaching and community outreach – the stature of Irish Studies as a discipline has been further enhanced in the national and international academic landscape.

It should be evident from the Canadian experience, then, that if Irish Studies scholars and practitioners are willing to embrace new topics and theoretical perspectives, if they offer courses that speak to Ireland but also to the forces shaping students' immediate reality, and if they demonstrate that their discipline is capable of straddling different fields of enquiry and possesses a genuine internationalist thrust, a sustaining interest can be maintained that will attract students from diverse ethnic and academic backgrounds. Furthermore, if the presence of hospitable scholarly journals readily allows students already committed to the discipline to move to the level of published scholars, they will, if pursuing academic careers, be poised to develop the parameters of Irish Studies still further. Given the demographics of the ageing population of university professors over the next ten to twenty years, such young scholars will be uniquely positioned to carry the torch for Irish Studies in innovative and exciting new directions.

NOTES

1. Houston and Smyth's earlier study explored the historical geography of the Orange Order in Canada (Houston and Smyth, 1980), a subject that has also been examined in the context of New Brunswick by See (1993).
2. Recent work done by various researchers associated with Canadian Irish Studies at Concordia University in Montreal demonstrates the enduring interest this island retains for researchers. See, for example, the essays by O'Brien, Blair and Gauthier in Valone and Kinealy (2002) and Richman Kenneally (2003).
3. Padraig O'Gormaile's work has dealt with the image of the Irish in Quebec literature, while Mary Haslam's research on the representation of the Irish in French journalistic texts of the early nineteenth century promises to unveil a hidden subject and suggest further topics. I am grateful to Mary Haslam for discussions in which she shared ideas on topics related to the Irish in Quebec that await research.

3
10,000 Miles Away: Irish Studies Down Under

Elizabeth Malcolm

The distinctive Australian identity was not born in the bush, nor at Anzac cove: these were merely situations for its expression. No; it was born in Irishness protesting against the extremes of Englishness. (O'Farrell, 2000: 12)[1]

When viewed in terms of the substantial numbers of Irish people who emigrated during the nineteenth century, mainly to the United States, and during the twentieth century, mainly to Britain, those who came either voluntarily or involuntarily to Australia were comparatively few. Yet, in terms of their proportion of the Australian population, the Irish and their descendants loomed larger than in any other major emigrant destination (Fitzpatrick, 1994: 6–7). Therefore, whether or not one agrees with the bold interpretation of Patrick O'Farrell (1933–2003) quoted above, it is indisputable that for some 150 years after European settlement of the Australian continent, the Irish-born and their descendants were the most influential non-British community in the country.[2] The Irish were, without doubt, a 'founding people' of modern Australia (Richards, 1998: 350–1).

Down Under, then, Irish Studies is not just about Ireland or the Irish, it is about how a collection of small British penal colonies developed over 200 years into an enduring nation-state. Given the undoubted importance of the Irish in the modern Australian story, one might suppose Irish Studies to be a thriving field.[3] But while the subject is growing, to characterise it as thriving would be to err on the side of optimism. Much ink has been shed in this book and elsewhere on what exactly constitutes, or should constitute, Irish Studies. Here is not the place to rehearse that debate; suffice it to say that in Australia at least, Irish Studies most commonly boils down to history, followed at some remove by literature. Irish Studies Down Under is thus not notably interdisciplinary, for the simple reason that it is barely multidisciplinary. Nor is it particularly adventurous in terms of its theoretical conceptions: postmodernism and postcolonialism have barely registered. In addition, it continues to be ethnically ghettoised to a worrying degree, in the sense that those who pursue it are almost exclusively of Irish birth or descent.

The history of the Irish in the Australian national story is a very incomplete narrative, and also a contested one (Bolton, 1986: 5–19). But before Irish-Australian history became contested, it was frequently ignored or at best treated in the context of religious history. The founders of Australian historiography were in the main of British birth. Historians such as the English-born George Arnold Wood (1865–1928) and Ernest Scott (1867–1939), both of whom were leading history professors during the first half of the twentieth century at the universities of Sydney and Melbourne respectively, had little to say about the Irish, other than to subsume the more successful of them under a British rubric and treat the less successful as a small problematic minority (Crawford, 1975; Scott, 1947). On the other hand, some of their Australian-born and more radical successors, such as Brian Fitzpatrick (1905–65) and Manning Clark (1915–91), tended to view the Irish primarily through a religious lens. Fitzpatrick, although of Irish descent himself and the father of a leading contemporary Irish historian, lumped the Irish into the 'British' category and only treated them separately as 'Catholics' (Fitzpatrick, 1951: 24, 28–9), while Clark conceived of the Australian story as fundamentally a struggle between Protestantism, Catholicism and rationalism, with the Irish representing Catholicism (Clark, 1995: 27–9). So if the Irish are mentioned at all in nineteenth- and early twentieth-century accounts of Australia, they are generally marginalised or stigmatised, usually as troublesome others: recalcitrant convicts; lawless bushrangers; murderous Fenians; superstitious Catholics in a rational Protestant society; and, disproportionately, the poor, the criminal, the drunken and the insane.

Interestingly, many Irish Australians themselves were inclined to accept rather than reject this prevailing image of the Irish as troublemakers, although they put a very different gloss upon it (Kiernan, 1954). They believed that most Irish convicts were transported, not for petty or mercenary crimes, but for their political beliefs. Some certainly were, but the majority were not. Around one quarter of convicts transported to Australia between 1788 and 1867 were Irish. It is much harder to determine how many were political or social rebels, but they certainly did not form a majority (Reece, 1989, 1993). Nevertheless, before World War II, the Irish were to the fore in many radical and dissenting political movements in Australia. They were the leaders of the one major convict rebellion, which occurred at Castle Hill in New South Wales in 1804 (Ramsay Silver, 2002). They were also disproportionately represented among the bushrangers. To the Irish, however, bushrangers were not thieves; they were rather the Robin Hoods of the antipodes. The Irish also led the miners, known as 'diggers', who founded Australian republicanism in 1854 during the rebellion at the Eureka Stockade on the Ballarat goldfields in Victoria (Currey, 1954). In addition, they played a major role in the development of trade unionism in Australia. They were among the founders of the Australian Labor Party (ALP) in the 1890s and have provided many of its leaders since then (McMullin, 1991). Furthermore, they successfully resisted English-supported attempts to introduce conscription into Australia in the wake of the slaughter of the ANZACs at Gallipoli in 1915 and the brutal suppression of the Dublin Easter Rising in 1916.

In this heroic narrative of political dissent, two iconic figures stand out: the Irish-Australian bushranger, Ned Kelly (1854–80), and the Irish Catholic archbishop, Daniel Mannix (1864–1963).[4] According to popular myth, Kelly's family were small farmers, battling against English-descended landlords in Australia, as his father, a transported convict, had done in Ireland. Like his father, Kelly was the victim of a corrupt Anglo-Irish police force and judicial system. His so-called 'crimes' were not venal, therefore, but were the result of his struggle to defend his family and community from persecution. Mannix, a president of Maynooth College and then for 50 years archbishop of Melbourne, was a nationalist who had condemned British rule in Ireland and continued to fight British attempts to dictate in Australia after his arrival in 1913. He stood up for the ordinary working man and later resisted communist efforts to take control of the Australian labour movement. Yet despite his political activism, he remained unpretentious and unworldly, and was always accessible to his flock. Kelly is thus the embodiment of the idealised Irish rebel and Mannix the incarnation of the idealised Irish priest – both translated Down Under.

Many of the early writings by Irish Australians endorsed and promoted this narrative, and indeed such works continue to appear today. Even recent academic histories continue to treat the Irish as little more than a troublesome minority (Atkinson, 1997). O'Farrell himself can be seen as part of this tradition, although his analysis was far more sophisticated and intensively researched than anything that preceded it. In addition, he drew attention to the irony that, although the Irish in Australia celebrated dissent, most of them, in practice, strove for respectability and acceptance by the British-Australian colonial establishment. Thus, there are decidedly less dramatic, and probably more typical, Irish-Australian narratives than those afforded by the likes of Kelly and Mannix. For example, there is a narrative, favoured by the Catholic church, focusing not on rebels and republicans but on the successes of working- and middle-class Irish Catholic men who became leaders in business, politics, the professions and the church (Cleary, 1933). There is, in addition, although much less well-known, a Protestant Irish-Australian narrative that emphasises the contribution of Protestant men, whether from Ulster or the South of Ireland, to the law, medicine, education and the various Protestant churches in Australia.[5] But most of the major works on the Irish tend to deal exclusively with Catholics, and indeed for many years the history of the Irish in Australia was synonymous with the history of the Australian Catholic church. Irish Protestants, who probably made up around 10 per cent of convicts and 20 per cent of later, assisted immigrants, were generally ignored.[6] These narratives of successful professionals, clergy and businessmen, whether Catholic or Protestant, are what historians sometimes term 'contribution' history: attempts to validate minority groups by highlighting their contributions to the existing political and social order. As such, they are profoundly conservative. O'Farrell, accurately if somewhat cruelly, dismissed them as little more than attempts to jump on 'the traditional bandwagon, driven by the establishment, with the cry: "The Irish are here too!"' (O'Farrell, 2000: 13).

Up until relatively recently, then, most accounts of the Irish produced by Irish-Australian writers tended to assign them to the categories of heroic political dissident, zealous upwardly mobile Catholic or, less commonly, middle-class Protestant professional. O'Farrell began in the 1960s, working largely in the second category, by producing studies of Australian Catholicism, and it was not until the 1980s that his focus shifted to a more wide-ranging and ambitious consideration of the role of the Irish in Australia in general. But in his work, and also in other earlier writings by historians, the Irish who appear are overwhelmingly male. Where is the story of Irish women in Australia? The Irish are also assumed to be exclusively heterosexual. Were they really? In these narratives too they are white. Where are the stories of Irish Aborigines and of Irish Chinese?

While there is a growing number of studies on issues of gender, sexuality and race in relation to the Irish in Britain and the United

States, a similar literature is not yet evident in Australia. There is only one collection of essays on Irish women in nineteenth-century Australia and a mere handful of articles about Aborigines and the Chinese (McClaughlin, 1998; Rule, 2000). In fact, the crucial issue of Irish-Aboriginal relations has not really been researched at all. Claims that the Irish treated the indigenous Australian population better than the British did during the colonial period amount to little more than wishful thinking on the part of Irish sympathisers (Reece, 2000a). Another major aspect of the history of Irish Australia that has not been adequately investigated is regional diversity. O'Farrell was dismissive of the impact of environmental and local circumstances, but recent studies of Irish communities in Britain and the United States have demonstrated how widely spread the Irish were, and also how varied were their experiences, depending upon where they settled (Emmons, 1989; MacRaild, 1998). With a few notable exceptions, studies of the Irish in Australia have tended to focus on Sydney and Melbourne or, somewhat more widely, on certain parts of New South Wales and Victoria (Campbell, 1997; Waldersee, 1974). Some significant work has been and is being done on the Irish in Victoria and Western Australia, but studies of Irish communities in other states are scarce (MacDonagh, 2001; McGinley, 1991; Reece, 2000b; Richards, 1991). We do not as yet have a detailed survey of Irish communities throughout Australia, and much local history connected with the Irish who settled away from the south-east of the country remains unexplored.[7]

There are, therefore, still glaring gaps in the history of the Irish in Australia in terms of gender, religion, race and region. Moreover, important general works on Australian history and historiography continue to exclude the Irish, suggesting that Irish-Australian history remains marginalised (Macintyre and Clark, 2003).[8] Patrick O'Farrell was the leading historian of the Irish during the latter part of the twentieth century. His major book *The Irish in Australia* (1986) went into three editions in less than 15 years and remains the standard work. O'Farrell was a fine scholar and writer, who devoted four decades to the study of Irish Australia and also New Zealand, where he grew up. Yet, in some respects, his work may have contributed to this evident marginalisation. He devalued issues of environment, economics, race, gender and class, and offered a sweeping clash-of-cultures analysis of the development of a distinctive Australian national identity. He characterised the Irish as 'a constant liberalising creative irritant', 'the force that made things change', even the 'fun factor' in nineteenth-century Australia that prevented English culture from becoming totally dominant (O'Farrell, 2000; 13, 19). To younger historians this seemed an old-fashioned, conservative interpretation, and one that flattered the Irish excessively. In addition, the fact that O'Farrell did not include footnotes in his book frustrated scholars, as this made it virtually impossible to interrogate the sources underlying his analysis. So, while his work is extremely stimulating, it has not entered mainstream Australian historiography and younger Irish-Australian historians have begun to challenge key aspects of it.[9]

But if there are major holes in the historiography, there are literally chasms in our understanding of the contribution of the Irish to Australian literature and culture. Certain writers of Irish birth or descent have been examined and their Irishness stressed, among the most notable of whom are the poets Charles Harpur (1813–68), Victor Daley (1858–1905), Bernard O'Dowd (1866–1953), Christopher Brennan (1870–1932), C. J. Dennis (1876–1938), P. J. Hartigan (1878–1952), James McAuley (1917–76) and Vincent Buckley (1925–88); the novelists Joseph Furphy (1843–1912) and Thomas Keneally (b.1935); and the essayist Gerard Windsor (b.1944). As yet, however, there is no comprehensive account of the complex links between Irish literature on the one hand and Australian literature on the other; and the contribution of Irish-Australian writers to the Australian literary canon has only been examined in a relatively haphazard fashion (Molloy, 2001, 2002; Windsor, 1983). In the field of literary and cultural studies, there is no book comparable to O'Farrell's *The Irish in Australia* – in fact, there is no book at all.

Once we move away from history and literature and consider fields such as geography, anthropology, sociology, art and architectural history, film studies, sport and music, Irish Studies Down Under becomes woefully thin and, in many instances, non-existent. Nevertheless, interest in Ireland among Australians was probably higher in the 1990s than it had been for 80 years. The peace process in Northern Ireland, cheaper and easier international travel, growing sporting links, the popularity of Irish music and dance, and the proliferation of so-called 'Irish pubs' all combined to make Ireland highly appealing, especially to the young. Yet this was very much an interest in contemporary Ireland – that tiny country 10,000 miles away – rather than an interest in the major role the Irish have played in Australian history and culture.

Australia was also influenced – albeit belatedly – during the final quarter of the twentieth century by the proliferation in the northern hemisphere of Irish Studies conferences, centres and chairs. Up until the 1990s, the study of Ireland in Australia was very much dependent upon the enthusiasm of individual academics and community groups.[10] But when teachers retired or voluntary groups dispersed, momentum was frequently lost. One major and continuing impetus for over 20 years, however, has been the Irish-Australian conference series, the first of which was held in Canberra in 1980 and the latest of which (the fourteenth) took place in Cork in 2005. The proceedings of every conference have been published and together they constitute an invaluable repository of information. Out of these conferences has grown a Centre for Irish Studies, established in 1998 at Murdoch University in Perth, which began the publication in 2001 of the *Australian Journal of Irish Studies*. In 2000 the first chair of Irish Studies in Australia, endowed by an Irish-Australian business family, was founded at the University of Melbourne, and at the time of writing the University of New South Wales in Sydney is fund-raising to establish another Irish Studies chair in the near future.

It is no coincidence that these initiatives have occurred during a period of severe government cutbacks in university funding on the one hand, and a growing interest in Ireland among the young on the other. These conferences, chairs and centres have received a substantial amount of private financial support, whereas Australian universities in the past have always been largely government-funded. The development of Irish Studies in recent years thus reflects the growing entrepreneurial nature of tertiary education in Australia. Universities are increasingly under pressure to teach popular courses, to attract large numbers of students – in particular, fee-paying students – and to solicit outside funding. Irish Studies has had some success in this regard, though it remains to be seen just how long Ireland will continue to be fashionable and attractive to students and sponsors.

It is, therefore, a hard task – indeed probably an impossible one – to draw up a reliable balance sheet of Irish Studies Down Under in the first decade of the twenty-first century. Given that Irish immigrants formed a far larger proportion of the Australian population during the colonial period than they did anywhere else, it is disappointing that Irish Studies remains well behind the northern hemisphere in terms of intellectual breadth and depth. But, to look on the positive side, this means that there is much exciting work still to be done, and the recent establishment of a new Irish Studies centre, chair and journal offers scope for more research and teaching, and the prospect of greater continuity in the future. Already the Irish Studies Centre in Perth is fostering work on neglected topics, such as the Irish in Western Australia and post-1945 Irish immigration; the Gerry Higgins Chair of Irish Studies in Melbourne is involved with projects investigating issues of gender, violence and health among Irish Australians; and at the University of New South Wales teaching and research are being undertaken on the influence of Irish literature on Australian culture.[11] Race, unfortunately, remains a sensitive issue that Irish-Australian historians still largely shy away from.[12] But by establishing a more secure base within the Australian academy, and by fostering a greater degree of cooperation through regular conference activity, it is to be hoped that Irish Studies Down Under will advance during the twenty-first century on a broader front, thereby filling in at least some of the substantial gaps identified above.

In his important 1993 survey of the Irish diaspora, Donald Akenson titled his chapter on Australia 'Coming Attractions', and predicted that 'in the next decade Australian historical writing will produce a major breakthrough relating not only to the Irish in Australia, but worldwide' (Akenson, 1996: 91). Over a dozen years later, this prophecy remains unfulfilled, but Akenson was right to highlight the *potential* for Irish history and Irish Studies more generally in Australia. His prediction may not have been realised, but this certainly does not mean that it was, or is, unrealistic.

NOTES

1. It has often been suggested that a distinctive Australian character was largely shaped by life in the outback – in other words, by a frontier experience – and also by the participation of Australian and New Zealand troops (ANZACs) in the disastrous Gallipoli campaign of World War I. See Ward (1966).

2. Miriam Dixson agrees with O'Farrell that it is 'scarcely possible to underrate Irish influence in shaping Australian identity', while at the same time taking him to task for focusing solely on ethnicity and ignoring the significance of class and gender. For her, the Irish influence has been 'ambiguous' and decidedly less 'creative' and 'benign' than O'Farrell suggests (Dixson, 1999: 95–6).

3. This chapter will deal only with Australia, as there is not space to do justice to Irish Studies in New Zealand, for which see Fraser (2000) and Patterson (2002).

4. There are numerous studies of Kelly, the most recent being Jones (2003), and several laudatory biographies of Mannix, but for a more critical assessment, see Keogh (1991).

5. For an account of the careers of the many Trinity College Dublin graduates who emigrated to Australia, see Ronayne (2002).

6. Although O'Farrell makes a point of stressing the importance of Irish Protestants, he in fact has little to say about them. The title of the other major general history makes abundantly clear who it considers the Irish in Australia to be (McConville, 1987).

7. For a preliminary attempt to explore the regional diversity of the Irish in colonial Australia, see Greiner and Jordan-Bychkov (2002).

8. This controversial account of recent debates in Australian history does not even list the words 'Irish' and 'Catholic' in its index, reflecting a worrying exclusion of the Irish from mainstream Australian historiography.

9. For a recent critique of O'Farrell, see Partlon (2000).

10. In terms of history, the two most influential late twentieth-century academics were Oliver MacDonagh (1924–2002) at the Australian National University, Canberra, and O'Farrell at the University of New South Wales, Sydney. The study of Irish literature was promoted by, among others, Vincent Buckley at Melbourne University.

11. For more information on these activities, see the following websites: for the Irish Studies Centre in Perth, http://wwwsoc.murdoch.edu.au/cfis; for the Irish Studies chair in Melbourne, http://www.history.unimelb.edu.au/irish/index.htm; and for the planned Irish Studies chair in Sydney, http://irishstudies.arts.unsw.edu.au.

12. The impact of white settlement on indigenous society has become a bitterly debated topic in Australian history, and more broadly in Australian politics, which has tended to deter historians from entering the field. For one side of the debate, see Manne (2003).

4

'Our Revels Now are Ended': Irish Studies in Britain – Origins and Aftermath

Shaun Richards

In 2003 *Irish University Review* published a special issue on the Irish Literary Revival. Featuring the work of 'an emerging generation of cultural critics', the gathered essays offered 'new scholarship' and 'new perspectives' on the Revival, one of the most significant moments in Irish literary history (Kelleher, 2003: viii). Adrian Frazier's *Irish Times* review acknowledged the quality of the collection but expressed surprise at the apparent consensus among the contributions, along with the absence of committed dispute and debate. Frazier's criticisms return us to the origins of Irish Studies in Britain, a moment when 'academic wars' raged and 'theory', new historicism, nationalism and revisionism were positions to be jealously defended and resolutely advanced. But now, he suggested, 'Only scraps of jargon remain' (Frazier, 2003). While the accuracy of Frazier's judgements is a moot point, his suggestion of comfortable critical conformity will be particularly acute for those in Britain (and the Irish Republic) who had fought to dispel what W. J. McCormack termed the 'quote-and-dote approach' to Irish literary studies in favour of an engaged and politically informed analysis (McCormack, 1994: 1). This critical realignment represented a decisive shift towards a fluid and creative interdisciplinary approach in which the complexity of the subject of study, rather than the interests of the discipline through which it was approached, was the primary concern.

McCormack's introduction to the revised 1994 edition of his *Ascendancy and Tradition in Anglo-Irish Literary History from 1789 to 1939*, originally published in 1985, enables us to apprehend the complex moment of disciplinary meltdown in the face of imported – and largely Francophone – theory in which Irish Studies emerged in Britain. McCormack's concern was to break down the sealed disciplinary boundaries by which analyses of Ireland's cultural–

political complexities were always incomplete. In his introduction, he anticipated that his approach would displease practitioners of two disciplines in particular: literature and history. Traditionally minded literary critics would, he suspected, deplore the book's 'abstractions and exotic allusions', while historians were liable to dismiss its 'directly cited matter as a crude survival from some pre-historic methodology'. Yet he remained staunch in his defence of a study that sought 'to negotiate a critical idiom through which quotation and abstraction might comprehend each other' (McCormack, 1994: 1–2).

Much British and Irish literary analysis in the period prior to the original publication of McCormack's study was a variant on the American New Criticism, inflected by I. A. Richards's earlier *Practical Criticism*, with a consequent emphasis on a strictly limited object of study: the 'verbal icon' of the text to which history, society and politics were deemed extraneous. However, this position was to be radically displaced. As Terry Eagleton phrased it in 1976:

Criticism is not a passage from text to reader: its task is not to re-double the text's understanding, to collude with its object in a conspiracy of eloquence. Its task is to show the text as it cannot know itself, to manifest those conditions of its making (inscribed in its very letter) about which it is necessarily silent. (Eagleton, 1976: 43)

This perception that an understanding of a complex text was always inadequate if it relied on discrete mono-discipline analyses was soon extended to the complex 'text' of Ireland. For the outbreak of the Troubles in Northern Ireland in the late 1960s had made increasingly untenable analyses of O'Casey and Yeats, let alone Seamus Heaney and Brian Friel, which did not engage with their texts' ideological implications for the political present. Now, context was no longer a means through which to explain the specifics of names and dates. Criticism was expected to state the unstated and analyse the excluded; the political preferences and textually elided allegiances with which a purely aesthetic analysis could not engage. In the words of Pierre Macherey's *Theory of Literary Production*, the 1978 translation of which fuelled many of these changes, criticism should reject the idea that 'the work encloses a meaning which must be released' (Macherey, 1978: 76). Rather, it should 'go beyond the work and explain it, must say what it does not and could not say', and this was always to do with its imbrication in ideology (Macherey, 1978: 77).

The nature of the rejected establishment position is best exemplified by a paper from one of the conferences of IASAIL (the International

Association for the Study of Anglo-Irish Literature), which had been established in 1969 to promote the teaching and study of Irish literature in third-level education, and to facilitate contacts between a worldwide network of scholars.[1] The conference in Graz, Austria in July 1984 featured a seminar paper by the late Robert O'Driscoll of the University of Toronto entitled 'The Irish Literary Renaissance in the Context of a Celtic Continuum'. G. J. Watson's *Irish Identity and the Literary Revival* (1979) had already delineated Yeats's poetic–political imperative of 'ignoring, or holding at arm's length, the coming into being of an Ireland in which his own cultural and class inheritances made him feel profoundly uncomfortable' (Watson, 1979: 115). However, O'Driscoll's paper fully subscribed to the publicly stated mystic mindset of the Yeats- and Gregory-inspired Revival as being 'outside all the political questions which divide us' (Gregory, 1972: 20) and which, if political at all, was so in the interests of humanity in general rather than a class in particular. Indeed, he asserted that the Revival 'was deliberately planned as a counter-movement to the Darwinian denigration of the spiritual origins of man' (O'Driscoll, 1987: 137). O'Driscoll glossed his position in the question period: 'The Celts could not have invented the refrigerator', and for that we were to be grateful, irrespective of the curdled consequences.

The significance of this conference and this paper is the extent to which they propelled its British-based Irish participants towards the establishment of a British Association for Irish Studies (BAIS) that would match the international reach of IASIL and the intradisciplinary dimension of the American Conference for Irish Studies (ACIS). However, there was also a wish to have the venture informed by the developments in cultural analysis advanced by the Birmingham University Centre for Contemporary Cultural Studies – founded in 1964 – whose Occasional Papers series was bringing the cultural analysis of Antonio Gramsci into a British context. The first step towards the setting up of an association were taken at a conference at St Peter's College, Oxford in 1985, which was hosted by Anglo-Irish Encounter, a body initiated by the British and Irish governments to promote 'mutual understanding, useful cooperation and good relations between their [the British and Irish] peoples' (Orr and Whitaker, 1985). The conference was addressed by the then Ministers of Education from the Republic of Ireland and the United Kingdom, Mrs Gemma Hussey and Sir Keith Joseph respectively, both of whom stressed the significance of the educational initiative within the context of what Hussey referred to as the 'serious efforts being made by our two Governments to lay the foundations for peace and stability in Northern Ireland' (Hussey, 1985: 28).

But while this approbation by the political establishment aided the development of Irish Studies in terms of an association (the draft constitution of which was determined at the conference) whose access to funds for development was significantly greater than that normally available to academic organisations, it also carried with it the suspicion of being a creature of that same establishment. One finds traces of the politicised moment in which Irish Studies in Britain emerged in the very inaccuracy of the record of its activities in Tim Pat Coogan's *Wherever Green is Worn* (2000). Coogan claimed that Ruth Dudley Edwards used her position as the BAIS's first chairperson to advance an agenda that served the interests of the British establishment. As the *Irish Times* reported on 15 December 2002, Dudley Edwards contested the allegation that she had 'grovelled to and hypocritically ingratiated herself with the English establishment' in an action in the London courts in December 2000, resulting in an apology, an award of £25,000, and the removal of all allegations of impropriety from the book. But the very existence of such a view illustrates the conflicts over the supposedly political subtexts that were often thought to inform the development of Irish Studies in Britain, when ideological commitment was felt to be more than simply a manifestation of the text.

As the published record of that 1985 Oxford conference makes clear, there was a widespread and eclectic number of academics in the UK involved in Irish Studies whose work encompassed archaeology, economics, geography, history, Irish language, music, religion, sociology, anthropology and the visual arts. All of these subgroups reported their positions and preferences with regard to the development of Irish Studies, but it is a comment from the literature subgroup, chaired by Vivian Mercier of the University of California, that strikes the discordant – but representative – note: 'Some of the participants in this session subsequently prepared a note setting out their thoughts on a number of important issues which had not in their view been adequately discussed during this session' (Anonymous, 1985: 12). What was felt to have been ignored were the 'political' ramifications of literature in both its moment of production and its contemporary consumption. In this statement of dissatisfaction we can see the germinating seeds of a theorised Irish Studies.

The originary moment of Irish Studies in Britain, then, coincided with and was centrally informed by crises in the UK's political realm consequent upon the Troubles – which gave a sense of both relevance and urgency to the venture – and in the discipline of 'English' itself, where the demand was also for relevance. Equally influential were the student revolutions of 1968 in terms of their demands for the social relevancy of university courses across the humanities and social sciences. Journals such as *Red Letters*, *LTP* and *Textual Practice* advanced an agenda predicated upon the demise of English as a 'privileged domain of acceptable texts' (Barker, 1982: 1). The objective was now 'to reshape the discourse of English itself' and introduce 'modes of teaching and learning which challenge the established power relations of class, gender and race' (Barker, 1982: 1). Central to this development was the drive towards a 'sociology' of literature as exemplified by the Essex Sociology of Literature conferences, which started in 1976. However, its relationship with Irish Studies is both instructive as to their shared methodological concerns and salutary as to the relative ignorance of British academics when it came to appreciating the extent to which Ireland was, in fact, precisely the local focus of the theories whose relevance and applicability they were so concerned to debate with regard to almost any other global location.

The introduction to the collection of papers from the Essex conferences defines the disciplinary crisis affecting literary criticism as a result of 'that global conjuncture which has become known as "1968" – the Vietnamese struggle against US imperialism, the Prague Spring, the Parisian *événement*, the anti-war and civil rights movements in the USA' (Barker *et al.*, 1986: ix). These conferences, along with the journals mentioned above, were a crucial part of the development of a theorised practice. However, irrespective of the critical position adopted, one looks almost in vain across the various journals and conferences of the 1980s for any reference to Ireland, a conspicuous absence that continued into the 1990s, when primers and readers in colonial and postcolonial theory appeared on the lists of major publishers. Robert Young's review of Williams and Chrisman's *Colonial Discourse and Post-Colonial Theory: A Reader* (1993) indicates how far this exclusion could go: 'Ireland, which from Edmund Spenser to the present has generated the most sustained corpus of colonial discourse in existence, does not even feature in the index' (Young, 1994: 78).

Given that the proceedings of the Essex conferences listed events in Vietnam, the US, Paris and Prague as catalysts for cultural change, the absence of any reference to events in Northern Ireland is striking.

Indeed, as instanced by John Wilson Foster's recollection of Dublin in 1974 when the prelude to a poetry reading by Seamus Heaney was the 'heart-stilling stereophony of two loyalist car-bombs [...] that killed twenty-two passers-by', one did not have to move as far as Paris or Prague to find the established order being variously, and violently, defended and attacked (Foster, 1991: 4). But Ireland appears to have been the blind spot in the eye of the politically aware critic. While papers on topics ranging from Artaud to Amerindians and countries from Australia to Algeria all found conference space at Essex, only four of some 170 papers presented were on Irish topics.

Given their clear socialist commitments, the Essex conferences are notable for their failure to include Irish issues on their agenda of critical engagements, but they are not alone in this omission. While *Literature and History* was less committed to imported French theory than other journals, its radical commitment to rereading the canon or recuperating lost and forgotten working-class writing retained an almost exclusively English focus, to the extent that its first article on Ireland did not appear until 1988. Since the late 1980s both this journal and *Textual Practice* have regularly included articles on Irish texts and topics, but that is itself a consequence of the revolt against the parochialism of the 'crisis' in English that largely limited its radicalism to rereadings of its own, still exclusive, canon. Writing in 1984, McCormack deplored the neglect of Anglo-Irish literature in general, and by Marxist critics in particular, before going on to lament the critical silence on 'the colonial or neo-colonial status of the Yeatsian or Joycean context, and a complementary excision of the colonial and imperialist dimension to that "English" culture upon which the New Left intermittently concentrates' (McCormack, 1984: 168–9). But prior to McCormack's lament it was Tom Paulin's 1982 attack on the Methuen New Accents series that marked a decisive moment in the definition and development of a British-based Irish Studies, most specifically in what Paulin advanced as its necessary conceptual framework.

Methuen launched the series with the collection titled *Re-Reading English*, but far from accepting the terms of this 're-reading', Paulin's review in the *London Review of Books* made a swingeing attack on the 'freewheeling nihilist[s] with a taste for sociology and anthropology and a disquieting resemblance to a character from a Glen Baxter cartoon' (Paulin, 1984: 9–10). A cause célèbre in the 'crisis' had been the failure of Cambridge University to appoint Colin McCabe to a permanent lectureship, a move that was interpreted as a direct result of McCabe's commitment to theory. Paulin, however, singled him out for especially scathing treatment, as while McCabe wrote nominally from the standpoint of a radical alternative to class and racial distinctions, the language in which he conveyed his opposition betrayed him:

McCabe's use of 'our' excludes everyone who has colonised ancestors rather than imperialist ones. In a reflex and unthinking manner, he appears to identify himself with a thin white band of pith helmets and ruling accents [...]. There is in his analysis an agonised or embarrassed sense of superiority which is deeply condescending. (Paulin, 1984: 11)

Paulin's pyrotechnic display of invective should not disguise the deeply considered position at the heart of his analysis; namely, that while the humanities were being radicalised, this was being effected within a narrow frame of reference that was largely constituted by class-consciousness and vaguely informed by 'some form of post-imperial guilt' (Paulin, 1984: 12). However, he did suggest a way forward: 'it seems to me that it is the term "English" which needs to be first deconstructed and then redefined. This involves arguing from and for a specifically post-colonial or post-imperial idea – it means that the critic must come out into the open and say "*credo*"' (Paulin, 1984: 15–16). Given the 'crisis' in English Studies that was generated by 'theory', Irish Studies seemed to hold out the promise of an indigenous source of cultural–political significance that was absent from other literatures. In this sense Irish Studies appeared to offer a partial redemption for its now 'effete' neighbour, 'English'.

But that was then. To what extent did Paulin's call for conviction, along with the energy driving the engagement with theory and its concomitant demand for interdisciplinarity, translate itself across the twenty years since Irish Studies in Britain declared its formal existence?

The sense of genuine excitement and commitment in the 1980s resulted in a number of third-level institutions establishing Irish Studies programmes at both undergraduate and postgraduate levels. The first of these was the Centre for Irish Studies at North London Polytechnic (now London Metropolitan University), which was founded in 1986 with a view to countering negative representations of the Irish 'by increasing knowledge and understanding of the Irish community in Britain' (Hughes, 1987/88: 21). This was followed by the establishment of the Institute of Irish Studies at the University of Liverpool, which initiated an ambitious programme extending beyond the university curriculum to that of primary and secondary education. To these two centres were added those at St Mary's College, Twickenham and Bath Spa University College. Major British publishers developed specific Irish lists, and doctoral studies that examined Irish subjects as more than simply subsets of other disciplines became established at a wide range of universities. Perhaps the most significant recognition of Irish Studies by the educational establishment, and one enabled by the BAIS, was the foundation of the Carroll Chair of Irish History at Oxford, with Roy Foster as its first incumbent. To add to these successes, Irish strands at major conferences became as established as those dedicated to other areas; the BAIS gained a membership of some 300 and the *Irish Studies Review* (funded initially by the Association) established itself as a major international journal. Moreover, in 2001 the Arts and Humanities Research Board (now Council) funded the foundation of the Research Centre for Irish and Scottish Studies at the University of Aberdeen, which expanded the range of the discipline through the comparative study of the two nations.

As this synoptic coverage of the past two decades suggests, the impulse to establish Irish Studies in Britain clearly gave rise to a number of significant developments. Yet now, at the beginning of the twenty-first century, the situation is one of limited, albeit capable, continuation rather than significant development. While the Centre at London Metropolitan University continues, as does the Institute in Liverpool, the degree programmes at St Mary's and Bath Spa have been progressively marginalised and threatened with closure. Irish Studies seminar series at the universities of London and Cambridge could be identified as signs of healthy regeneration, but the current funding-led crisis in British higher education effectively ensures that activities will be limited to small-scale events such as these, and occasional day schools and conferences organised by bodies such as the BAIS and the Women on Ireland Network. In such a context, the pressing questions in terms of the current state of Irish Studies in Britain are less to do with outputs and awards than with informing dynamics. In what, to return to Tom Paulin's 'credo', does Irish Studies believe?

One of the drivers behind Irish Studies in Britain was the political situation in Northern Ireland and its demand for an analysis that was both socially specific and historically and culturally wide-ranging. In this regard Irish Studies in Britain was dependent upon the political instability of at least part of its object of study, and a concomitant capacity to read that instability back into a fractured and divided culture across the island. The most obvious future implication of this approach is that as politics in Northern Ireland is distinguished less by violence than by standard democratic procedures, so the frisson of violence and transgression surrounding the discipline are correspondingly diminished. This is not to suggest that Irish Studies was, or needs to be, parasitic on catastrophe, but rather to argue that a discipline that does not occupy a guaranteed position at the heart of the academy needs to have a strong and immediate sense of purpose in order to engage both students and scholars in advancing its claims to relevance, rather than allowing it to become the Old Norse of contemporary academe.

As is clear from the above, a key force in the development of Irish Studies in Britain was the crisis in 'English', particularly as a discipline-specific engagement with theory pushed beyond text-bound limits into the complexity of history and politics. However, as Patrick O'Sullivan argued in 1997, this particular disciplinary driver finally failed to realise the stated goal of interdisciplinarity:

'Irish Studies', as it has emerged, is mostly literature – and a very limited canon at that – plus a bit of history – but mainly the bits of history that you need if you are to understand the literature [...]. These problems need not be as great as they seem to be – were it not that, for one reason or another, the study of literature has entered a strange hermetic and hermitic phase, which makes dialogue between the scholar of literature and other scholars [...] difficult. To say the least. (O'Sullivan, 1997)

Strikingly, while O'Sullivan saw Irish Studies as 'mesmerised' by the individual nation-state as rendered through one discipline, it was in the same year, 1997, that Terry Eagleton's 'The Ideology of Irish Studies' presented 'Ireland' as having become an all-purpose signifier that encompasses

on the one hand roots, belonging, tradition, *Gemeinschaft*, and on the other, again with marvellous convenience, exile, diffusion, globality, diaspora [...]. Irishness thus becomes a terrain on which some of the most typical, world-historical issues of our day can be seen to congregate. (Eagleton, 1997a: 11–12)

However, while Irish Studies in Britain might now be as limited in its range as O'Sullivan suggests, or as multiple in its interpretations as Eagleton argues, the social, political and cultural need for its presence is as strong as it was in the 1980s, at the moment of its formal emergence. Brenda Maddox's wide-ranging disparagement of Irish Studies in a 1996 *New Statesman* article denied its academic validity and asserted that it was 'riding the crest of a larger, more sinister wave known as "post-colonial studies". This is a politically correct vogue for elevating the grievances of newly independent nations to academic status' (Maddox, 1996: 21–2). This is a long way from the benign Arnoldianism of O'Driscoll's 1984 paper. Indeed, Maddox's questioning of 'Irishness' as a subject of serious study resonates with other, earlier evocations of the inferiority of the Irish, as pictured by *Punch* and analysed by L. P. Curtis (Curtis, 1971). Here we are verging on the depiction of Irish Studies as the refuge of the 'MOPE' ('most oppressed people ever'), the acronym by which Liam Kennedy sought to disparage the 'fatuous' claims for Ireland's postcolonial condition advanced by literary and cultural critics (Kennedy, 1996: 217).

Clearly, while the disputes within Irish literary studies might have subsided, the clashes of disciplines over their respective methodological superiority are as strong as ever, and full interdisciplinary cooperation remains unrealised. The degree-specific presence of Irish Studies has fluctuated as, paradoxically, its presence in key disciplines has multiplied, but the benign/malign misrepresentation and marginalisation of Ireland that it was formed to dispel has a continuing presence in academic debate, as has the acute question as to how, and by whom, Ireland's past and present can be most adequately represented. In her contribution to the 1985 Oxford conference, Mary Fitzgerald stressed that Irish Studies 'must now assemble the questions to which it must address itself' (Fitzgerald, 1985: 14). Irish Studies in Britain has made a major contribution to the clarification of the questions; providing the elusive answers is the challenge of the future.

NOTES

1. In recognition of the cultural diversity of Ireland's literature, the Association changed its name in the mid-1990s to IASIL: the International Association for the Study of Irish Literatures.

5

Teaching Irish Studies in Ireland: After the End

Michael Brown

The events of 28 July 2005 alter our perspective. If we are to believe the statements of intent, and all concerned pass this high test of character, the announcement by the Irish Republican Army that it will decommission its arms marks an end of the Troubles and, albeit less significantly, a defining moment in the Irish culture wars of the last 40 years. Perhaps this sanguine vision is deceptive and the protracted peace process will persist in being characterised by sporadic slides into crisis. If so, then this vision of an end to the culture wars will also deceive; but the moment is propitious for us to consider the nature of the intellectual dispute and its possible reconfiguration in the years ahead.

CONFRONTING THE CLASSROOM

I want to begin with an anecdote from my own classroom.[1] In the wake of a lecture where I had critiqued recent interpretations of the 1798 United Irish Rising, a visiting student approached me. She told me of how she had been taught one such approach at her home institution, by a prominent proponent of the thesis. She remarked that my lecture had pleased her precisely because she had always wondered what other views existed, and what criticisms might be made of the approach being offered. I tell this story not to cast aspersions on the teaching of my foreign-based colleague, but to highlight what is surely a crucial difference between the experience of teaching Irish Studies in Ireland and elsewhere. Outside Ireland, the common experience of teachers is that they are the sole member of staff in their department, perhaps even in their institution, interested in Irish matters. Thus they are a voice of authority, and are less likely to confront dissent in expounding their views. In contrast, the central fact of teaching Irish Studies in Ireland is that you are not alone; staff and students can and do offer up alternatives and criticise your stance from a position of informed commitment. The classroom is politicised by its very nature, so that a plurality of voices and a polyphony of interpretations are always present.

This fact makes the disjuncture between the interpretive content of Irish Studies and the experiences of many Irish students all the more perplexing. To caricature Irish Studies as practised in Ireland, it runs the danger of being considered insular, monochrome and temporally unambitious. It is insular in that Irish history often lacks any sense of the impact of external contexts; even Britain regularly remains an abstraction, seen only through the lens of an unchanging state. It is monochrome in its treatment of Irish society, perceiving it as divided into two great religious and political blocs – Protestant and Catholic; Anglo-Irish and Gaelic – giving little attention to other social categories or to comprehending the internal variations hidden beneath those hegemonic terms. Both of these tendencies are, to my mind, buttressed by the third characteristic, a tendency to concentrate on the period from the Act of Union of 1800 to the present day, to the detriment of earlier events. While these perceptions may be a result of my working in a history department, it seems to an outside observer that the hallowed triumvirate of Yeats, Joyce and Beckett similarly dominate the teaching of Irish literature in English, replicating the historical eclipse by obscuring earlier writers and trends.

Why is this so? At its simplest, it is a repercussion of the points' race that is an all-pervasive aspect of the Irish Leaving Certificate system that determines entry into third-level education. The very nature of this exam-based qualification produces an approach to education that favours recitation over revision, regurgitation of agreed truths over independent thought. It is education by rote. Secondly, we might apportion blame to a political vision of Ireland as predominantly rural, poor and populated by practising Catholics. It is surely of some import that the two historical events that attracted substantial state money in the past decade were the commemorative programmes surrounding the sesquicentenary of the Famine and the bicentenary of the 1798 Rising. One recollected the Ireland of rural poverty, the other the sectarian conflicts that germinated from a dysfunctional relationship with our nearest neighbour.

All this must strike the average Irish university student as strange, if not a little cloying in its romantic sentimentalisation of an untidy, often unpleasant, past. An eighteen-year-old student entering university in 2005 was a mere seven when the IRA called its first ceasefire; the Troubles do not impinge upon their consciousness in any direct way. They do not recall the mass migrations of Irish people to Britain and America that so marred the 1980s (our eighteen-year-old was born in 1987, the year Margaret Thatcher won her third successive British general election). Indeed, Ireland now experiences net immigration for the first time in its history. Nor does our Celtic cub remember the parching winds of poverty and unemployment that have long since been replaced by a sustained period of quite startling economic growth. Moreover, the fact that a majority of Ireland's population now lives in towns and cities renders versions of Irish pastoral increasingly anachronistic. In other words, political culture and our national tale no longer chime with the experience of our students. What should be done to bridge this gap? How might we reorient ourselves to engage the student body anew? And what might its experience tell us about what Irish Studies should be?

NARRATING IRISH STUDIES

For a long time after the achievement of Irish independence in 1922, the intellectual purpose of Irish Studies – though the term was not in use then – was clear: to define and defend the nation. Few men better epitomised this dual purpose than Eoin MacNeill, co-founder of the Gaelic League, chief of staff of the Irish Volunteers, first minister of education in the Irish Free State, professor of early Irish history at University College Dublin and the author of substantial scholarly works on the vexed period from the Norman invasion – which in the popular mind still marks the beginning of British imperial intervention in Ireland – to the Tudor age, when Ireland was declared a kingdom. Those who resisted this project found purpose in repeated acts of revision, opening up nationalist readings for scrutiny and reassessment. They were led by the revisionist preachers Robert Dudley Edwards and Theo Moody, proponents of a more thoroughly professional history, whose punctilious pronouncements found expression in the journal *Irish Historical Studies*, founded in 1938.

In the heat and intensity created by the eruption of the Northern Ireland Troubles in the late 1960s, and through the bitter and bloody 1970s and 1980s, the counterpoint of revisionism apparently warded off the demons of sectarianism and savagery, just as the melodies of nationalism seemed to summon them from the depths. But just as the national experience altered in the 1990s, so that decade complicated the apparent binaries of the nationalist–revisionist confrontation. Notably, the debate centred on an overt exercise in canon-creation:

the three-volume *Field Day Anthology of Irish Writing* published in 1991, with two further volumes added in 2002. Academics soon questioned the propriety of building such a monument to national identity at a time when much international energy was being directed towards the deconstruction and denuding of such grand architectural projects (Mulhern, 1998: 147–57). Importantly, the *Field Day Anthology* marked the ascendancy – the resonance of that word in an Irish context, where it is associated with the Anglo-Irish and not the Gaelic past, is worth remarking – of a postcolonial analytical perspective. Both the Field Day enterprise and the associated Critical Conditions series published by Cork University Press – projects sharing Seamus Deane as their general editor – espouse a vision of Irish culture forged within a colonial crucible. At once effecting and riding the back of a remarkable expansion in Irish Studies in the US, this thesis claimed that Ireland was not only worthy of scholarly attention, but demanded disproportionate attention because of its size and its status as an early and classic example of the colonial condition. Seen in this perspective, the country's historical experience foreshadowed and epitomised other nations' crises of incorporation into a global British Empire. In this vein, recent debate has been marked by the ritualistic publication of commemorative history, with substantial essay collections marking the bicentenary of both the United Irish Rising and the Act of Union (Bartlett *et al.*, 2003; Keogh and Whelan, 2001). Alongside these ventures lie two weighty mediations by Deane and Luke Gibbons on the most complex countervailing force of the 1790s, Edmund Burke, both of which portray him as an internal dissident who opposed the tyrannies of English, French and Ascendancy Irish imperial visions, making him a Jacobin in temperament if not in kind (Deane, 2005; Gibbons, 2003).

On occasion, such postcolonial claims to attention have been criticised for subsiding into a soft-focus neo-nationalism. The combustible and combative pronouncements of the historian Brendan Bradshaw, who declared that the scholarly pursuit of neutrality should be abandoned in favour of empathy for the 'catastrophic' aspect of the Irish historical experience (Bradshaw, 1994b: 215), have lately been overshadowed by the theoretically inspired readings of Declan Kiberd and Terry Eagleton, yet there remains a substantial subtext reconstructing and reclaiming a republican and non-sectarian vision of the nation. This often surfaces in the actual text, as when Kevin Whelan speaks of the 'redemptive potential' of his reading of the past (Whelan, 2001: 44). The period from 1798 to 1803 is a crucial battleground in the debate, not merely for its landmark events of rising, union and rebellion, but because the postcolonial vision of the Irish nation is consciously derived from the United Irishmen. As Whelan observes in the preface to *The Tree of Liberty*: 'Relieved of its oppressive weight the 1790s cease to be divisive, and become available in a fresh way, opening a generous space which has been artificially constricted' (Whelan, 1996: ix). It is intended to offer this republican, non-sectarian nation to unionist communities as a softer, kinder national identity. In turn, it is hoped that this might persuade them to shake off the shackles in their self-imposed false consciousness – to use old-fashioned Marxist terminology – and rediscover their Irish nature. In other words, that the Field Day project is undeniably culturally inclusive does not stop it developing a cultural politics in which unionism is made irrelevant.

The publication of the first three volumes of the *Field Day Anthology of Irish Writing* also marked the ascendancy of literature over history as the central discipline in Irish academic culture. Many historians, perplexed and puzzled by the postcolonial, postmodern and post-Marxist theories espoused therein, retreated, leaving the field to literary and cultural critics. In the face of this agenda-setting, the remaining revisionist residue was forced to redefine itself, and in doing so historians did more than merely effect an inelegant rearguard action. In the work of S. J. Connolly, Jacqueline Hill and T. C. Barnard a rather different reading of the contested eighteenth century emerged. Primarily, these authors responded by accentuating Ireland's correspondences with Europe, thereby resisting analogies with the native peoples of the Americas, Africa or Australia. In place of a colonial society they posited an *ancien régime*, organised through reciprocal privilege and duties, and at home with ethnic, if not religious, diversity. In literature, this shift in focus moved attention away from the national tale of Maria Edgeworth and the Celtic Twilight of Yeats and Lady Gregory towards Irish modernist writing and fresh readings of Wilde, Joyce and Beckett.

CIVIL SOCIETY

By the late 1990s, the old divisions had resurfaced, albeit in a new guise. Although the bombs had stopped exploding, the intellectual bombardment continued unabated. And now, in the immediate wake of the most recent IRA declaration, a moment of decision arises. How now do we begin again, after the end as it were, to refashion our past, our literature, our culture, our country? Two thoughts. First, if it is to flourish, Irish Studies must live in an open intellectual economy. We are a small community and we depend upon an international trade in ideas to spur local growth. We have benefited in recent decades from developments in critical theory and our increased consciousness of European and American academic trends, and there are still gains to be made. The New British History, first propounded by J. G. A. Pocock in the 1970s and now common practice among students of the seventeenth century, has as its central achievement the incorporation of Ireland into English understandings of their past (Pocock, 2005). The Irish, however, have remained relatively reluctant to accommodate regional variations and temporal developments within their analyses of the motives of British actors in Ireland's tale (Brady and Ohlmeyer, 2005). Historians have gained in thinking of 'the British problem', but if it shows anything it is that the British polity was a kind of accident, a construct as multiple and reductive as the nation-state (Bradshaw and Morrill, 1996). Thus, by thinking anew about Britain's internal complexity we can also rethink Ireland's. Projects to understand the Irish diaspora must be complemented by a reconsideration of the impact of émigré communities upon indigenous Irish culture. This is all the more necessary now that EU freedom of labour protocols have successfully diversified the Irish workforce, a fact increasingly reflected in the annual third-level student intake.

This leads me to my second consideration, which is that we must surely begin to consider our past, and its creative utterances, as a shared heritage in which violence devastated both communities, just as literature, art and culture enriched them. Irish, Anglo-Irish, Gaelic and Ulster-Scots literatures all germinated and grew alongside each other, oftentimes within the same artistic creation. Ireland has a deep and rich history of macaronic verse and of poetry written in local idioms, from *The Irish Hudibras* (1689), which features an English dialect of Tudor origin known as Fingalian, to the late eighteenth-century Ulster weaver poets, many of whom wrote in Ulster-Scots (Carpenter, 1998; Hewitt, 1974). Gaelic, it should also be remarked, has many regional manifestations, bowdlerised in the mongrel tongue of state-sponsored Irish, while its greatest literary exponents drew from diverse sources. To cite just one example: Brian Merriman's *The Midnight Court* (1780) not only draws from the wellspring of Gaelic aisling poetry, but also echoes the English pastoral verse of

Dryden and Pope and the bawdier elements of the French courtly love tradition.

In the face of these apparently contradictory injunctions – to internationalise and to localise our awareness – I want to add a third onerous task. We need to rethink ourselves out from under the theoretical umbrellas of the nation-state and empire. Ireland had a history long before their intervention and in capturing the complexity of our culture we might well be wary of their stark theoretical clarity. Given this, how then might we make sense of the polyphonic voices of our culture and our past? A proposition suggests itself. In rejecting the nineteenth-century dualisms of nation and empire, we can instead profitably interrogate other eras. The writings of Jonathan Swift and Laurence Sterne are not primarily shaped by national or imperial concerns, although criticism has been preoccupied by Swift's imaging of an Irish nation in the *Drapier Letters* (1724–5) and the colonial critique embedded in *Gulliver's Travels* (1726) (Fabricant, 2003; Hawes, 2004). So too, Sterne has been reclaimed as an Irish writer whose deconstructive imagination foreshadows Joyce and Flann O'Brien, becoming thereby a participant 'if not in *the* then at least in *one* Irish fictional tradition' (Campbell Ross, 1991: 684, original emphasis). Perhaps we have a moment in which their intellectual achievement and creative energy might be reassessed. Work situating Swift in the intellectual confluences of the early eighteenth century, or in relation to his religious investments, might offer fruitful avenues of approach (Fauske, 2002; Kelly, 2003). So might Jonathan Lamb's study of Sterne's debt to David Hume, which positions him neither as a heaven-taught Irish ploughman nor as an interloper in the English canon but as a vital figure in the Irish–Scottish nexus (Lamb, 1989). Perhaps even more significant is work done on the relationship between the writer and his marketplace, emphasising the mediation between the creative impulse and the capacity of civil society to disseminate ideas. In the case of Swift, Ann Cline Kelly has illustrated how he moved between polite and popular literature, and adopted authorial poses accordingly (Cline Kelly, 2002). Similarly, Thomas Keymer has shown how Sterne's perplexing masterpiece *The Life and Opinions of Tristram Shandy, Gentleman* (1759–67) emanated from a literary conversation with popular novels and humorous poetry of the 1760s (Keymer, 2002).

From this, a new theme emerges upon which we can play multiple variations. It is one scored in the eighteenth-century notation of civil society. At its simplest, civil society is where unrelated humans congregate for common purposes. Thus, it accommodates and displays difference, inscribes and revises itself in reflexive observation, and propounds a philosophy of politeness that precludes the intensities of uncivil war. It is at once, as the political philosopher Charles Taylor has noted, a location and a value system, a critical tool and a mode of life, a descriptive and a normative concept (Taylor, 1995: 208). And, importantly in this context, its habitat is not necessarily a nation-state or an empire; it can be found in both and in neither. Equally, it can provide for them too, placing them in relation to other organisational forms without utilising them as controlling metaphors. Mapped first by the Scottish literati of the eighteenth century, although its social origins are broader and deeper, the concept's potency was rediscovered by Eastern European dissidents under Communism (Keane, 1988, 1998). Those within it can topple kings and autocrats, or defend the validity of the status quo, but it is itself oblivious of political and religious convictions.

Thus, by disposing of our intellectual dependency on national and imperial contexts we can rethink the conundrum of sectarian conflict. The Field Day project was right to identify a need for a new meta-narrative that might do away with religious controversy, even if its admission of the nation-state as its controlling metaphor arguably doomed the project to unionist rejection from the start. So too, the revisionists were right to argue for a broadening of perspective on to a European plain, but they were too besotted with the grand project of European unification to see that the real alternative lay not in the state offices of Paris or Berlin but, less glamorously, in the coffee-shops of Prague and Warsaw.

INTO THE CLASSROOM

Given the challenge and the opportunity now opening for Irish Studies to re-imagine itself, what can be done in the classroom – the engine room of the discipline – to meet this objective? Two developments may help. First, the environment in which Irish Studies is taking place in Ireland is undergoing radical reform. Put at its simplest, many Irish universities are dismantling the old system of faculties in favour of a more decentralised model of administration based upon schools. Thus, old alliances and interest groups are being dissolved and new ones are being formed. This produces new challenges and new chances. The traditional relationship between departments of history and English, upon which Irish Studies was founded, is being threatened by their placement into distinctly competitive schools. In saying that, the importance of graduate and postdoctoral research centres maintaining dialogue should become clear. But equally, the possibility of intellectual interaction between colleagues in newly configured academic schools may lead to the emergence of fresh paradigms and methodologies. The formal relationship between history and art history, for example, offers the chance to explore Ireland's visual culture in a fully integrated fashion.

Interdisciplinarity, despite inherent dangers of eclecticism, offers a holistic understanding of Irish experience, combining and transcending the insights gleaned by the strict use of a single methodological approach. And it is in supporting interdisciplinary investigations within the university that technology has a role to play, mirroring its enabling role in the civil society beyond the bounds of academia. Moreover, this need not be limited to debate among the staff. Much more important in fact is the use of PowerPoint, the internet and related teaching technologies in the classroom. At its most basic, these tools enable us to convey information more easily and directly. PowerPoint, for example, allows complex comparisons to be made by visual means, so that multiple narratives can be illustrated and debated in the confines of a lecture or tutorial. With the use of the internet, such local dialogue can go global, allowing colleagues to trade ideas without the cost of travel. Irish Studies has much to gain from developing the use of virtual learning environments alongside more traditional face-to-face teaching methods. Nor should these developments be limited by geography or status; the system allows for global interaction at all levels of academia, breaking down the isolation of foreign-based Irish Studies scholars and the insularity of Irish-based scholarship.

Such technologies, used sensitively, can thus aid a dialogic model of teaching, enabling students to investigate Ireland's historical narrative for themselves. So too, the role of the academic is changing. No longer members of a priestly caste, enunciating truths and quelling disciplinary heterodoxies, they are now knowledgeable guides, inspiring and directing investigation into the past. The lecture itself has also evolved a new function as a focal point for a community of scholars to share their commitment to critical investigation. The tutorial becomes ever more important in this light. Although a costly means of disseminating knowledge, it is the heartbeat of the discipline, for only there, in the confines and comforts of a coterie of curious contemporaries, can students confidently articulate, test and temper their perceptions of the past. And given the capacity of the internet to host course-based chatrooms for students, neither geography nor cost is prohibitive.

MULTIPLE VOICES, CIVIL NARRATIVES

Just as I began, I want to end with an observation drawn from personal experience. In the late 1990s I offered a course on the European Enlightenment. Alongside a number of students from the Republic were two Northern Irish students, one from each side of the religious divide. But students also came from further afield. There was a Scot, two students from England and Germany, and one each from France, Italy, Spain and America. The regions that experienced the Enlightenment were thus represented virtually in full. What this highlights above all else is the changing character of the Irish classroom, which has become increasingly internationalised. And given the net immigration into the country in the last decade, the ethnic and cultural character of Irish universities is set to become even more diverse. The challenge of teaching this student body is intellectual as well as practical. Irish Studies must speak to these students if their imagination is to be sparked; equally, it must be prepared to have its own assumptions challenged. The two-way street that is the classroom has much to teach all within it, if we can find a language that resonates with our experience and with theirs. Civil society may provide just such a common tongue, allowing us to reinterpret our plural past, while giving students the conceptual tools to understand their present condition. The end has come, our Troubles may be gone, but even now the classroom hears new tunes.

NOTES

1. This chapter was written while I was Research Fellow in History at Trinity College Dublin

Part Two
Irish Studies in Critical Perspective

Part Two
Irish Studies in Critical Perspective

6

The Intellectual and the State: Irish Criticism Since 1980

Conor McCarthy

I

This chapter concerns critical authority, and the ways that critical authority has developed and changed in Irish criticism since the 1980s. The term *authority* is used here to refer to the position of the critic in his or her text regarding the work he or she is analysing; to the discursive location of the critic; to the critic's institutional location; and finally the relationship of all of these to the final source of authority in modern society, the state (Said, 1984). The case I wish to argue is that the political and economic condition of Ireland in the period in question has had a profound influence on the varieties of critical project – or the lack of variety – that have unfolded. The crucial matter, I think, is the fact that the 1970s witnessed a major *crisis of authority* in Irish society, North and South. At the turn of the 1970s, this was manifest in a number of forms, the most obvious of which was the recrudescence of violence in Northern Ireland, which culminated in the Bloody Sunday massacre in Derry in January 1972, and the consequent proroguing of the Stormont parliament: that is, the collapse of the Northern state. A few years earlier, the so-called 'Arms Crisis' in the Republic indicated the degree to which the Northern situation could affect the South, showing the extent to which the crisis in one state was both cause and effect of the crisis in the other. As Joe Cleary has argued, this is best understood as a shifting of the tectonic plates of the inter-state system of the British Isles, held in tension since 1922 but now released with alarming results (Cleary, 2002: 97–111). The point, then, is that these states had, since partition, developed or tried to develop sets of legitimating ideological and cultural narratives, and as the state system began to fracture, a palpable sense of crisis in the cultural and intellectual spheres emerged also (McCarthy, 2000: 11–44; McIntosh, 1999). This crisis of the state system was accompanied and augmented by economic slowdown. In the North, the crisis was partly precipitated by changes in the economic sphere that led to the erosion of Protestant privilege, thus narrowing the gap between the loyalist and nationalist working classes. As the Atlantic economy slowed during the 1970s, with the onset of the oil crises and the end of the great postwar boom, the situation in Ireland, both economic and political, only seemed to worsen.

In his *Prison Notebooks*, Antonio Gramsci writes with great insight on the crisis of authority affecting the state and civil society:

If the ruling class has lost its consensus, i.e. is no longer 'leading' but only 'dominant', exercising coercive force alone, this means precisely that the great masses have become detached from their traditional ideologies, and no longer believe what they used to believe previously, etc. The crisis consists precisely in the fact that the old is dying and the new cannot be born; in this interregnum a great variety of morbid symptoms appear. (Gramsci, 1971: 275–6)

What occurred in the Republic was a fracturing *within* the ruling class, revealed in 1970 when the Fianna Fáil government, led by Jack Lynch, was rent by accusations of conspiracy to import arms laid against three senior ministers, Charles Haughey, Kevin Boland and Neil Blaney. The charge was that these three had made up a 'government-within-the-government', a secret committee empowered to draw up policy and take action regarding the embattled nationalist minority across the border, and that they had sought illegally to import weapons to be smuggled into Northern Ireland. All three men were acquitted, but the fracture within state nationalism had been clearly and dramatically displayed.

This crisis of authority in the state system paralleled, even if it did not cause, the crisis of authority in literary and cultural criticism. It is worth distinguishing here between *criticism*, which is usually deemed to be concerned with relatively local and specific matters of description, exegesis and valorisation of cultural works, and *theory*, which is reckoned to deal with the challenging of existing or inherited forms of cultural authority. It is in the light of this formulation that one can perhaps look at the major theory/anti-theory divide that has occurred in Ireland over the last 20 years or so. For in Ireland, 'theory'[1] has meant chiefly postcolonial theory, as opposed to feminism, psychoanalysis, Marxism or post-Marxism, deconstruction or structuralism. This is because postcolonial theory has significant contributions to make to the rethinking of issues that have been troubling Irish humanist scholars for a long time before 'theory' appeared on the academic agenda, issues of national identity, the politics of modernisation and the role of narrative in history. But 'theory' and its emergence also have certain implications for the academy and the discipline of literary studies. 'Theory', we might say, is the meta-discourse of literary criticism, the discursive self-consciousness of the discipline. As such, it can have various manifestations – philosophical, methodological, ethical, political, institutional – through which, individually and collectively, the crisis of the discipline is figured. Here, I want to concentrate chiefly on the political and institutional areas most of all, and on the possible relationships between them, in order to explore how, in the light of the emergence of 'theory' in Irish academe – and the attendant crisis in literary criticism – the questioning of the state became an area of interest to literary scholars.

II

At the first 'New Voices in Irish Criticism' conference in Dublin in 1999, and then at greater length in his book *Irish Classics* (2000), Declan Kiberd produced a characteristically audacious formulation of the future of Irish criticism. Noting that Irish Studies, 'for all its hopes of academic objectivity, remains a crisis-driven discipline', he suggested that the nationalism/revisionism debate was finally over, thereby allowing for the possibility of a healthy, 'normal' criticism, which he welcomed (Kiberd, 2000: 620). This possibility was linked to the apparent end of the Northern Ireland conflict, as mapped out in the text of the Good Friday Agreement, which he regarded as a cultural document comparable to Charlotte Brooke's *Reliques of Irish Poetry* (1789): 'coded into it are many of the same ideas which animated people like Edgeworth and Carleton, Burke and MacDonagh' (Kiberd, 2000: 628). Containing as it does the disavowal of the Republic's constitutional claim to Northern Ireland, and the aspiration towards '"parity of esteem" for both languages and cultures', the Agreement amounts to a powerful rejection of 'political nationalism'. From this, Kiberd suggested, 'a truly comprehensive national culture may for the first time be born' (Kiberd, 2000: 630–1).

Kiberd's argument is among the latest – albeit the most ambitious and startling – in a series of commentaries, dating back to at least 1980, on the function of culture, and more specifically, criticism in Irish intellectual life. In fact, if we look carefully we will see that his suggestions have a substantial and varied lineage, and that throughout culture has always been prioritised over politics. For example, Seamus Deane (1986: 45–58) and John Wilson Foster (1991: 215–33), from their admittedly sharply differing viewpoints, both suggested nearly 15 years before Kiberd that the Northern crisis was one of language and criticism; that is to say, criticism has frequently figured the crisis in its own, literary-theoretical terms. Clearly, the conflict and criticism are related. The question facing us now is: what is the fate of criticism when the conflict is, or appears to be, coming to an end? To those who have lived through it 'bomb by bomb', the notion that one might regret the dissipation of the energy that the conflict gave to academic debate will doubtless seem repellent. Yet perhaps there is something more complicated involved in this conjuncture. What the end of the nationalism/revisionism debate might mean is the end of a context in which certain modes of criticism tended to be openly *contestatory* or *oppositional*. For if the Northern crisis is ending, at least in terms of open paramilitary and military violence, then what we are witnessing is a fundamental resettling of the system of inter-state relationships that was put in place at the time of partition.

This, of course, is a rather crude formulation. The Good Friday Agreement is what Brendan O'Leary terms a 'consociational' treaty, a delicate structure designed to balance and nuance various political aspirations and desires between the poles of movement and stasis, narrative and repetition (O'Leary, 1999). It is not merely a partitionist treaty; nor yet is it simply the slippery slope to some form of united Ireland. The point is that it tries to contain the forces that would effect violent or fundamental change to the inter-state structure of the British Isles. To that extent, the two states, British and Irish, are no longer in question. To put it less dramatically, one of the crucial elements of the 1922 settlement, the border, has not shifted, though the aim is to have it criss-crossed by a network of organisations promoting cultural relations, tourist initiatives, business enterprises, educational cooperation and so forth. But with the removal of the so-called 'territorial claim' from *Bunreacht na hÉireann*, and the acceptance by the republican movement of a Stormont legislature, the constitutional stability produced in and by the Irish Free State and the Northern Irish state has been locked in place.

III

In his 1991 essay 'States of Ireland' Liam O'Dowd suggested that while there had been much Irish social scientific writing on the subject of statehood, all too little of it had problematised either the Northern or the Southern states as such. This, he argued, resulted in a potentially unhistorical attitude to the state, whereby it becomes naturalised as a unit of research. The risk is then that researchers become 'unwitting and tacit ideologists for existing states, thereby obscuring the way in which states are constructed, maintained and challenged' (O'Dowd, 1991: 98). As O'Dowd says, this neglect is all the more remarkable when one considers the various and forceful ways in which state formations on the island of Ireland have been and continue to be challenged, whether by internal or external militant subversion, the political agency of EU laws and structures, the economic imperatives of multinational capital or by migration. This history ought to teach us that all states are radically contingent and dynamic, but part of the problem is the recent origins of the two state formations in Ireland, and the violence of those origins. Max Weber famously defined the state as the agency that has the monopoly on the legitimate deployment of violence in a society, though no state likes to admit this openly, as to do so is to expose that legitimacy to question.

To O'Dowd's warning one might append Edward Said's argument that all cultural production and intellectual activity takes place on terrain fundamentally mapped and regulated by the state (Said, 1984). Said's point is that culture and criticism are at base related to authority, and that in Western modernity, the central origin of authority is the state. This relationship may be more or less mediated, more or less obscured, but it is present nevertheless. Said derives this formulation from a typically unusual conjoining of Gramsci and Matthew Arnold. In another essay, 'Secular Criticism', he shows how, for Arnold, culture was very much a force for and of the state; it was the best that was known and thought by humankind, and the state was its institutional manifestation. So a triumphant and dominant culture is a form of hegemony. Thus, the power of culture is potentially that of the state itself, so that for an intellectual or writer to have the honorific title of 'culture' conferred upon his or her work is to be endowed with an authority originating in the state.

Said goes on to suggest that the coincidence of state authority and cultural legitimacy results in a sense of centrality, confidence, community, belonging and 'home' for the writer. Conversely, to fall outside this legitimate culture is to be 'homeless', irrational, anarchic; to be without, or beyond, representation. Thus, the processes by which certain practices are deemed culturally legitimate are as much a matter of exclusion as of inclusion (Said, 1984: 10–11). David Lloyd puts it even more forcefully: 'To the monopoly of violence claimed by the state [...] corresponds the monopoly of representation claimed by the dominant culture' (Lloyd, 1993: 4). Furthermore,

Control of narratives is a crucial function of the state apparatus since its political and legal frameworks can only gain consent and legitimacy if the tale they tell monopolizes the field of probabilities. The state does not simply legislate and police against particular infringements, it determines the forms within which representation can take place. Access to representation is accordingly as much a question of aesthetics as of power or numbers, and not to be represented often as intrinsically a function of formal as of material causes. (Lloyd, 1993: 6)

The point, then, is that intellectual and aesthetic activity are of interest to the state, since culture is one of the means by which, on the one hand, the state fleshes itself out – in Gramscian terms, *elaborates* itself – while on the other, culture is the realm in which ideological alternatives to the status quo originate. This assertion foregrounds the location of cultural and intellectual activity, and begs the key question regarding any 'art-for-art's-sake' notion of the autonomy of culture from the vulgar encroachments of the economy or the state: how has that autonomy been won and maintained?

This question has become all the more insistent in the period since 1980, though the origins of the problem can be traced to a much earlier time. Looking back to the Irish Free State in the 1940s, many of today's dominant cultural institutions simply did not exist then. The Arts Council, Aosdána, tax breaks for artists, writer-in-residence schemes – these were all developments of the postwar decades (Brown, 2004: 254–96). They were accompanied by the creation of RTÉ television, the relaxation of censorship, the expansion of education, and the rebirth of an indigenous publishing industry in the 1960s. Indeed, the public sphere altered radically during and after the Lemass era of liberalisation and 'modernisa-tion', transforming the terrain on which intellectuals engaged with society. Further, the declaration of the Republic of Ireland in 1949 and the country's withdrawal from the Commonwealth represented the dramatic culmination of the project of statist nationalism. But this culmination was also a period of declining economic fortunes and flooding emigration, the onset of the acknowledged failure of autarkic development. It could be said, therefore, that the high-water mark of the ideology of national self-determination and self-development was also the moment of its ensuing collapse.

In the 1940s Sean O'Faolain had been able (albeit eventually despairingly) to exhort readers of *The Bell* to contribute both critical prose and creative writing to what he called 'your magazine'. In this way, he was appealing to a version of what we might call the classical public sphere (Habermas, 1989). By this I mean that O'Faolain's appeal is subtended by a set of assumptions about the journal, its authors, its readership and its mode of addressing that readership. The public sphere, as theorised by Habermas and as developed by writers as different as Terry Eagleton (1984), Nancy Fraser (1989), Oskar Negt and Alexander Kluge (1993), lies between the state and civil society. It is a discursive realm, a subject's entry to which is predicated on the rationality and temperate character of the statements she or he makes there. Originally in seventeenth-century England, and also in O'Faolain's discourse, the public sphere was a place where an enlightened public opinion could be formed and eventually forged into a powerful – because rational – critique of the authority of the state.

The Lemass period (1959–66), however, was to see a radical alteration of this version of intellectual community, as the state began to expand in a less symbolic, more pervasive manner through investment in education and economic planning, and to move towards membership of the European Economic Community. O'Dowd offers the most useful account of the intellectual ramifications wrought by these changes. He points out how the evacuation from the national revolution of a significant class or social content, most especially through the land reforms culminating in the 1903 Wyndham Act, produced a conservative revolutionary elite, more concerned with the transfer of sovereignty than the redistribution of wealth (O'Dowd, 1988). So if issues of social justice and equality were being met by the government of the colonial power, the intellectuals of the national revolution were most likely to advance the new state's claim to difference on the grounds of cultural distinctiveness. This class had mostly been born into this new post-land reform economic dispensation, and its members were thus little disposed to question it. The result was that post-revolutionary intellectuals, whether those critical of the new status quo such as O'Faolain and Frank O'Connor or those closer to it such as Daniel Corkery, focused principally on matters of cultural identity. The economic sphere was left to those O'Dowd calls, after Foucault, 'specific intellectuals': government policy-makers and technocrats. Criticism therefore became a matter of exposure rather than of radical structural analysis.

This separation of spheres had various effects. In the intellectual arena, it allowed the chief quarrel of Irish literary criticism and of other humanistic disciplines to remain caught up in the remorseless undertow of a politics of identity – or, if you prefer, 'a rhetoric and politics of blame' (Said, 1993: 19) – that is, in what we now call the revisionism debate between nationalists, alleged nationalists and anti-nationalists. More specifically, the disjunction between the material and the cultural spheres inhibited the emergence of a critical intellectual Marxism in Cold War Catholic Ireland that might have interrupted and productively disrupted this quarrel. Consequently, we find the analysis of the material base dominated by economists, journalists, media pundits, policy-makers, administrators and European technocrats in the Lemass era and the decades that followed. This was, in effect, the Irish variant of the emergence of what Alvin Gouldner (1979) called the 'New Class' of professional intellectuals, in contrast to amateurs like O'Faolain and his allies. The overarching theoretical framework of these intellectuals was the theme of modernisation, chiefly understood in the terms of post-1945 American 'modernisation theory', a functionalist modular theory of development that saw industrialisation and technology as engines of progress, and the increasing convergence of societies, on a broadly North American model, as the end result. This convergence would be visible in the structure and division of labour, and borne out by the replacement of ideological struggle by bureaucratic bargaining, as social conflict changed from being about the fundamental nature of society to being about internal checks and balances.

Such modernisation was not only seen as the best explanatory framework for Irish society and politics; in its emphasis on meritocracy rather than charisma as the marker of leadership it also served as an agreeably self-justifying discourse for precisely those intellectuals who were both products and producers of this new arrangement (Clancy et al., 1986).[2] In his 1989 study of twentieth-century Ireland J. J. Lee noted the rise of a kind of economism of public discourse in the 1970s and the 1980s, a reification of political, social and cultural debates into the crude logic of profit and loss. What Lee fails to highlight, however, is the degree to which this economism was couched in the terms of the neoclassical models favoured by Irish academic economists. This perhaps should not surprise us, especially if we accept Tom Nairn's formulation of modernisation theory as an undialectical non-contestatory materialism. Thus, it has taken disciplinary outsiders such as Raymond Crotty (1986) and Peadar Kirby

(1997), political geographers such as Jim MacLaughlin (1994), and sociologists such as Denis O'Hearn (1998), Kieran Allen (2000) and O'Dowd himself to argue the usefulness of development economics and political economy in understanding the contemporary Irish economic situation.

Within university departments of English, a proximate form of literary or aesthetic functionalism was being practised during this same period. The dominant critical mode in 1960s Ireland was a *mélange* of Leavisism and American New Criticism, notably embodied in the powerful figure of Denis Donoghue at University College Dublin. Such critical approaches can reasonably be described as functionalist: both are principally concerned with the internal workings of a text, and rigidly exclude historical context. Both, moreover, combine a putatively non-ideological *method* with a quasi-religious Arnoldian cultural-ideological *project*, while insisting that literature is neither the realm of ideas nor of politics. More to the point, perhaps, this differentiation of spheres has facilitated the continuing idealism of Irish criticism. So when, to take one notable example, Terence Brown traces the attitudes of Field Day polemicists such as Deane, Kiberd and Richard Kearney back to Yeats and Joyce, through Thomas Kinsella, O'Faolain, O'Connor, C. P. Curran, Thomas MacGreevy and the ethnic nationalism of Corkery, he is not concerned to note that, in spite of their espousal of Joyce's egalitarianism and pluralism, they are pursuing a politics as *textual* as that of their supposedly reactionary forebears (Brown, 1988: 77–90). Such is the persistence of idealist polarities in modern Irish criticism, whether they be sectarian or ethnic.

IV

The strength of this idealist heritage is demonstrated even more powerfully when one examines the major innovative cultural-theoretical project in Ireland in the period immediately preceding the 1980s: the journal *The Crane Bag*, instituted and edited by the Benedictine Mark Patrick Hederman and the philosopher Richard Kearney. *The Crane Bag* first appeared in 1977 and quickly acquired as contributors all of the major figures in Irish humanistic intellectual life, among them Deane, Kiberd, Lee, Conor Cruise O'Brien, Edna Longley, W. J. McCormack, Dorothy Walker, Louis Le Brocquy and Anne Madden. Published twice-yearly, it ranged widely over Irish life and culture; literature, visual art, film, philosophy, social thought and political theory were all discussed in its pages. This interdisciplinary emphasis was bold and new, as was the journal's non-academic determination that culture was a matter important enough to warrant attention from the broader public sphere. McCormack has suggested that the magazine 'displayed a pluralism of approach going beyond generosity to begin to resemble hesitancy. Or caution' (McCormack, 1986: 50). Yet *The Crane Bag*'s fundamental philosophical underpinnings were very far from these apparently worldly concerns, derived as they were from the phenomenological tradition. The journal's opening manifesto was expressed in somewhat Heideggerian terms:

The Crane Bag [...] is not a tangible object. It exists only as a metaphor or symbol. [...] The full 'content' of the symbol cannot be expressed in other words. There can be no definitive exegesis. [...] *The Crane Bag* is a container rather than a content in itself. [....]

The Crane Bag is really a place. It is a place where even the most ordinary things can be seen in a peculiar light, which shows them up for what they really are. There must be a no-man's land, a neutral ground where things can detach themselves from all partisan and prejudiced connection and display themselves as they are in themselves. (Hederman and Kearney, 1977: 3–4)

One of *The Crane Bag*'s defining concerns was with the nature and function of 'myth' in Irish society, as the contributions of Kearney, Hederman and some others demonstrated. This preoccupation was related to a kind of psychohistory – the journal was characterised by an express wish to plumb the 'depths' of the Irish psyche in order to release whatever negative mythic legacy was there sedimented – and had definite effects on the analyses offered. There was, for example, a comprehensive evasion of material or structural factors in the journal's critique of Irish culture and society in favour of a marked emphasis on 'identity' and a concomitant wish to explain the Northern crisis in terms of clashing identities. Allied to this was a Manichaean opposition between regressive tradition – generally held to be characterised by 'atavism' – and progressive modernity, typically conceived in terms of Enlightenment values. But the concept that lay at the core of the magazine's cultural programme was that of the 'fifth province', defined as the meeting-point of the four historical provinces of Ireland, seen as either the geographical county of Meath or a Euclidian punctual space. This non-political space was concep-tualised as a counterweight to Tara, the centre of political power in ancient Ireland.[3] As the editors explained:

It seems clear to us that in the present unhappy state of our country it is essential to restore this second centre of gravity in some way. The obvious impotence of the political attempts to unite the four political and geographical provinces would seem to indicate another kind of solution, another kind of unity, one which would incorporate the 'fifth' province. This province, this place, this centre, is not a political position. In fact, if it is a position at all, it would be marked by the absence of any particular political and geographical delineation, something more like a disposition. (Hederman and Kearney, 1977: 4)

The function or value of such a space was as a locus of reconciliation – it would be 'the place where all oppositions are resolved' – and finding it was the role of artists and poets:

Thus, the constitution of such a place would mean that each person must discover it for himself within himself. Each person would have to become a seer, a poet, an artist. The purpose of *The Crane Bag* is to promote the excavation of unactualized spaces within the reader, which is the work of constituting the fifth province. From such a place a new understanding and unity might emerge. (Hederman and Kearney, 1977: 4)

This, of course, is the language of the Romantic aesthetic: an idealist and idealised zone of reconciliation between subject and object, where the divided self can be reunited and thus empowered to act back upon the world. One crucial problem with such a formulation is its aestheticist tendency, its wish to see the aesthetic as a zone of compensation for the rough games of the economic and political worlds. Another is that, in the act of plumbing the 'depths' of the mythologies and 'atavisms' of nationalism, unionism and other Irish 'traditions', *The Crane Bag* was always already presupposing the philosophical ground it purported to investigate. The journal, that is, was clearly indebted to the Romantic aesthetics and politics it wished to analyse.

The Crane Bag eventually collapsed under the burden of its own contradictions and those of Irish public intellectual discourse. Deprived of Arts Council funding because of an interview with Seamus Twomey, then Chief of Staff of the Provisional IRA, the journal closed itself down in 1985, just as it showed signs of shaking off the invidious legacy of identity thinking, with its 'special issues' on development, ideology and Latin America. But its idealism and culturalism had already found a new outlet in the Field Day project, an altogether more ambitious scheme for cultural investigation and renewal (Richtarik, 1994). Field Day started as an ad hoc theatre touring company, assembled in 1980 by Brian Friel and Stephen Rea to bring Friel's *Translations* to provincial venues around the country. It soon instituted its pamphlet series, which initially drew on the talents of such *Crane Bag* alumni as Kiberd and Kearney, and later imported three major Anglo-American literary theorists, Eagleton, Said and Fredric Jameson.

Yet in spite of its practical experience of running a theatre company and publishing work by the two most influential Anglophone Marxist literary critics of recent times, Field Day remained a resolutely idealist/culturalist operation. Seamus Deane, the most intellectually coherent and forceful of its major figures, argued that the Northern problem, while a 'colonial crisis', was also '[i]n a basic sense [...] stylistic. That is to say, it is a crisis of language – the ways in which we write it and the ways in which we read it' (Deane, 1986: 46). The exposure of the stereotypes that were both symptomatic and causative of this crisis were central to the company's mission, working within the established discourse of identity and retaining an interest in unearthing the 'fifth province'. Friel suggested as much in a 1982 interview when he argued that the company was adumbrating 'a cultural state, not a political state' out of which 'a possibility of a political state follows' (O'Toole, 1982: 21). This formulation reconfirms the Romantic basis of the thinking behind both *The Crane Bag* and Field Day; it could even have been quoted from Schiller's *On the Aesthetic Education of Man*. And while Field Day's dramatic productions were unusual in their willingness to deal with ideas, it must be said that they were formally highly conventional. Further, the company's major publishing venture, *The Field Day Anthology of Irish Writing*, is a magnificent but essentially academic achievement (Bourke *et al.*, 2002; Deane, 1991).

V

My argument, then, is that the separation of intellectual spheres in Ireland has allowed a pervasive idealism to suffuse literary and cultural criticism. This separation is all the more regrettable when one considers that the theoretical mode that has recently seemed most powerfully applicable to the Irish situation, and the one that was placed firmly on the agenda by the Field Day Company and its confederates, is 'the postcolonial'. Postcolonial approaches to Irish culture have found rich and varied expression not only in the work of Deane, but also in Kiberd's (1995) ebullient Fanonian history of Irish literature since the Revival; in David Lloyd's (1993, 1999) highly elaborated theoretical investigations of the fragmentary and the marginal in Irish writing, which draws on Walter Benjamin and the Indian subaltern studies project; in Luke Gibbons's (1996) astonishingly fertile and varied work that spans film, literature, mass culture and the visual arts, but returns most frequently to the disinterring of alternative modes of Enlightenment thinking; in John Wilson Foster's (1991) eccentric reading of Albert Memmi which, coming from outside the Field Day orbit, posits Northern loyalist identity as being under threat from the nationalist South; and in the recent work of younger scholars such as Joe Cleary (2002) on partition, Gerry Smyth (1998) on criticism and Colin Graham (2001) on the 'deconstruction' of Irish identities. Yet in all of this work there has been almost no engagement with Irish political economy, with the varieties of economic as well as political dependence we find in both the Republic and the Northern statelet. It is this absent context that explains why, for example, Graham is wide of the mark when he suggests that the postcolonial theorist most congenial to Kiberd would be Aijaz Ahmad (Graham, 1996). What this claim fails to take account of is the fundamental disparity between Ahmad's orthodox and economistic Marxism and Kiberd's culturalism and textualism, his ascription to creative artists of the power to shape the nation and society through their discourse.

Whatever distaste Ahmad's attacks on figures such as Rushdie, Bhabha and, most notably, Said may engender, his work has been salutary in its placing of political economy, and the political economy of criticism, firmly back on the agenda. But if one looks at the work of the Irish 'postcolonial' critics named above, one does not find any explicit engagement with development economics or with the issue of development conceived in wider sociological or political terms, with the exception of Gibbons who teaches in the area of cultural studies. In fact, it fell to David Cairns and Shaun Richards to read contemporary Irish culture within the framework of dependent development in *Writing Ireland* (1988), one of the earliest and most theoretically explicit contributions to this debate, written from the perspective of British post-Williamsite cultural materialism. Even then, the narrative of cultural history they provide has its *telos* in the Northern conflict, as if it were from the North that the crisis of development in the Republic can best be understood. Of course, in a way this is true, since the Northern crisis served to expose the ambivalences of Southern partitionism, notably, the reluctance to allow Southern economic, political or social stabilities to be affected by relationships with Northern unionists or nationalists. To that extent, the Northern conflict also served as an awkward reminder of the disjuncture between the legitimating state nationalism of the Republic and its desire to protect its own borders. The isolated figure of Conor Cruise O'Brien apart, it has fallen to Northern writers and critics, whether nationalist or unionist, to provide a critique of the Southern dispensation.

The point is, therefore, that for all the variety and intelligence of the work of Deane, Kiberd and Lloyd, and those who have followed in their wake, we find them still engaged chiefly with the literary and the superstructural, with the discourses of the nation rather than the structures of the state. The idealisations of identity thinking (or their negation) continue to preoccupy them, as opposed to the material institutions that produce and benefit from such thinking. This represents a clear continuity with, rather than a radical break from, the modes of criticism such writers might have aspired to overcome. That said, it is nevertheless true that postcolonial theory offers a more properly dialectical mode of negotiating between modernity and tradition than the nationalist Zhdanovism of Daniel Corkery or the Arnoldian New Criticism of Edna Longley or the revisionism of historians such as F. S. L. Lyons and R. F. Foster.[4] It is also true to say that Lloyd's work has issued in the most searching analysis Irish criticism has yet produced of the role culture plays in producing citizen-subjects of the nascent or emergent postcolonial state. However, his work has concentrated on the subaltern and the fragment, issues that fall beyond the coercive or representational capacity of the state, to the extent that one senses that he dismisses the state as a site of struggle altogether.[5]

More recent work by Joe Cleary (2002) and Ray Ryan (2002) focuses more on what Said called the cultural 'elaboration' of the state, the way that cultural forms may give expression to the fundamental ideas of the state: 'culture serves authority, and ultimately the national State, not because it represses and coerces but because it is affirmative, positive, and persuasive' (Said, 1984: 171). But what all these tendencies lack, and what makes them vulnerable to the charge of producing what Said called 'oppositional debate without real opposition', is, in Marxist terms, a theorisation of the relationship between base and superstructure, and the Lukácsian idea of totality (Said, 1984: 160). By the former I mean an attempt to provide a critical sociology of cultural production as it relates to the forces and relations of production in the era of the Celtic Tiger. By the latter I mean that revolutionary apprehension of an entire economic and cultural system *as a system*, in the manner famously described by Lukács (1971). The risk is that the variously inflected forms of criticism practised by our most intelligent critics are no more attuned to flushing out the Saidian 'affiliations' between literature, economy and the state than Leavisite or New Critical 'close readings'. Further, the very intensity of the debate tends to disguise the institutional normality and normalisation of the work produced by critics on either side, a state of affairs that, for example, allows Terry Eagleton (1997b) to point out the obsession of both the 'liberal' Joep Leerssen and the 'radical' Seamus Deane with concepts such as national character and ethnic stereotyping in their work.

This situation is all the more extraordinary when one takes account of the fact that, in the moment of the Celtic Tiger, cultural and intellectual production has become more imbricated with capital than ever. Now that the Tiger has proven to be a transient visitor, critics have begun to take stock of what it has meant as an historical phase, an economic moment and a cultural turn. To date, most studies of the new economy have been uncritical, whether of the Left or the Right, with a couple of notable exceptions.[6] This serves to point up one of the most striking elements of the current situation: the disappearance of politics as we have known it since the inception of the state. By this I mean that the two great issues that confronted the independent Irish state – the 'national question' and the economy – have ceased to be areas of serious contention. All significant political parties are agreed as to the developmental path the Republic is set upon: creating an export-led, high-technology economy based on foreign capital investment. Few stand outside this neo-liberal economic consensus. Equally, all political parties are agreed that the Good Friday Agreement provides the solution to that aberration in the inter-state system in these islands that was the Northern Ireland conflict. Further, the form of corporatism that is now known as 'social partnership' has largely evacuated whatever Left and Right splits there ever were in Irish politics. The system of forging national agreements, which involve not only the government but also trade unions, major lobby groups and business organisations, has had the effect of making conventional party politics increasingly irrelevant. This change has implications for the politics of cultural debate, and for the public sphere into which that debate sometimes spills.

The crucial matter here is the interpenetration of culture and economy. The sociologist Michel Peillon has pointed out that we have moved from a position whereby the sphere of culture offers a vantage point from which a social critique can be mounted, to one where culture is so invested with capital that, as Adorno and Horkheimer predicted, a great deal of it offers little more than 'enlightenment as mass deception' (Adorno and Horkheimer, 1979). This situation has profound implications for the elaboration of any critical project, whether that be of the Left or the Right, whether in the service of Arnoldian humanism or Foucauldian anti-humanism or whether it be advanced by New Critical aestheticism or Marxist ideology-critique. It means that any revivalist model of the literary/ intellectual avant-garde is now hopelessly outdated, as is the liberal identity-critique offered by writers such as O'Faolain and his allies in *The Bell*. Instead, we have writers who rarely take positions of public dissent, which means that the public sphere is dominated not by writer-intellectuals but by celebrity pundits – Conor Cruise O'Brien, Kevin Myers, Fintan O'Toole – of the kind Regis Debray has described in France. These figures are highly competent media 'commentators', more at home in a television studio or the pages of a mass-circulation newspaper than in any erudite journal. Culture, in short, has been collapsed into economy, high culture into mass culture, and commentary into literature.

As a structural concomitant of this reification of the public sphere, we now have the institutionalisation of a distinctly attenuated notion of theory. The subjection of the public sphere to the most crudely commercial and instrumental imperatives has been paralleled by the corporatisation and professionalisation of theory itself. The result is, arguably, the further *de-politicisation* of criticism. One mark of the condition of a discipline is the emergence of the 'reader', the collection of 'important essays', which gives student and teacher alike a handy repository of material for easy reference, but which also stands as a freeze-frame image of a rapidly flowing stream. Claire Connolly's *Theorizing Ireland* (2003) is the first such reader of Irish criticism, bringing together work by some of the most familiar voices – Deane, Gibbons, Lloyd, Eagleton – and slightly less prominent or newer ones – Cleary, Graham, Richards, Christopher Morash, Richard Kirkland, Clair Wills, Angela Bourke and Patricia Coughlan. What is notable are the form and assumptions underlying the collection. The first thing to be said is that such a book represents a kind of 'coming of age' of Irish Studies: it implies that there now exists a substantial body of work in cultural theory regarding Ireland, and that this has achieved institutional prominence and stability. The key question, however, is whether such 'maturity' is simply an achievement to be celebrated or a development requiring critical interrogation. After all, there is an unacknowledged Whig narrative that underpins such 'progress', which sits oddly with the professed anti-foundationalist and anti-teleological impulse of much current cultural and literary theory.

It is interesting to note, then, the exorbitance of literary and cultural theory implied in this reader. All of its contributors, save the extraordinarily versatile Gibbons, are primarily literary critics. This suggests that literary/cultural work has monopolised the entire field constituted by 'theorizing Ireland'; there are no sociologists, historians, political theorists, anthropologists, geographers, philosophers or political economists in the collection. But literary and cultural theory is not the only kind that the humanities in Ireland have absorbed, nor indeed the first. As I mentioned earlier, modernisation theory and structural functionalism were important forces in Irish sociology in the 1960s and 1970s, and also informed historiography, economics and political science. Irish Studies, we are fond of telling ourselves, is an interdisciplinary field but unsurprisingly, the old disciplinary boundaries die hard. Perhaps as a consequence, *Theorizing Ireland* contains little evidence of meta-disciplinary reflection; the issue of disciplinarity itself is ignored, as are the institutional locations in which this 'theorizing' takes place. It is surely striking, though hardly unusual, that a volume dedicated to 'theorizing Ireland' should contain no examination of the grounds of its own possibility.

The absence of non-literary/cultural work in the collection also implies that 'theorizing Ireland' began only when 'theory', in the sense of the intellectual formation that is now everywhere found in Anglophone literature departments, arrived in Ireland. This reveals the assumption that, say, New Criticism or Leavisism had no conception of what 'Ireland' was. It is to assume also that a Kantian or empiricist aesthetic has no broader conception of the relationship of culture and society, and it is to neglect entirely a journal such as *The Crane Bag*, which was, as we have seen, replete with 'theory'. This seems to point to a rather unhistorical notion as to what 'theorizing Ireland' might involve. After all, an apparently 'untheoretical' critic such as Edna Longley has offered a highly articulated model of the relationship between Irish culture and society in her famous polemic 'Poetry and Politics in Northern Ireland' (Longley, 1986: 185–211). It seems short-sighted, therefore, to assume that 'theorizing Ireland' can only be accomplished with the assistance of 'theory'. Furthermore, contemporary 'theory' provides opportunities for valuable rearticulations of criticism of an older generation: it would be fascinating, for example, to reread Vivian Mercier's *The Irish Comic Tradition* (1962) in the light of Bakhtin's *Rabelais and his World* (1965). Equally, it seems odd to assume that Corkery or O'Faolain were without theoretical resources. The point is that one has only to scratch the surface of our contemporary arguments to find these much older figures lurking beneath. In the context of various critical historicisms, it seems a mistake not to historicise criticism itself.

VI

The sociologist Desmond Bell noted in the late 1980s that contemporary Irish historical experience was marked by a series of absences:

Such are the contradictions of Irish modernisation that we have prematurely entered the postmodern era. We are experiencing for example – in the sphere of economic ideology, 'monetarism' without a prior social democracy; in politics a 'new right' without an old left, 'postnationalism' with the national question materially unresolved; at the social level, a return to 'family values' without the advances of feminism; at the cultural level, the nostalgia and historicist pastiche of 'post-modernism' without the astringent cultural purgative of modernism. We are entering the future, as some wag has commented, walking backwards. (Bell, 1988: 229, original emphasis)

One can freely concede the datedness of this formulation (and the fact that Bell's 'wag' was surely Walter Benjamin) while noting that, in the sphere of Irish criticism, it holds that the emphasis has passed to ethnicity, gender and sexual orientation as analytical categories, without a Marxist criticism having ever been experienced, and that the category of social class is one that has little critical currency (Benjamin, 2003). The danger, therefore, is that postcolonial theory could turn, if it has not already turned, into merely one more intellectual subject-position in the academic ideological state apparatus. Criticism once again validates the terrain of discussion – which, as Said reminded us, is demarcated by and suffused with the authority of the state – by demonstrating that terrain's capacity to contain and recuperate a dose of 'radical' theory. This is true whether criticism is defending nationalism from revisionists or scouring its discursive recesses for radical traces that can be blown out of the continuum of history in some Benjaminian gesture. Therefore, critical theory of culture in Ireland must find a way to question that very terrain, to articulate itself with a critical theory of the state and of the economy, if it is not to repeat the gestures of the debate it fancies itself as deconstructing.

This task is made more urgent still by the sense that the Irish university sector, like many others in the West, is undergoing profound changes. Its shifting role leads us to conclude that the internal crisis represented by the 'theory' wars is in fact a structural analogue of the wider external crisis. This crisis has been named by Bill Readings as the 'ruin' of the university, whereby the decline of the nation-state leads to a decline in its socio-cultural mission. As he puts it: 'the University is becoming a different kind of institution, one that is no longer linked to the destiny of the nation-state by virtue of its role as producer, protector, and inculcator of an idea of national culture' (Readings, 1996: 3). Accordingly, the centrality of the traditional humanistic disciplines in the self-definition of the university is no longer assured. More sweepingly, 'the University [...] no longer participates in the historical project for humanity that was the legacy of the Enlightenment: the historical project of culture' (Readings, 1996: 5). Into the void left by 'culture' rushes the model and the rhetoric of 'excellence': the university as corporate technocratic centre of knowledge-production for the market, with the attendant apparatuses of 'research assessment', 'quality assurance' and the consequent burgeoning of a new management/ administrative stratum.

The specifically Irish version of the changes Readings analyses is expressed in *The University Challenged* (2001), Malcolm Skilbeck's report on the tertiary education sector, which advocates a wholehearted acceptance by Irish universities of the corporate model Readings describes. What is striking is that this report emerged at the same moment as Declan Kiberd's confident assertion of the centrality of culture discussed earlier. But Kiberd is hardly alone: the most powerful and brilliant critical projects outlined or alluded to in this essay, for all their varying degrees of *discursive* reflexivity, evince no explicit *institutional* or *material* reflexivity; that is, Irish criticism, of whatever kind, shows next to no interest in examining its own conditions of possibility, even as those grounds become ever more hedged about by the requirements of the state on one side and of capital on the other.

Accordingly, and by way of conclusion, it may be helpful to outline some of the questions that it seems to this writer Irish criticism is *not* asking:

1. What does it mean to pursue 'postcolonial' studies in a state and an economy that is so thoroughly dominated by extraterritorial political and economic institutions?
2. What does it mean when even a putatively 'radical' body of theory is overwhelmingly mediated through the academic-political complex of the last true imperial power?
3. What does it mean to pursue 'cultural politics' in a context where there is no affiliation to an active political movement, let alone to a viable left-wing party?
4. What is the fate of the Irish intellectual in these conditions? Do Irish literary-academic intellectuals have responsibilities beyond the ivory tower?
5. How might criticism acknowledge and then negotiate its relations with power, be that state power or corporate power?
6. What are the implications for Irish criticism of the origins of English literary studies as an explicitly hegemonic project?
7. What are the implications for Irish criticism of the great strength – intellectual, financial, archival – of Irish literary studies in the American academy?

It is not that contemporary Irish criticism lacks the resources to begin thinking about these matters; indeed, it now plays host to several highly impressive *oeuvres* and projects that have every potential for further radical and imaginative development. Nor can one deny the intelligence, erudition and stimulus that the major movements or trends analysed in this chapter have brought to Irish literary and cultural studies. Most simply and fundamentally, this argument, though it is critical, would have no terrain on which to operate without the genealogy it has tried to outline and critique. But this does not obviate the need to posit the preceding questions. An Irish criticism moving to answer these and other, proximate questions will be following the logic of its own best impulses to their unsettling, but crucial, conclusions.

NOTES

1. The quotation marks refer to the generalised discourse that we all, to a greater or lesser degree, have been swept up by, as opposed to specific and therefore legitimate theories.

2. For critiques of modernisation theory in the Irish context, see Gibbons (1996) and McCarthy (2000).
3. It says much about both the vagueness of the term, and the continuities of Irish cultural and political thinking, that this same idea would subsequently be pressed into service by both the Field Day project of the 1980s and Mary Robinson's presidency in the 1990s.
4. Andrei Zhdanov was the most powerful (and infamous) cultural administrator during the period of Joseph Stalin's rule of the Soviet Union.
5. For a critique of Lloyd's analysis of the state, in the context of his reading of Joyce, see Nolan (2000).
6. The exceptions are Kirby, *et al.* (2002) and Coulter and Coleman (2003).

7

Forty Shades of Grey?:
Irish Historiography and the
Challenges of Multidisciplinarity

Mary E. Daly

Historians place considerable value on the perspective given by the passing of time, so there are obvious difficulties in trying to assess major developments in the writing of modern Irish history over the past 15 to 20 years. But having entered this caveat, there are some trends that can be identified, including a significant expansion in the number of books and articles; greater diversity in research topics; increased specialisation and the concomitant emergence of historiographical debates that are accessible only to experts in particular fields; an end to the belief that it is possible to arrive at an objective – and therefore a definitive – account of historical events; a much greater involvement of scholars who do not describe themselves as historians; and the growing influence of modern media, such as television and film – though not yet the Web – on historical debates. Irish history was never the sole preserve of the historical profession, but in recent years this has become more evident than ever before.

The proliferation of publications is perhaps the most striking of these developments. In 1980 the 'Select Bibliography of Writings on Irish Economic and Social History', published in *Irish Economic and Social History*, listed 254 items.[1] By 1990 this had risen to 371, and eleven years later the bibliography had grown to over 1,250 items. Although access to new historical sources – oral and visual as well as written – has been a major driving force in fields such as twentieth-century Ireland, labour history, the history of emigration and women's history, most research has concentrated on re-examining topics that have long figured in narratives of the Irish past: Tudor Ireland, war, politics, changing land ownership and settlement in the seventeenth century, the 1798 rebellion, the Act of Union, the Great Famine and the Anglo-Irish war. The first 70 years of the eighteenth century, which traditionally attracted little attention, has emerged as a major area of interest in recent years (Dickson, 2000: 231–40), whereas the nineteenth century, with the exception of the Famine and emigration, appears to be marking time. With university education in Ireland and Britain increasingly driven by research agendas, measured by publications, conference presentations and completed doctorates, and the new funding opportunities provided by the Irish Research Council for the Humanities and Social Sciences and the Programme for Research in Third Level Institutions in the Republic, and the Scheme for Promoting University Research and the Arts and Humanities Research Council in Northern Ireland, there is every reason to expect that the volume of publications will continue to rise for the foreseeable future.

In view of this rapid growth in research and publication activity, it is impossible to provide a comprehensive guide to recent Irish historiography in a short chapter such as this. Instead, I propose to concentrate on certain key areas, beginning with the revisionist debate and the ensuing backlash, and then proceeding to examine the impact of the commemorations of 1798 and the Famine, and the growing tendency to place Irish history within an international framework. I will also analyse the methodological and ideological clashes between historians, who continue to emphasise contingency and ambiguity, and cultural critics, who tend to favour more generalised meta-interpretations of history and society. In addition, I will discuss a number of expanding areas in historical research, notably, emigration, women's history and twentieth-century Ireland. My analysis is premised on the view that despite the onslaught of criticism directed at Irish academic history during the 1980s, most historians continue to respect the broad principles laid down by T. W. Moody and R. D. Edwards in the 1930s. Framed by these principles, recent writings on modern Irish history show evidence of both change and continuity. The range of topics has expanded far beyond the traditional preoccupation with high politics, the comparative and international dimensions of Irish history have been increasingly recognised, and defining events have been subjected to new interpretive and methodological approaches. These approaches, however, have tended to remain the preserve of scholars who would not describe themselves as historians, so that much scope for interdisciplinary dialogue and research remains.

REVISIONISM AND ITS DISCONTENTS

During the 1980s, it became impossible to escape the issue of revisionism, which centred on the debate over the possibility of producing 'value-free' history, and claims that the outbreak of violence in Northern Ireland had exerted so great an influence on Irish historiography that it had thwarted the writing of history, which could in anyway be deemed patriotic (Boyce and O'Day, 1996; Brady, 1994). This often acrimonious debate was prompted in part by two key anniversaries: the fiftieth anniversary in 1986 of the founding of both the Ulster Society for Irish Historical Studies and the Irish Historical Society, and the fiftieth anniversary in 1987 of *Irish Historical Studies*, the premier journal in the discipline. These anniversaries were bracketed by the deaths of the founding editors of *Irish Historical Studies*, T. W. Moody in 1984 and R. D. Edwards in 1988, which inevitably prompted a reassessment of their scholarly achievement (Mulvey, 1984–85; Dudley Edwards, 1988–89; Clarke, 1988–89). Edwards, Moody and their associates set out to establish an Irish historical profession whose training and standards would conform to the best academic practice at the time. They placed considerable emphasis on establishing the facts by scrupulous use of primary sources and stressed the importance of writing 'value-free' history. One consequence of this approach was to move away from a simplistic narrative of Irish history as '800 years of English misrule' towards a much more nuanced story that emphasised contingency, incongruity and complexity.

Edwards's and Moody's academic initiative must be seen from the twin perspectives of international historical practice and the intellectual climate of Ireland in the 1930s, which was characterised by state censorship, intolerance towards minority views and introverted forms of nationalism and unionism. Their mission respected and reflected the first influence and transcended the second. Most remarkably, they managed to create an Irish historical profession that was *not* polarised by politics or religion, one where Northern and Southern scholars met and collaborated on a regular basis, at a time when such links were uncommon in other spheres of Irish life. One of the major shortcomings of the tradition inaugurated by Edwards and Moody, however, was the privileging of certain sources, such as official papers, over others, such as folklore and literary records. This promoted the writing of 'history from above' and gave little scope for the kinds of historical discourse found in ballad or popular memory, except as something to be, in the main, refuted.[2]

In the less hierarchical, more international scholarly community of today, no one person or publication has the status once accorded to Edwards, Moody and *Irish Historical Studies*. The expansion in historical scholarship, coupled with the emergence of a more open and diverse society, have resulted in the fracturing of historical consensus in Ireland. Moreover, the 1980s vogue for deconstruction and discourse analysis – a mode of intellectual enquiry originating in literary and cultural studies that raised new questions about the objectivity of any text, including sources such as official papers – had an undoubted influence on the revisionist controversy, resulting in the interpretation of texts and documents as a reflection of the ideological stance of the author, and a blurring of the lines between fact and fiction. But the majority of Irish historians are relentless empiricists, and few came to grips with this aspect of the debate. The revisionist debate also reflected an unhealthy introversion in Irish historiography and a failure to recognise that the difficulties involved in writing the history of a country with a troubled or contentious past, that may still have an influence on contemporary events, are not unique to Ireland (Daly, 1997a). Many of the issues raised, indeed, apply equally to Germany – even more so since reunification – and to France, where research into the Vichy years or the war in Algeria present questions for contemporary French society that are at least as troubling as anything that Irish historians have had to address.

The debate about revisionism also promoted what might be termed 'armchair history'; lengthy and at times tendentious discussions about the reinterpretation of events such as the 1916 rebellion, conducted without the benefit of any new research, became a comfortable alternative to long hours spent in the archives. Ironically, this was a development that was entirely contrary to the spirit of Edwards's and Moody's mission. In addition, the debate served to reinforce an already excessive concentration on high politics. In no other national history does the political narrative dominate as much as in Ireland; social, cultural and economic history has tended either to be ignored or treated as a specialist discipline worthy of no more than peripheral attention in the general historical narrative. Ronan Fanning has suggested that the vogue for social and economic history was a response to the eruption of the Northern Ireland crisis, implying that scholars who concentrated on these topics were failing to confront key issues relating to Ireland's past (Fanning, 1994: 153). Yet topics such as land ownership and settlement, emigration, population decline, religion and economic development are as central to the interpretation of Irish history as, say, Conservative policy towards Ireland during the Balfour years.

The period after 1945 saw a significant expansion of social and economic history in most countries, as historians emulated the *Annales* School, which sought to counter the predominant emphasis on political and military history with a more comprehensive approach to phenomena and their underlying causes. Although this trend can be detected in Ireland, it did not happen to the same extent (Cullen, 1981). Since the late 1980s political history has been revitalised in North America and Europe, partly in reaction to the gradual passing of a postwar generation of academics who were identified with social history and their replacement with scholars from the Reagan–Thatcher generation. There has also been a renewed interest in historical biography – driven in part by commercial publishers – an activity previously regarded as a lesser form of scholarship. In the case of Irish history, the effect of these trends has been to reinforce rather than reverse established practices. For example, J. J. Lee's bestselling *Ireland 1912–1985: Politics and Society* (1989) is centred on a chronological political narrative, with considerable emphasis on the personalities of political leaders, whereas his earlier book, *The Modernization of Irish Society, 1848–1918* (1973), consciously sought to break away from this narrative. Indeed, a substantial amount of the historiography of twentieth-century Ireland has focused on political personalities and personality conflicts, such as the rivalry between Eamon de Valera and Michael Collins, and on other key figures such as Noel Browne, John Charles McQuaid and Seán Lemass. As if to underline this trend, R. F. Foster, holder of the only chair of Irish history in Britain, dedicated what should arguably have been his most productive years to writing a biography of W. B. Yeats (Foster, 1997, 2003). This tendency to read Irish history through the life-story of a major political or cultural figure tends to diminish the significance of larger social, economic and cultural trends, and the far-reaching societal impact of ideas, thereby reinforcing the isolationist tendencies in Irish historiography.

FROM REVISIONISM TO REVIVALISM AND COMMEMORATION

In 1988 Foster noted that in the world of Irish history 'academic revisionism has coincided with popular revivalism' (Foster, 1994: 143). Popular revivalism flourished during the 1990s, thanks to the commemoration of the sesquicentenary of the Famine (1995–97) and the bicentenary of the 1798 rebellion, although the seventy-fifth anniversary of the 1916 rising passed largely unnoticed in 1991.

This flowering of revivalist activity was not confined to Ireland; it also flourished in North America, Australia, Britain and elsewhere in Europe.[3] Famine commemoration took many forms, including candlelight processions to former workhouses and graveyards; the commissioning of sculptures and memorials in Ireland – notably on Dublin's Custom House Quay, directly in front of the International Financial Services Centre – and overseas; efforts to restore disused workhouses; the building of two replica 'famine ships'; attempts to include the event in US educational curricula dealing with genocide, as well as conferences, lectures, television documentaries and a host of publications. A comparable flow of publications and documentaries attended the commemoration of 1798, as well as the opening of a new museum in Enniscorthy and a parade of thousands of pikemen and women in snow-white shirts and dark trousers through the streets of Wexford. Such commemorative fervour was strongly influenced by the elaborate celebrations that marked the bicentenary of the French revolution nine years earlier, and by a renewed interest in the Irish diaspora that was a major feature of the presidency of Mary Robinson. Moreover, the resurgence of nationalist energy that it engendered was skilfully choreographed and managed by the Irish government to boost the Northern Ireland peace process and promote an international tourist drive among the Irish worldwide.[4]

This flurry of commemorative activity certainly made the history of the Famine more accessible to the general public and resulted in a number of important publications, including analyses of the impact on British government policy of 'providentialist' ideology, the role of the Catholic church, and the impact of the Famine in Dublin and overseas (Gray, 1995; Kerr, 1994; Neal, 1998; Ó Gráda, 1999). Remembering the Famine also reminded scholars of the daunting array of source material that has yet to be digested and revived Mitchelite arguments that Ireland had more than enough food to feed its population at the height of the disaster, although there is substantial evidence to refute this.[5] The Famine commemorations also encouraged comparisons with contemporary famines in the 'developing world', which, however financially beneficial for relief programmes, probably detracted from the understanding of the Famine *per se*, because the scale of food deprivation and excess mortality in 1840s Ireland was immensely greater than anything experienced in recent decades in Africa or Asia. The appropriate, if less politically attractive, comparisons are with other famines in nineteenth-century Europe. Another feature of the commemorations was the large volume of publications by literary and cultural critics, whose contributions tended to highlight themes drawn from Holocaust studies, such as the experience of trauma, the alleged suppression of memories and the consequences of such phenomena for later generations (Eagleton, 1995; Kelleher, 1997; Morash, 1995; Morash and Hayes, 1996).

Given that it took place shortly after the signing of the Good Friday Agreement, the bicentenary commemoration of 1798 had a more explicit political dimension and was, notably, an all-Ireland event. A travelling conference circuit opened in Belfast before moving to Dublin Castle, and the Ulster Museum staged an impressive exhibition, most of which subsequently transferred to the National Museum in Dublin (Parkhill, 2002/03; Ulster Museum, 1998).[6] The dominant message was that 1798 was an egalitarian, all-Ireland, non-sectarian rebellion, a failed attempt to create the kind of Ireland that, it was hoped, would follow from the 1998 Agreement. Sectarian aspects, which figured prominently in the centenary celebrations of 1898, were played down. The official, pluralist message was effectively expressed by Minister Síle de Valera at the opening of the 1798 exhibition in the National Museum at Collins Barracks in which she said:

Firstly, we must continue never to entertain a sectarian version of '98. Secondly, we must stress the modernity of the United Irish project, its forward-looking, democratic dimension. Thirdly, we must emphasise the essential unity of the 1798 insurrection: what happened in Wexford was of a piece with what happened in Antrim and Down.[7]

The mammoth volume of essays that issued from the bicentennial events followed the official line in minimising the sectarian dimension of the rising, but it also highlighted local diversity (Bartlett *et al.*, 2003). Indeed, one of the real strengths of 1798 historiography is the range of excellent local studies, something that cannot be yet said about the historiography of the Famine. Irish local history has flourished in recent years, as evidenced by the publication of an impressive series of county histories and the Maynooth local studies series. However, much more needs to be done if Irish history is to replicate the depth of local studies in France or Britain, to name only two examples.

In Ireland as elsewhere, commemoration has recently emerged as a research topic in its own right, with essays on the nature and politics of historical and contemporary commemorations. The alleged failure to commemorate the Irishmen who fought in the

1914–18 war, for example, has prompted considerable attention, but if this neglect is attributed to the triumph of Sinn Féin and the 1916 generation, how then can we account for the even greater absence of memorials to the Irish civil war or the fact that the Irish Free State spent £50,000 on the First World War memorial at Islandbridge, and less than £1,000 on a cenotaph to commemorate Arthur Griffith and Michael Collins on Leinster Lawn (Dolan, 2003; Jeffery, 2000; Leonard, 1996)? Again, while there was no formal commemoration of the Irish Famine before 1995, it would not be correct to equate this official silence with forgetting. Irish political speeches from the 1850s until the 1960s contain countless references to the Famine, references that presume a common knowledge and understanding of that event among Irish people.

Memory and commemoration – what Roy Foster (2001) has dubbed 'the Irish story' – offers a mechanism for re-examining historical writings in the past, and for exploring the part played by historical memories, real or imaginary, in the formation of nationalist and unionist identities (Geary, 2001; McBride, 1997, 2001). Memory opens the door for a more inclusive scholarly approach to oral and written sources and the long-neglected topic of popular culture. The use of Irish-language sources in particular has greatly enriched the study of both 1798 and the Famine, as evidenced by the work of Cormac Ó Gráda (1994) and Cathal Portéir (1995a, 1995b). The records of the Irish Folklore Commission, held in the Department of Irish Folklore at University College Dublin, have gained a new standing and are now more widely known to the general public. Irish-language sources have also assumed a much greater importance in the historiography of early modern Ireland, though their use has not been without controversy (Leersson, 1986, 1996). Given that most of this material is in the form of verse written by Irish *filí* – poets who were paid by Gaelic or Old English families to sing for their supper – rather than more conventional historical sources, its interpretive use has given rise to a heated debate. Do these verses, praising Gaelic chiefs or Stuart monarchs, represent a precocious proto-nationalism or should they be read as a form of courtly literature, produced by a dispossessed Gaelic elite who were clinging desperately to past glories? (Bradshaw, 1994a; O'Riordan, 1990).[8] While historians offer different answers to such questions, it is clear that these Irish-language sources have on the whole resuscitated a more nationalist version of eighteenth-century Ireland than that provided by S. J. Connolly, who argued that it should be regarded as an *ancien régime* society. However, Louis

Cullen's (1988) revisionary essay on Daniel Corkery's *The Hidden Ireland* (1924), which makes extensive use of Irish-language material, provided a major corrective to Corkery's romanticised view of a vibrant scholarly tradition surviving among the Irish peasantry (Daly and Dickson, 1990; O Cíosáin, 1997). Underpinning this ongoing debate is a growing realisation that Gaelic and English-language cultural traditions were not hermetically sealed, and the future undoubtedly lies in attempts to analyse this interaction in more detail.

LOCATING IRELAND IN AN INTERNATIONAL CONTEXT

Despite my earlier criticism of the isolationist tendency within Irish historiography, it must be acknowledged that there has been a significant increase in scholarly writings that place Ireland within a wider international context. This development reflects contemporary Ireland's engagement with global society, in contrast to the isolationism of earlier decades, and contemporary Irish historians' broader scholarly perspectives and career aspirations, as a means of opening up new opportunities for international dialogue, debate and publication.[9] At first sight it might seem that placing Irish history within a transnational context would inevitably entail a refutation of the traditional nationalist picture of conquest and colonisation, but this is not necessarily the case. Although historians such as Stephen Ellis see the Gaelic world of the Middle Ages as localised and dynastic, with no sense of national identity, and English lordship in Ireland as 'part of a much wider group of territories, in which the English crown and court culture acted as a strong centralising force' (Ellis, 1994: 171), it is also possible to interpret medieval and early modern Ireland as an example of British colonisation within an archipelagic context. Many historians, indeed, do not regard the two models as necessarily exclusive. Although a sense of colonial superiority can be detected among Anglo-Norman/British settlers in Ireland from at least the time of Giraldus Cambrensis, many Irish residents, including a significant number of native Irish leaders, were happy to accept British rule and kingship, so that few historians would now regard Hugh O'Neill (Earl of Tyrone and The O'Neill) as a clear-cut exemplar of Irish nationalism or see religion as constituting a definitive mark of political allegiance (Brady and Gillespie, 1986).

The examination of the Irish past in terms of 'four nations' history has probably been most fruitful in analyses of the seventeenth century, where the period from 1640 to 1660 is increasingly seen in terms of 'the War of the Three Kingdoms', having due regard to the importance of Ireland, Scotland and England (Ohlmeyer, 1993; Russell, 1990). While some claim that the 'new British history' is little more than the history of England dressed in new clothes – a disguised form of intellectual colonisation – such accusations cannot be made about Scottish-Irish historical studies, which are proving particularly productive for intellectual history, especially in relation to Irish nonconformity (Bradshaw and Morrill, 1996; Connolly, 1999).[10] Another aspect of the archipelagic model concerns the links between settlement and colonisation in Ireland and the Americas, a topic pioneered many years ago by D. B. Quinn, and now flourishing in the hands of Nicholas Canny and others, working in conjunction with leading scholars of colonial America such as Bernard Bailyn and Jack Greene. This research is also open to multiple interpretations: whereas Canny has highlighted the fact that Scottish settlement in Ulster meant that fewer Scotsmen figured among the early colonial settlers in the Americas, others, especially scholars with a background in cultural and literary studies, have examined colonial discourse in the writings of Edmund Spenser and other British settlers in early modern Ireland (Canny, 1994, 1998; Palmer, 2001).

An alternative approach to the early modern period examines Ireland in a more European context, as part of the militant counter-reformation or as yet another *ancien régime* (Connolly, 1992; Ó hAnnracháin, 2002). This Eurocentric analysis is being advanced by research into Irish immigrants in Spain, France and the Holy Roman Empire, including mercenaries, military leaders, statesmen and clergy. This revisiting of old and half-forgotten histories of 'the Wild Geese' and the Irish colleges in Europe, using modern research tools such as computer databases, appears to confirm and even strengthen traditional claims of Irish influence and links with Catholic Europe. Clearly, then, Irish society in the early modern period was not isolated. Rather, it was integrated into several overlapping worlds – the Atlantic, the British Isles, Catholic Europe, and a British Empire extending from the Americas to India – and this integration extended to the Gaelic community. This picture of interwoven networks is confirmed by recent works on economic history, which show Irish involvement in the French wine and brandy trades and highlight the extent of Irish trade links with the Americas (Cullen, 2000).[11]

In recent years the study of Irish emigration has benefited enormously from the work of scholars based outside Ireland, and from the growing interest in Irish history and Irish Studies in Britain,

North America and Australia. As research on Irish connections with colonial America is extended up to and including the American War of Independence, it is becoming easier to detect the links and discontinuities between that period and the mass emigration of the nineteenth century (Kenny, 2000). The key influences on the evolution of this historiography have been Arnold Schrier (1958), Kerby Miller (1985) and D. H. Akenson (1996). Schrier pioneered the use of emigrant letters, which was later taken up by Miller in his controversial *Emigrants and Exiles,* a book that contrasted the pragmatic ambition and successful adaptation of Scots-Irish emigrants to the USA with the passivity and fatalism of Catholic exiles who continued to pine for home. The debate over Miller's use of emigrant letters inspired David Fitzpatrick's *Oceans of Consolation* (1994), a much more upbeat story of Irish emigration that reproduces all the letters *in extenso,* thereby enabling the reader to assess the evidence alongside Fitzpatrick's own interpretation.[12] Akenson has challenged Miller's distinction between Catholic and Protestant Irish emigrants, suggesting that significantly more Irish settled on the land than is generally assumed, while David Doyle has taken issue with both Akenson and Miller, showing that the Irish were among the urban pioneers in the USA, and that they were much more successful and upwardly mobile than Miller had suggested (Akenson, 1988; Doyle, 1990). A flourishing historiography of Irish-America and Irish-Australia is increasingly linking settlement and occupational patterns in North America with specific parts of Ireland, but this scholarship has not yet resulted in reciprocal studies of the local Irish background. The history of the Irish in Britain, especially in the period since 1920, is also unfolding, with regional and local aspects again emerging as critical areas of enquiry (Delaney, 2000; Swift, 2002).

COLONIALISM, POSTCOLONIALISM AND IRISH EXCEPTIONALISM

By definition, every nation has a unique and exceptional history. In Ireland, however, there is a longstanding belief that the country's history has been uniquely miserable, resulting in what Liam Kennedy has termed the 'MOPE' ('most oppressed people ever') syndrome. At a scholarly level, the less isolationist perspectives discussed above have gone some way towards eroding this point of view. Studies of emigration to North America, for example, or of Irish mercenaries in continental armies lead naturally to a comparative dimension, and to the realisation that Scottish and English immigrants, and German and Swiss mercenaries, also existed. Tim Guinnane's study of post-Famine Irish demography, for example, showed that several regions in continental Europe had late and low marriage rates similar to that of Ireland (Guinnane, 1997). But despite these correctives, the belief that Ireland's history has been exceptionally bleak has in recent years acquired a new lease of life and a fresh vocabulary, featuring terms such as colonialism, violence and discontinuity.

This renewed emphasis on these aspects of Irish history was prompted in large part by the Troubles. Presenting the Northern Ireland crisis as a war against colonialism has the attraction of placing the conflict in an international framework and providing an alternative to the rather passé image of a sectarian struggle between Catholics and Protestants. Colonial discourse analysis was also employed during the 1980s to draw loose comparisons between economic conditions in the Irish Republic and the 'Third World'.[13] The most eloquent recent statement on the theme of Irish exceptionalism is that by Seamus Deane in his introduction to *The Field Day Anthology of Irish Writing* (1991), in the course of which he rationalises his reordering of Ireland's literary tradition as follows:

It is important to do this now because the political crisis in Ireland, precipitated in 1968, but in gestation for many years before that date, has exposed the absence within the island of any system of cultural consent that would effectively legitimize and secure the existing political arrangements. There has rarely been in Ireland any sustained coordination between prevailing cultural and political systems; indeed, when this has existed, its oppressive nature and function has always been visible. The fact that Ireland has been colonized through conquest and invasion several times and in several ways is obviously central to an explanation of this phenomenon. [...] Versions of Ireland and its history and culture were created by many groups within the island – colonists and colonized – in attempts to ratify an existing political and economic system or to justify its alteration or its extinction. The failure of these cultural versions to achieve hegemony in alliance with the political system is more remarkable in a European country than it would be in those parts of the world that have been subject to European domination. That is part of the interest of and reason for this project. (Deane, 1991: xx)

It shouldn't surprise us that this is written by a leading literary critic since references to Ireland as a postcolonial society are more common among literary and cultural scholars than among historians, reflecting the vogue within English Studies for works originating in India, Africa and other former colonies, and the impact of Edward Said's influential

Orientalism (1978). In *Inventing Ireland* Declan Kiberd expressed regret that an earlier study of postcolonial literatures paid only cursory attention to Ireland, and expressed the hope that his book might initiate a reassessment, on the grounds that 'the introduction of the Irish case to the debate will complicate, extend and in some cases expose the limits of current models of postcoloniality':

What makes the Irish Renaissance such a fascinating case is the knowledge that the cultural revival preceded and in many ways enabled the political revolution that followed. This is quite the opposite of the American experience, in which the attainment of cultural autonomy by Whitman and Emerson followed the political Declaration of Independence by fully seventy-five years. In this respect, the Irish experience seems to anticipate that of the emerging nation-states of the so-called 'Third World'. (Kiberd, 1995: 5)

But the more valid comparisons are those between Ireland and states that achieved independence during the early twentieth century, notably Poland, Finland (whose history also includes famine and civil war), Czechoslovakia and other former colonies of the Austrian and Turkish empires, rather than with African and Asian countries, which achieved independence after World War II. Furthermore, Kiberd's claim that a cultural revolution preceded the political revolution in Ireland is equally true of many European nations. In fact, nineteenth-century Irish nationalist movements such as Young Ireland and the Fenians were strongly influenced by similar groups in Germany and Italy. And the discontinuities of Irish history surely pale in comparison with many parts of Central Europe that have experienced occupation, war, major population movements and numerous boundary changes over the centuries. In short, violence, discontinuity and occupation are fundamental parts of the history of all Western European states, with the exception of Britain, Switzerland and Sweden.

There is, however, one interesting instance of Irish exceptionalism that is rarely noted, one identified by Eric Hobsbawm in *Age of Extremes*: 'the only European countries with adequately democratic political institutions that functioned without a break during the entire inter-war period were Britain, Finland (only just), the Irish Free State, Sweden and Switzerland' (Hobsbawm, 1994: 111). Good luck was probably a major factor in the Irish case, but so too was Ireland's democratic traditions, which, however flawed, were firmly embedded during the nineteenth century, though not in isolation from more militant forms of politicisation. The more mundane aspects of Irish political life during the 1800s have been brilliantly summarised in Theo Hoppen's claim that in periods not dominated by major political campaigns, the main motivating force was not nationalism or unionism but the parish pump (Hoppen, 1984). Hoppen's work has highlighted a major continuity in Irish political life; most post-partition activity in Leinster House and Stormont was concerned with jobs, grants and other forms of patronage rather than ideological issues. In a series of works that were undoubtedly influenced by contemporary political developments in Northern Ireland, Paul Bew has tried to detect other possible outcomes for post-partition Ireland by examining the Irish Party in the period from the fall of Parnell to the rise of Sinn Féin (Bew, 1987, 1994). His work is complemented by Patrick Maume's broad study of Irish nationalism, and by analyses of nationalist and unionist parties in the late nineteenth and early twentieth centuries (Maume, 1999). The cumulative impression is that Irish political parties were more diverse in their views than is generally suggested, and that the post-1920 political outcome was by no means inevitable.

In the light of events in Northern Ireland it is not surprising that historians have been keen to re-examine the Anglo-Irish war and the long history of the IRA (Bowyer Bell, 1987; English, 2003). On the whole, their accounts have replaced the heroic narrative found in republican classics such as Dorothy Macardle's *The Irish Republic* (1937) and Ernie O'Malley's *On Another Man's Wounds* (1936) with a more complex and darker story that is more attentive to the experiences of the victims of nationalist struggle. The tone and tenor of Peter Hart's analysis of IRA activity in Cork is representative of this new narrative: 'This dirty war was waged largely by small bands of gunmen, young, tough and barely under the control of their superiors. The "active squads" on both sides did what they liked, undeterred by orders or discipline from further up the organization' (Hart, 1998: 18). Hart's book is one of a growing number of local studies of the Anglo-Irish war – all of them influenced by David Fitzpatrick's outstanding monograph on Clare, *Politics and Irish Life, 1913–1921* (1977) – which illuminate the complex factors that brought about a change in nationalist sentiment. Yet it is important not to ignore the complex state-building efforts of Dáil Éireann at both a local and a national level during the 1919–22 period, efforts that were coterminous with and strongly influenced by violence and warfare (Daly, 1997b; Garvin, 1996; Mitchell, 1995).

While in no way denying the horrors of the Irish civil war, the early 1920s could easily have resulted in an even more violent conflict between unionists and nationalists or even in a military dictatorship. The survival of democracy in independent Ireland was a close-run thing, achieved at the cost of restrictions on civil liberties, financial stringency and cultural conservatism. The strong hand of the Catholic church was invoked to assist in restoring law and order and frugal budgets were used to balance the books, albeit at the cost of continuing emigration and high levels of poverty. Some of the Free State's greatest successes were in foreign relations, but this ranked low with most voters (Kennedy, 1996; Murray, 2000; O'Halpin, 1999; Regan, 1999). Other aspects of the domestic political story are being filled in by recent studies on the 1937 Constitution, Fianna Fáil's social and economic policies and its relationship with the Labour Party, the Blueshirt movement of the 1930s, and Irish involvement in the Spanish civil war (Allen, 1997; Cronin, 1997; Dunphy, 1995; Farrell, 1988; McGarry, 1999). However, we still lack a major biography of Eamon de Valera and detailed histories of Fianna Fáil governments, although we now know a lot about the first inter-party government of 1948–51 (McCullough, 1998).

Irish neutrality is a topic with considerable contemporary relevance. During World War II de Valera's government went to considerable lengths to assist the Allies, but evidence of this cooperation was carefully concealed at the time. Contemporary documents show that Ireland's 1949 rejection of an invitation to join NATO was couched solely in terms of partition, and that during the Lemass years Ireland's United Nations policy – often seen as an example of principled neutrality – was skilfully tailored to promote the country's application for EEC membership (Fanning, 1982; O'Halpin, 1999; Salmon, 1989). In overall terms, however, the years from the early 1920s until the late 1950s continue to be seen as a time of socio-economic gloom and cultural backwardness that magically disappeared with the publication of T. K. Whitaker's *Economic Development* in 1958 and Lemass's succession as taoiseach in 1959.

One of the major dilemmas for anyone writing a history of Ireland since partition is whether to adopt an all-Ireland perspective or to write the history of one state. Lee (1989), Jackson (1999) and Townshend (1999) choose the partitionist approach, with separate chapters for North and South, whereas Keogh (1994) focuses almost exclusively on independent Ireland. The only history written from an all-Ireland perspective is Fitzpatrick's *The Two Irelands, 1912–1939* (1998). While this book throws up some interesting comparative insights, such as the similarities in the attitudes of both governments towards censorship or the much greater suspicion of public spending in Belfast than in Dublin, the overall impression is of two equally rotten states that 'for all their cosmopolitan millennial glitter, have yet to escape the shadow of their revolutions' (Fitzpatrick, 1998: 243). Yet despite the fact that in both states 'the consolidation of majority rule was secured through extensive coercion, abuse of the rights of minorities, and widespread infringement of religious, moral and personal liberty' (Fitzpatrick, 1998: 238), one survived and could even be said to have prospered, whereas the other collapsed. For those interested in the Troubles, the key issues are whether the premiership of Terence O'Neill could have brought about an accommodation between the two communities in Northern Ireland, and the significance of the first formal contact for almost 50 years between the governments in Dublin and Stormont in 1965. That said, it is clear that the outbreak of violence in Northern Ireland in 1969 caught the Dublin government completely unprepared, and that the initiative rested with Whitehall (Fanning, 2001; Kennedy, 2000; Mulholland, 2000).

It is notable that most studies on post-1960 Ireland, North and South, have been written by political scientists and journalists. Irish historians themselves have been slow to take up the challenge of writing contemporary history; the ghosts of Edwards and Moody and their emphasis on sources is undoubtedly a factor in this reluctance. Yet a daunting research agenda is emerging in relation to twentieth-century Ireland, an agenda determined not only by events in Northern Ireland but also by current affairs in the Republic, including the various public inquiries and tribunals into political corruption, the scandals relating to the sexual abuse of children by Catholic clergy, the treatment of children in industrial schools, and questions posed by books such as Frank McCourt's *Angela's Ashes*, which opens with the claim that 'Worse than the ordinary miserable childhood is the miserable Irish childhood, and worse yet is the miserable Irish Catholic childhood' (McCourt, 1996: 1). Is it true? We do not know because we still lack a comprehensive history of Irish childhood (Raftery and O'Sullivan, 1999).

Women's history has also broadened the research agenda with its interest in topics such as poverty, sexuality, work and religion, in addition to more conventional political themes. This breadth of focus is evident in the database of sources produced by the Women's History Project (Luddy *et al.*, 1999), in Maria Luddy's (1995) documentary history of Irish women, and in the very wide range of material included in volumes four and five of *The Field Day Anthology of Irish Writing* (Bourke *et al.*, 2002). Nevertheless, Irish women's history replicates some features common to Irish historiography as a whole, notably the 'MOPE' syndrome and a tendency to view the history of women in isolation. Furthermore, the close association between women's studies and women's history has resulted in a tendency to view the past in presentist terms, as if the priorities of women 100 years ago were those of women today; hence the concentration on topics such as divorce or married women in the workplace, rather than on women in the home or in farming.[14] And while today's scholars are careful to incorporate women into studies of the 1798 rebellion or the Anglo-Irish war, women's history continues to operate at arm's length from general narratives of Irish history.

To conclude, let me recapitulate the three major characteristics of recent Irish historiography that set it apart from what has gone before. Firstly, the range and diversity of subject matter and methodology; secondly, the shift from seeing Ireland in exceptional terms towards more comparative and more globalised interpretations of the country's past; and thirdly, the contrast in emphasis and approach between mainstream historians and cultural and literary scholars. It is also evident that while historians in general have moved some way towards embracing broad analytical frameworks for the study of Irish history, they continue to place considerable weight on complexity and contingency, and to eschew grand narratives. Most of their work could be characterised as forty shades of grey, rather than black and white or orange and green. By contrast, the meta-narratives of recent years have come from non-historians, the Field Day collective being the most noteworthy example. By the same token, cultural critics, literary scholars and sociologists have been more willing to employ the discourse of postcolonialism when analysing Irish culture and society. Multidisciplinarity appears to be flourishing in the form of Irish Studies programmes and journals or societies that adopt a multidisciplinary approach to a specific historical period, but it is unclear whether such initiatives and dialogues extend beyond polite conversation. In all of this, it is important to remember that many academic disciplines only emerged in the late nineteenth century, and may not survive the end of the twenty-first, so the future may well rest with inter- and multidisciplinary research. The other force to be reckoned with is the technological revolution; the printed word is only one medium for transmitting knowledge, hence the importance of audio-visual and multimedia resources for future scholarship on Ireland's past.

NOTES

1. In practice this bibliography covers all aspects of Irish history.
2. It was also the case that *Irish Historical Studies* did not accept papers relating to post-1921 Ireland during the early decades of its existence, partly because of the editors' stringent requirements regarding sources and partly because of their desire to avoid controversy. Although this policy changed gradually during the late 1970s and early 1980s, under the editorship of Ronan Fanning and David Harkness, officially, *IHS* does not publish articles on events that are less than 30 years old.
3. While the mood reflected the feel-good sentiments of the country's new prosperity, Ireland was not unique in seeking out good old-fashioned 'comfort history': witness the popularity of Simon Schama's television series on the history of Britain and the efforts by the US National Endowment for the Humanities to promote the writing of American history that emphasises patriotism.
4. During the commemoration of the Famine, despite the emphasis on local events, most of the discussion concentrated on the role of the British government and a tendentious debate as to whether Britain was guilty of genocide. Thus, shortly after coming to power in 1997 Prime Minister Tony Blair issued a statement about the role of the British administration that came close to an apology. See Kinealy (2001: 1–30).
5. Kinealy (1997) is the major supporter of the Mitchelite case. For a critique, see Daly (2002).
6. The Ulster Museum organised visits by community groups from both nationalist and unionist backgrounds as a means of making both communities aware of their shared history.
7. Speech by Síle de Valera at the opening of the 1798 exhibition in the National Museum, Collins Barracks, Dublin, 25 May 1998.
8. Brendan Ó Buachalla's (1996) important study of Jacobinism has shown significant links with the Defender movement that played a key role in the second wave of the United Irishmen.
9. For example, recent writings (Kearney, 1989; Pocock, 1975) have investigated medieval and early modern Ireland as part of what J. G. A. Pocock termed 'the Atlantic archipelago', seeing it as both part of Europe, albeit on the periphery, and as a colonial or postcolonial society.
10. There have been regular conferences devoted to comparative studies of Scottish and Irish history since the 1970s. See Cullen and Smout (1977).
11. Research on Irish links with continental Europe is being promoted by a PRTLI-funded programme based at Trinity College Dublin, and by the Micheál Ó Cléirigh Institute for the Study of Irish History and Civilization at University College Dublin.

12. See also Miller *et al.* (2003), which gives extensive excerpts with detailed notation and commentary.
13. On Northern Ireland as an anti-colonial struggle, see Howe (2000), Crotty (1986) and Jacobsen (1994). For a more measured analysis of the Irish economy and society in recent decades, see Nolan, *et al.* (2000) and Goldthorpe and Whelan (1992).
14. For a comprehensive examination of the Irish women's movement and an excellent bibliography, see Connolly (2002), Clear (2000) and Bourke (1993).

8

The Religious Field in Contemporary Ireland: Identity, Being Religious and Symbolic Domination

Tom Inglis

Ireland is an anomaly in more ways than one.[1] On a map of the world, it appears as a small island stuck out in the Atlantic on the edge of Europe. In global terms, it seems insignificant. Yet for two years in a row at the beginning of this century the Irish Republic appeared at the top of the globalisation index compiled by the US *Foreign Policy* journal, which declared it the most globalised society in the world. This was mainly because it had the most open economy, though the survey also showed that the Irish tend to travel more internationally and communicate more often with people from other parts of the world. Following Weber, there is a tendency to associate industrialised, globalised, capitalist societies with the dominance of a rational, scientific *habitus* or mentality. Such a *habitus*, it is argued, is inimical to the type of magical-devotional oriented religion associated with traditional forms of Catholicism (Fahey, 1992).[2] Certainly, if capitalist societies are going to be religious, one would suspect that they would be more Protestant than Catholic. The anomaly here, therefore, is that while the Irish Republic is designated the most globalised society in the world, it is also one of the most Catholic. In the 1990s, when the Republic had one of the fastest-growing economies in the world, it also had one of the highest levels of religiosity, particularly in terms of adherence to traditional devotional practices.

There is one further anomaly to note. Although quite a small island, Ireland is divided politically between the Northern six countries, which are part of the United Kingdom, and the remaining 26 counties, which form the Irish Republic. This political partition of the island is a function of a religious division. In most developed Western societies, tensions – let alone conflicts – between Catholics and Protestants tend to be minimal. In Northern Ireland, conversely, they are quite high, a fact that has been closely linked to the importance

111

of religious identity in different social fields (Bruce, 1986; Coulter, 1999; Hickey 1984; O'Malley, 1990). In the North, being identified as Catholic or Protestant has had important consequences outside the field of religion, particularly in the areas of housing, employment, education, health and sport.[3] The situation is somewhat different in the Republic, where the impact of religious identity is less marked, though Southern Protestants still tend to intermarry, attend separate schools, engage in different sports and, in some respects, are seen as ethnically different (as Anglo-Irish or British). Many Southern Protestants, moreover, are the remnants of an established class that exists in little social bubbles or enclaves around the country and who are perceived – and see themselves – as outsiders (Mennell *et al.*, 2000).[4] What makes Ireland different, then, is that religious identity and being religious have not become compartmentalised from the rest of social, political and economic life.

In this chapter I explore what religious identity and being religious mean in contemporary Ireland, both theoretically and empirically. My explanations will be sociological and will, I hope, help to elucidate some of the anomalies mentioned above. I will concentrate on describing and analysing the structure of the religious field and the hermeneutics of religious identity and being religious. I argue that to understand why Irish people have so often seen and understood themselves so readily in terms of religious difference – that is, as being either Catholic or Protestant – it is necessary to understand how the religious field is a social arena of relational differences, opposition and competition. However, to understand why the level of religious identity is so strong, and why being a good Catholic or Protestant is so important, we must go beyond the religious field and examine how religious affiliation has influenced people's success in other social spheres. What is happening is that while there are still strategic struggles between the Catholic and Protestant churches to maintain their competitive position in the religious field, the significance of religious identity and the importance of being a good Catholic or Protestant are declining owing to the devaluation of religious capital, which is linked to secularisation and the increasing significance of other forms of social and personal identities. But before exploring these issues, it is necessary to reflect critically on writing on religion in Ireland and, specifically, to provide a sociological explanation for the issues of religious identity and being religious.

The first important point to recognise is that most of the writing about religion in Ireland is done by people operating and working within the religious field. A vast array of material is produced each year, from books, journals, magazines, pamphlets and newspapers to television documentaries, films, music and art. Most of this is produced by religious professionals – bishops, priests, ministers – but also by members of the laity. Much of this material is denomination-ally based and often revolves around how to lead a spiritual and moral life. However, there are many others – journalists, intellectuals, academics – who have helped develop our understanding of religion in Ireland, but who do not write or comment out of a religious interest. They describe and analyse the way religion operates in institutions and everyday social life, and have created insights and understand-ings about, for example, what it is to be Catholic or Protestant in Ireland. What connects these diverse cultural 'texts' is their emphasis on critical reflection. Together, they seek to identify and examine the way things are religiously, and how they came to be the way they are. What is of interest for us here is the question of when, where and among whom this critical reflection first began to emerge.

While debates about religion within Irish Studies have tended to contain this element of critical reflection, the fact that the subject is made up of different academic disciplines, each of which have their own conception of what constitutes knowledge and their own rules of discourse production, presents particular problems that are not shared by other disciplines.[5] So although there will always be internal feuds about what constitutes good historiogra-phy, for example, most historians adhere to orthodox methods and, particularly among specialists, tend to write for other historians. The same is true of sociologists; while there are many who refer to historians and anthropologists in their work, there are few who cite poets, novelists or filmmakers. This lack of reference to other cultural texts and producers may also help to explain the general absence of a sociological strand within Irish Studies. Just as Irish sociologists have been slow to refer to literary and artistic sources, Irish Studies practitioners have been similarly neglectful of sociology. This begs the question: how is the field of Irish Studies constituted, regulated and controlled? An analysis of conference programmes, journals and books would suggest that some disciplines and subjects are more prominent than others. That is to say, Irish Studies tends to be associated with history, literature, language and the arts rather than with economics, political science, geography, sociology and anthropology. What arbitrary, artificial boundaries have come to constitute the subject as it is?

To answer these questions it might be useful to undertake an analysis of the field of Irish Studies. As in the present chapter, this would mean identifying the key institutional players who, through their critical discourses, practices and processes of inclusion and exclusion, structure the existing *habitus* – the often unquestioned orthodoxy – of the subject. Although these discourses, practices and processes are essentially arbitrary, they have the very real material consequence of exercising a form of symbolic domination. What makes this domination fascinating is the critically unreflective manner in which it has taken place. One of the characteristics of Irish Studies is the almost automatic, intuitive way in which the key players constituted the field of investigation, and instituted policies and practices of exclusion based on this configuration. Challenging this orthodoxy means recognising that there are always new players entering the field who struggle to achieve status and recognition by doing things differently, by not exercising the same processes of inclusion and exclusion, and by questioning existing boundaries.

RELIGIOUS IDENTITY AS SOCIAL IDENTITY

Identities have to do with a sense of belonging, of 'we-ness'. They are founded on people seeing themselves as being similar to a particular group of people and, at the same time, as being necessarily different from others. Identities can be usefully divided into social and personal types. Social identities tend to be broad, inherited and fixed. They are bound up with gender, race, ethnicity and religion; for example, being male, white, Irish and Catholic. Social identities also relate to occupation and social class. Much social life revolves around one's work, the class to which one belongs, and the way the classes are distinguished from one another. This is where social and personal identities begin to overlap. Personal identities have more to do with individual tastes, lifestyle choices, preferences and orientations. But as Bourdieu has shown, it is these personal tastes and preferences that define and delineate social classes (Bourdieu, 1984). There is, however, another way in which social and personal identities overlap: both are constructed around the stories that people tell about themselves. These stories reveal the sense of belonging, the strength of mutual identification, and the emotional intensity that underpin particular identities, and it is the levels of feeling that such factors generate that make social identities personal.

Identities are also systems of classification that are central to everyday social life, and as such are both inherently relational and culturally constituted. Although they are often seen as essential – as defining who one is – they are always, in effect, 'culturally arbitrary' (Bourdieu and Passeron, 1977: 8).[6] In other words, there is no inherent or necessary reason why people should divide themselves into Catholics and Protestants. Furthermore, owing to the lack of personal, face-to-face contact with all members of a particular faith, religious affiliation will generally be more imagined than real. This is not to say that the consequences of church membership are imagined. In fact, they are very real. As Anderson points out, membership of an arbitrary and imagined community can arouse 'deep attachments', which generate 'profound emotional legitimacy' for behaviour and can inspire people to be 'ready to die' for their community (Anderson, 1983: 13–14, 129).

Identities are not fixed. They are fluid processes that are embodied and presented differently depending on the social contexts that people inhabit. How people present themselves, therefore, and the stories they tell about themselves depend on the social environment in which they operate and, in particular, on the other people who are present within that environment. This sense of fluidity, of process, is at the heart of the difference between identity and being. Identities become fixed because there are interested groups and organisations who want to define them in a certain way. There are, for example, social, political and cultural organisations that specialise in defining what it is to be Irish, and there are also numerous bodies that regularly speak on behalf of the Irish people. But such statements and definitions are different from the actual ways in which Irish people live their lives, and from how they express their sense of Irishness. Similarly, definitions of what it is to be Catholic – whether those of the church itself or of Catholic organisations – do not often correspond with the lived experience being Catholic or with the Catholic way of life (Brubaker and Cooper, 2000). It should also be noted that social and personal identities, the labels and processes through which we announce our similarities and differences, can be distinguished from the more permanent, ongoing, ontological sense of self that constitutes being a particular individual in the world. However, it is through social and personal identities that an ongoing sense of self is constituted, cultivated and presented. So identity is the process by which a particular self is announced and described as being the same as others. As Ricoeur argues, 'identity lies in the distinction between sameness and selfhood, in the narrative dialectic between sameness and selfhood' (Ricoeur, 1992: 130).

Identity, then, is the anchor that links individuals to the social world. It is a process, a cognitive mechanism, through which individuals develop feelings of belonging, mutual identification, 'we-ness', and a sense of being part of a distinct group (Brubaker, 2001: 16). This process in turn becomes a way of reading and understanding the world in terms of who is similar and who is not. For most people, identity formation begins in the family. Children develop a sense of sameness and difference, first in relation to other members of the family, and then in relation to other people and bodies with which they come into contact. Social identity effectively begins with one's name, since it is through one's family name that identity within society, the state and the legal system is established. In everyday life and the various social fields within which people operate, it is a person's proper name that classifies and differentiates them from others. Personal names constitute the unity of an accumulated life history. They are the essential constants in everyday life, in moving in and between different social fields. As Bourdieu notes: 'Through this quite remarkable form of *nomination* constituted by the proper name, a constant and durable social identity is instituted which guarantees the identity of the biological individual in all possible fields where he appears as *agent,* that is in all his possible life histories' (Bourdieu, 2000: 299). Through one's name, then, self and social identity become merged. One's name not only implies constancy, it implies normalcy, a unification of self that is intelligible and predictable and has a well-constructed history of social integration. Names give people formal identity, legal status and recognition; their signature is the essential social statement of who people are.

It is within the family that particular forms of social identities are transmitted. One develops, for example, an identity as a male; as a member of a particular race, nationality or family; as being from a certain locality or county; as being middle class, Catholic and so forth. However, people can distance themselves from their ascribed social identities. They may, for example, have a weak sense of belonging to or mutual identification with the family in which they grew up, or they may have little contact with or emotional feeling for other family members. On the other hand, there are many emigrants who may not have set foot in Ireland for years, but who still see themselves not only as Irish but as, for example, a Mayo man or a Dublin woman. Something similar can happen with regard to religion. Most people in the Irish Republic are brought up Catholic. However, their identification as Roman Catholic tells us little about the strength of their loyalty to the church or the sense of bonding they feel they have with other Catholics. There are, moreover, many people, especially in Northern Ireland, who are identified as Catholic even though they no longer believe in or practise their religion and have no personal identification with other Catholics or the Catholic church. Finally, it is important to recognise that religious identity can often be more latent than manifest (Merton, 1957: 51). People may see themselves as Catholic or Protestant, but their sense of belonging to and participating in church activities may be low. However, in times of crisis or conflict, this latent identity may become more manifest, and may even lead to a renewed sense of religious self-identification.

The religious field is made up of different organisations – churches, denominations, sects, cults – which produce discourses about what it is to be religious. These in turn determine people's spiritual and moral outlook, and define the characteristics of being, say, Catholic, Protestant or Jewish. As already mentioned, religious social identities are ascribed and reinforced by gatekeepers and guardians who maintain existing classifications and divisions between people. Moreover, one of the key tasks of any religious organisation is to generate what Durkheim refers to as a sense of collective consciousness that unites people into a single moral community. This is necessary because for a church or sect to survive it has to persuade its members that they are, for certain purposes, 'identical' with one another (Brubaker and Cooper, 2000: 3). In other words, for religious professionals, the maintenance of a sense of religious identity and belonging is closely connected with the perpetuation of a sense of difference – and with it a sense of fear and anxiety about the religious 'other'. As Bourdieu explains:

What is at stake here is the power of imposing a vision of the social world through principles of di-vision which, when they are imposed on a whole group, establish meaning and consensus about meaning, and in particular about the identity and unity of the group, which creates the reality of the unity of the identity of the group. (Bourdieu, 1991: 221)

Religious social identity, then, is maintained through the expression of similar views and attitudes; that is, by embodying a particular religious *habitus*. This can be understood as an adaptable, almost automatic way of reading, understanding and acting in the world that is structured but not determined by church teachings (Bourdieu, 1990b: 52).[7] *Habitus* becomes embodied in the way people present and speak about themselves, and becomes objectified through representations such as icons, artefacts, emblems, badges and forms of dress. (In this way, maintaining religious identity is similar to maintaining ethnic identity.) But while we can say that Catholic identity is maintained through people embodying a Catholic *habitus*, the question arises as to how a collective identity is maintained among Protestants, particularly in Northern Ireland, where there are different Protestant denominations – Anglicans, Presbyterians, Methodists, Baptists – rather than a single Protestant church. In a situation where these denominations can only survive by distinguishing themselves from each other, what is it that creates a unifying Protestant identity? The reality is that Protestant identity as a whole is maintained more by political parties such as the Democratic Unionist Party and politico-religious organisations such as the Orange Order than by individual religious denominations. In effect, this is what distinguishes religious identity from ethno-religious identity. Members of the different Protestant churches and sects may effectively operate in terms of a competitive struggle with one another in the same way that Northern soccer teams compete in a domestic league. However, this opposition is overcome when the Northern Ireland team is competing against other countries. It is somewhat similar when Protestants compete against Catholics in the North.

It is also the case, however, that social and personal identities attain personal meaning and social significance not only because they are tied to social bonding and a sense of belonging, but also because they are related to power (Bourdieu and Passeron, 1977: 24–31).[8] In Ireland, being Catholic or Protestant impacts on marriage, family, education, social networks, sport and employment. In this way, religious identity affects people's life chances and their overall position in society. To understand how and why religious identity and being religious have remained strong in Ireland, it is necessary to understand how they are linked to social and occupational success, maintaining class position, attaining political power and gaining social respect. The fact is that many people invest time, money and effort in being Catholic or Protestant as an instrumental strategy rather than as a mere means of social bonding. Thus, being spiritual and moral means that they are seen as good people, which in turn helps them to secure and legitimate their power and position, not only in the religious field, but also in other spheres. Through attending religious services, saying prayers and reading the Bible, as well as by following priests' and ministers' advice about how to live a good life, people can accumulate religious capital (Inglis, 2003: 51–9). This then provides access to other forms of capital such as cultural (education), social (social networks), symbolic (honour and respect), political (high office) and economic (employment). In short, the more religious professionals help their followers to achieve and maintain other forms of capital, the more successful they will be in maintaining church membership. In this way, therefore, religious identity and the fulfilment of religious interests are fundamentally linked to the fulfilment of social, cultural, political and economic interests. In Ireland, overt and strong identification with the Catholic church has often been central to obtaining good positions in many Catholic and semi-Catholic organisations, especially in areas such as education, health and social welfare. Indeed, for most of the twentieth century the accumulation of religious capital was central to the creation and maintenance of an Irish Catholic social elite that permeated the fields of commerce, government, the civil service, the professions and the semi-state sectors. The history of this linkage and how it operated has yet to be written.

RELIGIOUS IDENTITY AS PERSONAL IDENTITY

Personal identity derives from two main sources. The first is the level of emotional and personal commitment an individual has to their different social identities. Thus, some people are passionately committed to their identity as a Catholic or Protestant, and in this way their personal and social identities become linked. The second source of personal identity lies in the various choices people make and the preferences they express within the different spheres of their everyday lives. So Catholics, for example, may engage in discourses and practices that confirm their affiliation with their fellow Catholics, while also doing things that mark them out as different. They may, for example, have preferred forms of prayer, develop close links with a certain religious order or charitable organisation, practise devotion to a specific saint or gravitate towards particular places of pilgrimage. In other words, the particular way in which they are religious and the way they attain religious capital defines their personal identity. What is of interest for us, of course, is the way in which personal religious identity combines with other forms of personal identity such as the sports people play, the way they dress, their preferences in food and drink, and the television and radio programmes they like. All of these are personal choices, but they are also, in effect, signs of individual identity by which we define ourselves as both similar to and different from other people.

Although we can make these conceptual or analytical distinctions about different forms of identity, it is important to recognise that in everyday life there is a fluidity between them, that the extent to which one form of identity is dominant depends on the field in which a person is operating, the particular social context and the people involved. This is where identity becomes a process through which the self is announced and presented. As a cultural actor, an individual will bring some identities to the forefront of what he or she says and does, and leave others in the background of their self-presentation (Goffman, 1969: 114–15).[9] There are two other important considerations to mention here. Since religious identity is linked to non-religious interests and outcomes, what is of interest in any religious field in any society is the extent to which people change their religious affiliation. In other words, what is the level of religious conversion and when, where, why and among whom does it take place? What makes people change their religion or stay with the church, denomination or sect into which they were born? To pose such questions is to acknowledge that, while they may not advertise in the marketplace, different religious organisations are effectively in competition with one another to provide access to religious capital and to offer the best chance of attaining salvation. But religious organisations can also compete by offering access to non-religious capital. However, what is striking about Ireland, North and South, is the low level of religious conversion and, at the same time, the low level of atheism and agnosticism. This reluctance to change or renounce one's inherited religious identity demonstrates how religion operates in terms of a cultural legacy and heritage. People see their religious identity as part of what they are, even though they may have little or no allegiance to the institutional church to which they belong. Indeed, while many Irish people see themselves as Roman Catholics, there does not seem to be a strong sense of defending the institutional church.

The ability of a church, sect or cult to satisfy the religious interests of its members is related to its ability to be independent and to avoid challenges from, on the one hand, other religious groups and organisations and, on the other, non-religious institutions such as the state and the media. One of the major recent transformations that has affected the Catholic church in Ireland has been the decline in its ability to play an influential role in the areas of health, social welfare and education. At the same time, it has been unable to prevent both state and media from prying into what was previously regarded as its private, sacred affairs. So while the Irish Catholic church devoted considerable energies in this and previous generations to fending off challenges from the Protestant churches, the real threat to Catholic religious affiliation has come from the increase in liberal, individualist behaviour associated with sexuality, the media and consumer capitalism in general.

There are two final factors I wish to mention in relation to religious identities in contemporary Ireland. The first concerns the ways in which the political sphere, or more properly the sphere of the state, impinges upon the religious field. This is seen primarily in the fact that, as already mentioned, the island is divided politically, and that the reproduction of this division is rooted in religion as much as in politics and economics. In the twentieth century there developed what was effectively a semi-Protestant state in the North and a semi-Catholic state in the South. Secondly, there has been a steady growth in number of new – and mostly Protestant – religious movements, sects and cults in Ireland in the last 20 years. There has also been a gradual increase in the numbers of people attracted to other world religions, due mainly to the rise in immigration, though these numbers remain comparatively small. However, because of differences in the religious complexions of the Northern and the Southern Irish societies, and variations in the way churches, sects and cults fulfil non-religious interests, the religious fields in both regions require separate description and analysis.

THE RELIGIOUS FIELD IN THE IRISH REPUBLIC

The religious field in any society is best outlined through a description of the different churches, denominations, sects and cults and the relative strength of their following (Aldridge, 2000: 39–46). These are the main institutional players who, as in any market, are competing to attract and maintain allegiance. Over the last 300 years there has been a shift away from religions trying to attract conversions from each other, towards maintaining whatever members and allegiance they have against the tide of liberal individualism, materialism and secularism. Indeed, in terms of religious affiliation, the picture over the last 150 years has been one of very little change. The proportion of Roman Catholics in the 26 counties has not changed significantly between 1861 (89 per cent) and 2002 (88 per cent). And while there have been some important socio-cultural changes during the years since 1991, which coincided with a period of sustained economic growth, the overall picture is of little substantial change. In terms of religious affiliation, then, the Catholic church still holds a monopoly position in the religious field, as is clear from the data produced by the 2002 Census (see Table 8.1).

Table 8.1 Religious affiliation in the Republic of Ireland, 2002

Religious affiliation	1991	%	2002	%
Roman Catholic	3,228,327	91.6	3,462,606	88.4
Lapsed Roman Catholic	3,749	0.1	590	0.01
Protestant				
Church of Ireland (incl. Protestant)	89,187	2.5	115,611	3.0
Christian (unspecified)	16,329	0.5	21,403	0.5
Presbyterian	13,199	0.4	20,582	0.5
Methodist	5,037	0.1	10,033	0.3
Jehovah's Witness	3,393	0.1	4,430	0.1
Baptist	1,156	0.03	2,265	0.05
Lutheran	1,010	0.02	3,068	0.1
Latter Day Saints (Mormon)	853	0.02	833	0.02
Evangelical	819	0.02	3,780	0.1
Quaker (Society of Friends)	749	0.02	859	0.02
Orthodox	358	0.01	10,437	0.3
Apostolic or Pentecostal	285	0.01	3,152	0.1
Brethren	256	0.005	222	0.006
Other religions				
Muslim (Islamic)	3,875	0.1	19,147	0.5
Jewish	1,581	0.04	1,790	0.04
Buddhist	986	0.02	3,894	0.1
Hindu	953	0.02	3,099	0.1
Baha'i	430	0.01	490	0.01
Pantheist	202	0.005	1,106	0.02
Other stated religions	2,197	0.06	8,920	0.2
No religious identification				
No religion	66,270	1.9	138,264	3.5
Not stated	83,375	2.4	79,094	2.01
Agnostic	823	0.02	1,028	0.02
Atheist	320	0.01	500	0.01
Total	3,525,719	100	3,917,203	100

Source: Census of Population, 2002.

There are three other significant features to emerge from this analysis. Firstly, the proportion belonging to the mainstream Protestant churches – Church of Ireland, Presbyterian and Methodist – increased from 3 per cent in 1991 to 3.8 per cent in 2002. Overall, the total number of Protestants grew from 132,631 to 196,675, an increase of 48 per cent. Secondly, there was a striking increase in the number identifying themselves with other religions, up 276 per cent from 10,224 to 38,446. Islam witnessed the most dramatic growth within this category, with the proportion of Muslims rising by an astonishing 394 per cent, up from 3,875 to 19,147. Thirdly, and perhaps paradoxically, the number reporting themselves to be atheists or agnostics is very low, particularly when compared to the number who declared themselves to have no religion or did not state that they had any religion. The latter category rose from 150,788 in 1991 to 218,886 in 2002, an increase of 45 per cent. The overall proportion of people identifying themselves with a particular religion, however, does not give any indication of the strength and depth of identification. In other words, affiliation with a particular faith does not tell us anything about the level of bonding or emotional sense of belonging that people feel. Many Irish Catholics may identify themselves as such in the Census and accept the fundamental tenets of the faith, but an increasing number rarely or never attend church rituals and disregard some of the church's basic moral teachings. So while there is a strong level of religious identity that may be emotionally quite deep and which may manifest itself on certain occasions, the bonding is weak on a regular basis. Although the analogy is not completely satisfactory, it is rather like a golfer who identifies strongly with a particular club, but rarely goes there, only plays golf on special occasions and, when he does, has no qualms about breaking the rules (Bruce, 1986: 57).

There are two main ways of assessing the level or depth of religious identification. The first is by describing and analysing the different dimensions to being religious and, in particular, the level of religious belief, practice, knowledge and experience. The second way is to assess the extent to which religious identification and being religious permeate other social fields. What is of importance here is the extent to which people display or portray their religious identity in everyday life and how relevant it is to them in developing and maintaining social networks, attaining honour and respect, obtaining a good education, gaining employment, getting elected and achieving promotion. The level of religious identification can be ascertained by the extent to which, for example, Catholic teachings and regulations influence behaviour and strategies in other fields and, most significantly, the extent to which people would still adhere to their religion if it clashed with the demands of family, work, politics, sport or friends (Inglis, 1980; Nic Ghiolla Phadraig, 1976).

Survey results in the Republic over the last 30 years indicate that while the proportion of people who formally identify themselves as Catholic has remained relatively stable (around 90 per cent), there appears to have been a significant change in the strength and depth of this identity. In 1973–74, 91 per cent of Irish Catholics attended Mass at least once a week (Nic Ghiolla Phadraig, 1976: 129). Thirty years later, a 2003 opinion poll indicated that this had declined to 50 per cent (RTÉ Prime Time/TNS MRBI, 2003). The decline was most evident among young people and those living in cities. The poll also indicated that only a minority – between a quarter and a fifth – accepted basic church teachings such as the prohibition on the use of artificial contraception, divorce, clerical marriage and women priests. It would seem, then, that for most Catholics, identity with the church is no longer linked to a strict adherence to its moral teachings, nor is it the major source of moral religious capital that it once was. This is further reflected in the marked decline over the last 30 years in the number of Catholics who believe in hell and attend confession (Inglis, 1998: 207). However, there is evidence from the same poll that there is still a high proportion (over 70 per cent) of Catholics who accept basic Christian beliefs such as the existence of God, the divinity of Christ, transubstantiation and the Virgin birth. Yet, this poll also indicated that just over half of Irish Catholics prayed on a daily basis and encouraged their children to pray at bedtime. Nevertheless, these findings would suggest that approximately the same number (50 per cent) have a strong social and personal identification with the church. For the remainder, it may be that their religious identity is more latent than manifest, only emerging strongly during rites of passage such as births, deaths and marriages.

Moreover, while there is definite evidence that many Catholics now distance themselves from a rigid adherence to church teachings and practices, and display a more individualistic approach to morality, there are also indications that Irish Catholic identities still extend to the traditional magical or devotional type of religiosity (Inglis, 1998: 24–30). For example, in the course of eleven weeks during the summer of 2001, it was claimed that as many as three million

Irish people turned out to view the relics of St Thérèse (Healy and McCaffrey, 2001). And despite recent changes in the nature of their religious identities, Catholics still tend to be married and buried in the church, to bring up their children within the faith, to celebrate christenings, first Holy Communions and confirmations, and to send their children to Catholic schools. In other words, while the importance of the Catholic church as a source of moral capital may be in decline in the Irish Republic, it still appears to act as a conduit for the supernatural and as a source of religious capital. There is also a sense that while Catholics are becoming more Protestant in terms of making up their own minds about morality and goodness, the majority can still be said both to believe in and belong to the church, in contrast to their Protestant neighbours in Britain.[10]

The level of religious identification can also be assessed by the extent to which the pursuit and accumulation of religious capital has importance in the pursuit and accumulation of capital in other social fields. If, for example, certain Catholics place an emphasis on being spiritual and moral and obtaining religious capital, it may benefit or impede their pursuit of power in other social areas. This relates to what Goffman refers to as the public presentation of self in everyday life, which involves presenting one's religious identification, beliefs and practices as front-stage behaviour. Such Catholics openly display their faith by making religious references in everyday communication, praying in public places, blessing themselves when passing a church and wearing religious insignia. In this way, their religious principles and ways of understanding and being in the world – that is to say, their Catholic *habitus* – permeate and guide their behaviour in other social fields. In short, there is a continual presentation of oneself as being first and foremost a Catholic.

This portrayal of self is central to religious professionals wearing clerical dress, for example, but also pertains to the laity working in other social fields, as doctors, teachers and politicians. In a national survey in 1973–74, more than six in ten (64 per cent) of Catholic respondents said that their religious principles always guided their behaviour with regard to their occupation (Nic Ghiolla Phadraig, 1976: 126–7). Even more significant, perhaps, is the proportion of Catholics who actively pursue and promote their religious beliefs in other social fields and whose primary loyalty, if there was a clash, would be to their religious principles. This is what the late Archbishop of Dublin, Dr Kevin McNamara, demanded in 1985 when he declared: 'For the Church a major challenge today is to help people make a closer connection between their religious practice and their daily lives; between worshipping God in church and serving Him in the world of work, recreation and culture' (Inglis, 1998: 82). Certainly, the social history of the extent to which being Catholic permeated other areas of Irish life, and of how, when, and where it took place, has yet to be written.[11] But it must be remembered that this permeation of other social fields was linked not only to a strong identity with the church – the sense that 'us Catholics should always stick together' – but also to the ways in which it helped people to accumulate other forms of capital and higher social positions. In effect, the decline in the strength of identification with the Catholic church is a function of the decline in the importance of religious capital in other social fields, particularly among the professional classes and the Catholic social elite.

In addition to this decline in the importance of religious capital among Irish Catholics, the waning of religious identification is closely related to the increase in the significance of other forms of personal identities, most of which stem from the growth of technology, the capitalist market and the commodification of social relations. For generations, the Catholic church strove to stem the tide of what it generically referred to as 'materialism'. However, it would seem that while identification with the church is still quite strong, the souls of many Irish Catholics are being lost to liberal individualism. This is evidenced by the extent to which many are becoming more Protestant, insofar as they are developing more personal paths to morality and salvation. In addition to trying to counter the rapid spread of materialism and liberal individualism, therefore, the church has had to contend with creeping Protestantism. And although the number of Irish Catholics converting to Protestant denominations is very small, the church has been anxious – its ongoing rhetoric of ecumenism notwithstanding – to draw rigid boundaries between the two faiths. This effectively means that despite having won the nineteenth-century war of attrition with the Church of Ireland, the Catholic church is still engaged in a symbolic twenty-first-century struggle to maintain its monopoly position in Irish society. At times, the church's struggle to establish its moral superiority verges on a denigration of the opposition. In some respects, little has changed from the 1950s approach of Archbishop John Charles McQuaid, who constantly warned against ecumenism and of Catholics becoming involved religiously with Protestants (Cooney, 1999: 365–7, 387–91).

THE STRUGGLE FOR SYMBOLIC DOMINATION

To understand Catholic religious identity and being in Ireland, it is necessary to remember that there is a long history of Catholics struggling to be allowed to worship in public, to participate in civil society and to exercise religious freedom. Once Catholic emancipation was achieved in 1829, there was an ongoing campaign by the Irish clergy not only to build churches and develop a Catholic system of education, health and social welfare, but also to engage in a symbolic struggle to demonstrate the spiritual and moral superiority of Catholicism over Protestantism (Inglis, 1998: 117–40). Thus, the Catholic church maintained a policy and practice of social exclusion, prohibiting Catholics from attending Protestant religious services, particularly weddings and funerals, and preventing them from entering Ireland's oldest Protestant university, Trinity College Dublin. More important, under the 1907 *Ne Temere* decree, Protestant partners in mixed marriages had to agree that any children born would be raised as Catholics. Viewed in this context, many of the incidents of religious discrimination that have punctuated the history of post-independence Ireland, such as the appointment of a Protestant librarian in County Mayo in 1931 and the Fethard-on-Sea boycott of 1957, can be seen as attempts by the Irish Catholic church to symbolically dominate Protestants (Fuller, 2002; Mennell *et al.*, 2000; Whyte, 1980).

There is, moreover, much evidence of the continuation of such symbolic domination in contemporary Ireland. In December 1997, as one of her first official acts, President Mary McAleese went to Christ Church Cathedral in Dublin and took Holy Communion (O'Leary, 2000). The event, which received front-page media publicity, was widely interpreted as an ecumenical act between a Catholic President and a Protestant church that demonstrated McAleese's campaign pledge to 'build bridges' between the two religious communities in Ireland. Her actions were warmly welcomed by the Church of Ireland Archbishop of Dublin, Most Reverend Walton Empey, as well as by some leading Catholic theologians and priests. However, inter-church Communion is not permitted for Roman Catholics, and within a matter of days the Catholic Archbishop of Dublin used the word 'sham' in a radio interview to describe the actions of Catholics who took Communion in a Protestant church. In a later article published in the *Irish Times* on 20 December 1997, Archbishop Connell explained that he had not used the word to mean 'cheap or shoddy' but rather to describe that which 'is not what it appears to be', which, he maintained, is the problem when Catholics take Communion in other churches.

Connell's tactics in this case can be seen as part of a long-term offensive strategy by the Catholic church and the Vatican against Protestantism in Ireland. In 1998 the Irish Conference of Catholic Bishops produced a document entitled *One Bread One Body*, which banned Catholics from taking Communion in Reformed churches and refused to allow non-Catholics to receive Communion, except in rare circumstances. Two years later the Vatican published *Dominus Jesus*, which described Reformed churches as 'not churches in the proper sense' as they 'had not preserved the valid Episcopate and the genuine and integral substance of the Eucharistic mystery'. It further argued that their ministries were invalid. Most recently, the late Pope John Paul II issued a 2003 encyclical, *Ecclesia de Eucharistia*, in which Protestant denominations are referred to as 'ecclesial communities' rather than 'churches'. This document also reaffirms the impossibility of Catholics sharing Communion with Protestants. As the Church of Ireland Bishop of Clogher, Right Reverend Michael Jackson, explained in an *Irish Times* article of 29 August 2003, these documents together sapped Protestant morale and revived the worst memories of *Ne Temere*.

The ongoing attempts by the Catholic church to symbolically dominate its Protestant counterparts is more than just a theological dispute, therefore. For example, in an *Irish Times* interview published on 31 October 2001, Archbishop Connell said that his Church of Ireland counterpart, Archbishop Empey, 'wouldn't have much theological competence' and was not one of his church's 'high flyers'. While there is always a gap between church teaching and people's beliefs and practice, institutional discourse does structure the way Catholics, especially those of the orthodox variety, read and understand the world in general and their relationships with Protestants in particular. The influence of institutional church rhetoric on maintaining boundaries between Catholics and Protestants may be small in the South, but in the North – particularly among Protestants who see Catholics as being ruled from Rome – its impact could be long-lasting. This is partly because in the North religious identity has not been swamped by secularisation and individualism to the same extent as it has in the South.

RELIGIOUS IDENTITY IN NORTHERN IRELAND

One of the problems of treating Northern Ireland and the Republic of Ireland as distinct entities when discussing religious identity and being religious is that it perpetuates the very ethno-political division which is being studied.[12] Nevertheless, because of the length and depth of the conflict between Protestants and Catholics in Ireland, and because religious identity is so closely interwoven with ethnic and political identities, being Catholic or Protestant has quite different meanings north and south of the border. Indeed, one of the factors that makes Northern Ireland unique is that while there are substantial shifts and divisions among the Protestant population on theological issues, politically speaking, they are united in their determination to maintain the Union with Britain (Brewer, 1998; Megahey, 2000).

Table 8.2   Religious identification in Northern Ireland, 2002

Question: Do you regard yourself as belonging to any particular religion? If yes, which?

Religion	Percentage
Catholic	41.0
Protestant	
Anglican/Church of Ireland	15.8
Presbyterian	21.7
Methodist	2.4
URC/Congregational	0.3
Baptist	0.9
Free Presbyterian	1.1
Brethren	0.6
Other Protestant Sect	1.1
Protestant – no denomination	2.4
Christian – no denomination	1.3
Non-Christian	0.6
Not stated	1.0
Independent	9.9
Total	100.0
[N]	[1,800]

Source: Northern Ireland Life and Times Survey, 2002.

A recent survey showed that while the proportion of Catholics in the North has risen steadily in recent years, from 35 per cent in 1991 to 41 per cent in 2002, the proportion of Protestants in mainstream churches – Church of Ireland, Presbyterian and Methodist – has dropped from 47 per cent in 1991 to 40 per cent in 2002 (Brewer, 2003a: 23).[13] In effect, this decline in mainstream Protestantism has been happening since 1926. Each generation has seen a loss of membership among the young and, with it, an ageing of the population. There is a corresponding decline in the number of Protestants marrying in church and having their children baptised. This is linked to a fall-off in religious practice generally, and in the loyalty and commitment of Protestants to their churches in particular. It is also connected to a decline in religious orthodoxy, a liberalisation of belief and the dwindling influence of religion in other areas of Protestants' lives. However, this general trend of Protestant diminution is complicated by the fact that some Protestants have been switching to conservative evangelical churches such as the Baptists and Free Presbyterians, as well as to more liberal, charismatic and independent house churches (Brewer, 2003b: 5–7).

There is, then, quite an amount of diversity and change within Protestantism in Northern Ireland. To outsiders it may appear that there is very little difference between the theology, teachings and practices of the various churches and sects, but to those involved there is a world of difference. However, as Brewer (2003a: 22) points out, while there is a general decline in religiosity among Northern Irish Protestants, they are still much more religious than their British counterparts. This is primarily because of the links between religion and politics in the North. Bruce (1986: 264–5) has argued that strong Protestant identities survive in the North mainly owing to the ethnic political threat posed by Catholics. In this regard Brewer notes: 'The violence used in ethnic defence has tended to reinforce identities by polarising people, thus giving religion as the boundary marker a seemingly impenetrable and absolute quality, like race, even though religion is socially constructed and contingent' (Brewer, 2003b: 10). He goes on to argue that because being Protestant is such an important ethnic marker in the North, religion has not yet been privatised, as it has in other parts of the UK. Indeed, there are still many Protestant associations and interest groups operating in civil society, which act as promoters and gatekeepers of Protestant identity through sermonising and engaging in public discussion and debate. Moreover, Protestant identity is regularly put on public display, particularly in the form of mass protests and annual parades. Thus, religion in Northern Ireland is closely related to political action, and as such can be used to legitimate as much as to condemn sectarian violence (Brewer, 2003b: 11–12).

Northern Catholics, on the other hand, tend to be more orthodox and conservative and to have higher levels of religious belief compared both to their Protestant counterparts and to Catholics in other parts of Europe, including the Republic (Mitchell, 2003: 2–3). The question, however, is to what extent this high level of religiosity is related to ethno-political identity. It has been argued that whereas for many Northern Protestants, the conflict with Catholics is rooted in theology, Catholic grievances against Protestants have more to do with political, economic and social inequality than with religion *per se* (McGarry and O'Leary, 1995: 205–7). However, the notion that Catholic religious identity is not linked to ethno-political identity has recently been challenged on the grounds that there is substantial evidence of a symbiotic relationship between nationalist politicians and Catholic clergy in the North (Mitchell, 2003: 3–5). Not only do they share the same *habitus*, they are also mutually dependent upon maintaining the allegiance of the Catholic community. While this symbiotic relationship may seem more tenuous in working-class nationalist areas, and while there have been many disputes between the Catholic church and Sinn Féin, both organisations are careful not to allow any disagreements to descend into an open conflict that could alienate either organisation from their mutual constituents. Moreover, territorial disputes within the Catholic community about the boundaries between religion and politics have rarely threatened their united opposition to Protestant unionism.

The issue of social class is also important in this context as it permeates behaviour in all social fields including the religious, and influences the extent to which people are willing to forefront their religious being and identity in their everyday lives. As already mentioned, to understand religious being and identity in the North, we have to appreciate how an individual's sense of belonging to a church or denomination permeates, if not dominates, other forms of identification. In every social field there will always be processes at work that cause people to form various kinds of alliances – some small and contingent, others large and institutionalised – through which they divide others into 'us' and 'them' (Jenkins, 1996; Southerton, 2002). The question posed by the Irish situation, especially the North, is to what extent religious identity transcends other forces such as class, family and locality. As Bell (1990) discovered, Protestant identity can lead to young people transcending their membership of the Church of Ireland and identifying themselves with Ian Paisley and the Free Presbyterians. But Protestant identity is also tied in with being British, unionist and perhaps a member of the Orange Order. What is crucial in this process is the extent to which people wear religious insignia, join marching bands, display the Union flag and signal their support for paramilitary groups. So to understand the meaning of Northern Irish Protestant identity one has to take account of the extent to which it permeates social behaviour and the presentation of the self in diverse areas of public life.

Following Benson (2004), it can be argued that there are psychological as well as physical and political boundaries by which being Catholic or Protestant in Ireland is maintained. One of the ways in which individuals sustain their sense of religious belonging is by defining what they will and will not do when it comes to engaging with members of other religious groups. Thus, for example, Northern Catholics might define themselves through announcing that while they will live in the same street as their Protestant neighbours, work in the same organisation and visit the same shops, they will not date Protestants, follow the same soccer team or frequent the same pubs. Decisions about whether or not to engage in such activities are based on notions of loyalty to one's personal honour – to what people see as belonging to them – and to one's social honour, to the group to which individuals feel bound and socially responsible. In other words, Catholics and Protestants know and understand themselves negatively, in terms of what they could not do. The very idea of engaging in some activity with a member of the opposite religion, therefore, produces emotions of guilt, shame, remorse and self-disgust. Hence the continuing belief among some traditional sections of the Northern Protestant community that the Catholic papacy represents the Antichrist (Barkley, 1966; Higgins and Brewer, 2003). These emotions are often linked to a pervasive fear and uncertainty that can underlie social interaction between the two communities. Thus, there is a recognition that unless these emotions are controlled and a religious and political correctness rigorously maintained, the thin ice on which cross-community sociability rests could easily break.

CONCLUSION

Ireland is a religiously divided island, the border between north and south being closely connected to the divisions between Catholics and Protestants. These boundaries are in turn perpetuated through a strong sense of mutual identification and 'we-ness'. Over generations, these religious boundaries and identities have been maintained largely because the fulfilment of social, cultural, political and economic interests has been intimately linked to religious affiliation. It is also evident that, despite the rhetoric of ecumenism, the clerical elites within both dominant religions have a continuing vested interest in maintaining these boundaries, as recent pronouncements by senior members of the Irish Catholic hierarchy attest. However, although the strength of religious identification and being religious is perhaps stronger in Ireland than in any other part of the Western world, it would appear that it is beginning to wane, the main force of change being the growth in significance of personal identities, especially those related to class, occupation and consumer lifestyles. At the same time, the link between religious affiliation and the attainment of power and influence in other social fields has gradually weakened, with the result that it is becoming less and less necessary to be a good Catholic or Protestant in order to gain access to proper housing, a decent education, a good job or membership of a social club. Nevertheless, being Catholic or Protestant is still seen by most Irish people as an essential part of who they are. We must conclude, therefore, that religious identity continues to play a significant role in the cultural heritage of many Irish people, whether it manifests itself privately as a latent sense of denominational affiliation or more publicly in times of personal trauma, social celebration or communal conflict.

NOTES

1. This study is part of the Identity, Diversity and Citizenship Research Programme within the Institute for the Study of Social Change at University College Dublin.
2. Fahey (1992) points out that it is commonplace in social theory to link industrialisation, technical rationality, large-scale urbanisation and institutional differentiation with secularisation. He argues, however, that institutional Christianity continued to thrive in Western societies during industrialisation and that Catholicism flourished in the United States throughout the twentieth century. He suggests that the church may have acted both as source of social capital and, through offering transcendental consolation, as a bulwark against the alienating affects of modernity.
3. The concept of social field used here derives from Pierre Bourdieu. For a description and analysis of how the religious field in the Republic of Ireland overlaps with other social fields, see Inglis (2003).

4. For an opposing view, see Coakley (1998).

5. In this respect, while Irish Studies may have been beset, as Eagleton (1997a) argues, by various forms of ideology, he fails to acknowledge that a central component of the subject – and indeed of late modern Irish society – is this element of critical reflection.

6. However, Bourdieu (1990a: 180–1) insists that although cultural beliefs and practices, including religion, are arbitrary, this does not mean that are all relative or equal to one another. Cultural beliefs and practices, and the institutions, organisations and classes that perpetuate them, necessarily involve symbolic domination.

7. Each field produces its own *habitus* at the heart of which is an unquestioned orthodoxy, which Bourdieu refers to as *doxa*. This, in turn, produces an *illusio*. In the religious field, the *illusio* is that there is nothing more important than being spiritual and moral; everything else, including power, wealth and status, is secondary.

8. Weber (1978: 400) argues that 'religious or magical behaviour or thinking must not be set apart from the range of everyday purposive conduct, particularly since even the ends of the religious and magical actions are predominantly economic'.

9. There is also an interchange between social and personal identities that links into Goffman's notion of self-presentation.

10. This is adapted from Davie's (1994) notion that the persistence of religious belief in Britain as well as in almost all Western European countries, together with the decline in churchgoing, is best summed up not as secularisation, but as 'believing without belonging'.

11. In a letter to the *Irish Times* published on 9 October 2003, a former civil servant remarked that while working in 'the middle ranks' of the service from 1979 to 1990, he attended a meeting in which a senior official in the Department of the Taoiseach openly declared that he was a 'Catholic first and foremost, a public servant thereafter'.

12. On the issue as to whether sociologists perpetuate the social divisions they claim to study objectively, see Bourdieu (1991: 226–7).

13. It should be noted that the 2001 Census indicated that 44 per cent of the Northern Irish population saw themselves as Catholics. However, this figure included those who originally said that they had 'no religion' but in a supplementary question stated they felt closer to Catholicism.

9

'A Decent Girl Well Worth Helping': Women, Migration and Unwanted Pregnancy

Louise Ryan

In the autumn of 2003 I was invited to a conference in a British university during which there was a lively discussion about Irish Studies. I found it thought-provoking but also a little frustrating. I concluded that the primary reason for my frustration was the lack of clarity and agreement about what constituted Irish Studies. The subject that was being discussed and critiqued did not reflect my experiences of teaching and researching in an Irish Studies Centre and, as I listened, I became increasingly aware of just how capacious a concept Irish Studies is. Perhaps that is one of its strengths. It has a broad focus and can encompass a diversity of subject matter and a range of methodologies. What's more, different people 'do' Irish Studies very differently. Perhaps this also explains why I had initially found this chapter difficult to write. I could not decide what I wanted to write about and where I wanted to start. The arena of Irish Studies just seemed far too wide and all encompassing to provide an easy point of entry. So in the end I decided that it would be best to start by locating myself and my particular interests within this expansive – and expanding – disciplinary field.

Since completing my PhD studies and leaving Cork in 1992 I have worked in academia in Britain. My published work spans a range of topics: the Irish suffrage movement, women and nationalism in Ireland, the Irish press in the 1920s and 1930s, infanticide, female sexuality in the Irish Free State, the oral narratives of Irish women migrants to Britain and, most recently, the health of Irish migrants in London. If I were working in an Irish university these research interests might be seen as somewhat eclectic and could be defined as being broadly interdisciplinary, encompassing history, sociology, media studies and women's studies. However, because I work in a British university, my research can be located under the broad umbrella of Irish Studies, since within this context the most striking thing about my work is that it is focused on Ireland, Irishness or the Irish in Britain. This is not to deny the influence of sociology, history and women's studies on my writing, but rather to highlight the importance of institutional contexts to perceptions of a scholar's profile and categorisation.

As a sociologist, my approach to Irish Studies has always been very materialist and somewhat structuralist. Teaching Irish Studies in Britain to a group of predominantly first- and second-generation Irish students, my approach to the subject was influenced not just by my sociological background, but also by these students' experiences as Irish migrants in Britain. In a society where Ireland and Irish people are rarely the subject of serious academic research and analysis, Irish Studies provides a welcome and much-needed space in which students can discuss the complex and diverse realities of being Irish in Britain. The discipline also provides a space for academics to come together and discuss their research interests in a way that is not possible if you are the only person in the faculty who is interested in Irish issues. Thus, in my experience Irish Studies has been an empowering and enabling educational and institutional force. Like women's studies, it has helped marginalised groups to carve out a space in which they can grow in confidence and strength, and challenge their erstwhile invisibility within the curriculum. For me, however, this is not just about challenging the invisibility of the Irish in Britain in the British university curriculum, but equally about confronting the continuing absence of the Irish in Britain from the Irish university curriculum.

During the 1980s, when I was a student in Ireland, emigration, although a daily reality for many of my friends and ultimately for myself also, was only mentioned within my academic syllabus in a historical context, usually associated with the nineteenth-century Irish exodus to America. Later, in the 1990s, as an academic and an emigrant living in Britain, I found that my research on Ireland and Irish women was continually being framed by my experiences of migration and the persistence of this theme in the evolution of twentieth-century Ireland. For example, during my first collaborative project with Breda Gray in the mid-1990s, which focused on gender and national identity within Ireland, it became clear that our location in the north-west of England was influencing our attitudes to and understanding of Irish society. In this way, it became increasingly apparent to us that issues around migration had to be an essential part of how Ireland was understood. In particular, the question arose as to how a focus on migration, specifically the movement of people between Ireland and Britain, might be conjoined with an interdisciplinary Irish Studies framework to explore some of the hidden social phenomena and taken-for-granted dynamics of Irish civic society. This chapter seeks to elaborate such a conceptual approach, with particular reference to one of the most covert forms of migration between Ireland and Britain.

Migration takes many different forms – temporary and long-term, individual and familial, internal and external – and is often conceptualised in terms of permanent separation and loss. However, as I have argued elsewhere, such a representation minimises the ongoing emotional and financial impact of migrants on the friends and families who remain behind, and overlooks the continuing social, cultural, economic and political effects of migration on the nation as a whole (Ryan, 2002a, 2002b). Emigration continues to impact on Ireland in so many different ways, from government economic policy and legislation to social and cultural attitudes (Delaney, 2000; Gray, 2000; A. Smyth, 1992; Walter, 2001). Since at least the nineteenth century it has been a safety valve, a way of dealing with unpalatable problems such as high unemployment, urban overcrowding and rural poverty. As Moser (1993) has observed, all Irish political parties have condemned emigration, while doing little or nothing to regulate or stop it. In fact, it has been suggested by some commentators that emigration became 'an asset to the ruling forces', as poverty and unemployment were exported elsewhere, and with them the potential for social discontent or revolt (Bracken and O'Sullivan, 2001: 48).

These were not Ireland's only social exports, however. One of the least discussed and most secretive dimensions of Irish emigration has been the ways in which both long- and short-term forms of departure have been used to deal with unwanted pregnancy. Long before the contemporary abortion trail to England, pregnant Irish women were arriving in London and Liverpool seeking help, advice and support (Ryan, 2002a: 59). And while we must acknowledge that women's migration is complex and involves numerous, overlapping decisions and choices (or lack of them), the fact that this aspect has been so rarely spoken about has enabled the state to avoid, ignore and flatly deny a problem whose existence is both embarrassing and politically challenging. In this context, I believe that an Irish Studies approach that is informed by an awareness of the interconnections between

Ireland and Britain, and of those between the Irish in Britain and the Irish in Ireland, can provide a very valuable and much needed space within which to explore the secret migrations of pregnant Irish women. My primary aim in this chapter, therefore, is not to discuss abortion *per se*, but rather to focus on the wider picture and the long-established Irish practice of using migration, both temporary and permanent, as a way of dealing with unwanted pregnancy. Despite the fact that Irish reproductive politics are often constructed as a way of maintaining national boundaries (Martin, 2000), I am more interested here in examining the significance of travelling *beyond* the national boundary. In particular, I wish to explore the questions of how Irish *national* policies and practices have been shaped and defined through the possibility of women's *international* travel to Britain to avail of abortion services, and how this most secret form of migration has acted as a safety valve for reproductive practices within Ireland.

GOING TO ENGLAND: SECRET JOURNEYS AND UNTOLD STORIES

Soon after my arrival in Britain in 1992 I saw the front page of the 19 February edition of the *Irish Times* and stopped dead in my tracks (Fig. 9.1). The featured cartoon by Martyn Turner was to become one of the most powerful and talked-about images in the Irish media that year. It depicted a small, vulnerable child with a teddy bear standing on the island of Ireland, surrounded by barbed wire. Trapped and fearful, the young girl was unable to escape her confinement.

This, of course, was a pictorial representation of the 'X case', the shorthand term for the controversy provoked by the Irish Attorney General's decision to prevent a 14-year-old rape victim from travelling to England for an abortion. This powerful image captured the mood of many people about this highly sensitive and deeply emotive issue. But what lay behind the cartoon and many of the public debates that followed was a particular assumption about the way the problem should have been dealt with, an assumption based on the historic practice of dispatching Irish problems to England. If only this young girl could have gone to England, have had her abortion quietly and secretly, and then returned home to get on with her life, everything would have been alright. Of course, for this particular girl and her family, obtaining an abortion was the most expedient way of dealing with an urgent and tragic situation. In the wider context, however, 'going to England' was and is a time-honoured Irish

Fig. 9.1   Cartoon by Martyn Turner, *Irish Times*, 19 February 1992
(Reproduced by kind permission.)

'solution' to an Irish problem, one that saw 6,625 Irish women travel
to Britain for an abortion in 2001 alone. This number has risen
steadily over the last 20 years – in fact, the figures have doubled
since 1980 – so that abortion rates per 1,000 women aged 15–44 are
now 7.5. In all, at least 98,565 Irish women have travelled to British
abortion clinics during that 21-year period.[1]

The issue of Irish women travelling to Britain for abortions must
be understood against the background of the 1983 constitutional
referendum on abortion, which provoked one of the most bitter and
divisive Irish public debates of recent decades. Even though abortion
was illegal, in the early 1980s a campaign was launched to amend
the Irish Constitution in order to copper-fasten the right to life of
the 'unborn'. The high-profile and well-resourced pro-amendment
lobby was made up of some of the most powerful figures in Irish

society, among them church leaders, doctors, politicians and an array of vocal lay Catholic organisations. These groups, which have been described as 'masterminds of the right' (O'Reilly, 1988), quickly occupied the moral high ground and demonised their opponents as 'baby killers'. As a schoolgirl at the time of the campaign, I can well recall the brutal and disturbing images of bloody aborted foetuses that were distributed by the pro-amendment side. Within this highly charged context, it became virtually impossible to voice a pro-choice viewpoint (A. Smyth, 1992: 16) and, in the event, the amendment was passed by a 70:30 majority in September 1983. Consequently, Article 40.3.3 of the Irish Constitution obliges the state to defend the right to life of the unborn with due regard to the equal right to life of the mother.

In the wake of the referendum, as the site of conflict shifted to the question of access to abortion information, Irish feminist strategies 'pragmatically concentrated on providing information and support services for those women who were travelling to Britain for legal abortions' (L. Smyth, 1998: 65). Linda Connolly notes that it is remarkable that the rights of Irish citizens to international information about abortion services should have become so contentious, but perhaps it is not so remarkable after all, merely an acknowledgement that unwanted pregnancy could only be dealt with beyond Irish national boundaries (Connolly, 2002: 168). Although pro-choice campaigners used EU law to argue that citizens should have the right to information about medical services in other European states (Fletcher, 2000), the Irish High Court denied the EU courts any jurisdiction over Irish legislation and outlawed counselling services and abortion referral agencies operating in the Republic. Even access to something as basic as a phone number of an abortion clinic became contentious. As a university student in the late 1980s, I remember regularly seeing British telephone numbers mysteriously appearing on toilet walls, only to be scribbled out the next day. Nevertheless, despite such difficulties, almost 4,000 Irish women travelled to Britain for abortions in 1988.[2]

Throughout this chapter I wish to draw upon my own research on Irish migrants in Britain to illustrate how unwanted pregnancy has been an underlying but mostly unspoken aspect of Irish migration for much of the twentieth century. Since 2000 I have been involved in two research projects with Irish migrants in London, in the course of which I have interviewed several hundred men and women across the city. Here is a brief extract from an entry in a research diary I wrote after one particularly upsetting interview:

Today was a bad day, I have interviewed a woman who told me a harrowing story. I am feeling very upset not just about the woman but also about the terrible things that have gone on in Ireland and from which young women have had to escape, coming to London alone and without any support.

The woman in question, 'Maura', had travelled to London in the 1960s. During the interview she seemed hesitant and unsure of herself; her answers were guarded and a little puzzling. She had left Ireland alone at the age of 15, not telling her family that she was going to London. I asked her, as I did all my respondents, about her main reasons for leaving Ireland. After a long pause, she answered that she became pregnant outside of marriage, was abandoned by her boyfriend and sent by her parents to a convent where she gave birth in secret. Once the baby was born, she was forced to give her up for adoption. Even then her parents refused to allow her back home and so she set off for London without any means of support. There she got a job in a department store and eventually married and had other children. However, it was clear that she felt very sad for the baby she had given away and was very resentful towards the parents who had rejected her when she needed them most.

Maura's story of migration was far from unique. Another interviewee, 'Sinead', a professional woman in her forties, also told me that she had left Ireland because of an unwanted pregnancy. As a teenager in the 1970s she had become pregnant only to be shunned by her boyfriend and literally thrown out of the family home by her father. She travelled to London alone for a termination and decided to remain in the city, despite having little money and no support network. Although these events had occurred almost 30 years ago, it seemed that they still defined Sinead's relationship with Ireland and her family insofar as she retained a deep bitterness about the way she had been treated and the choices she felt forced to make.

Such stories are by no means confined to contemporary women. There is evidence that Irish women travelled to Britain for illegal abortions as far back as the 1930s, though travel restrictions during World War II resulted in a significant but temporary rise in backstreet abortions in Ireland (Conroy Jackson, 1992: 128). Of course, not all pregnant women who went to Britain did so for the purposes of abortion; many, indeed, sought to have their babies adopted. In his work on the British adoptions of Irish babies in the 1950s and 1960s, Garrett has suggested that the Irish authorities were not wholly displeased by this phenomenon, since the fact that such babies were being born and adopted in England served to artificially reduce Ireland's illegitimacy rates. He goes on to observe:

Clearly, the extent of women's right to reproductive self-determination and their migration are related issues. Indeed, perhaps some similarities exist in terms of the crossings made to England, prior to the late-1960s, and the journeys to England made today to abortion clinics. Perhaps the 'silences' associated with 'secret' births and adoptions in the 1950s and 1960s, and 'secret' abortions following brief migrations today are not entirely dissimilar. (Garrett, 2000: 40)

From the 1992 'X case' back to Sinead in the 1970s and Maura in the 1960s, I am struck by the ways in which Britain has acted as a disposal ground for Irish women's unwanted pregnancies. Ailbhe Smyth chooses a related metaphor when she claims that 'Britain has become a vast laundry for human "dirty linen" that Irish morality refuses to handle' (A. Smyth, 1992: 21). In the next section I wish to explore these issues further in the context of Irish nationhood.

WOMEN AND THE REPRODUCTION OF THE NATION

The establishment of the Irish Free State in 1922, with its predominantly Catholic, rural ethos, marked a new phase in the construction and institutionalisation of Irish national identity. The nation-building project emphasised a narrow, exclusive definition of the Irish as a distinct 'race', based on the assumption that 'the sameness of Irish people was defined in relation to the assumed uniqueness of Irish culture, language, sports, and lifestyle that made Irish people different from all other "races"' (Gray and Ryan, 1998: 126). A male-dominated state and church foregrounded the common characteristics of the Irish 'race' while also emphasising gender differences. Women's roles were defined through mothering, nurturing and domesticity in order to ensure that an idealised 'Irishwoman' would guarantee the biological reproduction of the 'race' and the cultural continuity of the nation. Thus, the gendering of national identity and the use of female symbols to embody Ireland led to the constant overlapping and intersection of 'images of Ireland, images associated with the Catholic church and the ideal of Irish womanhood' (Innes, 1993: 60; Lentin, 1998; Meaney, 1991; Sharkey, 1993).

In her work on the politics of abortion in the Irish Republic, Angela Martin argues that because women are expected to personify national and religious ideals, their bodies are policed by the church, 'colonised by the state judicial apparatus and disciplined by state laws and the carceral system' (Martin, 2000: 81). However, as I have argued elsewhere, while one must acknowledge the legal constraints that have been placed on women in Ireland, it is also important to distinguish between constructions of mythic woman and the diverse realities of Irish women (Ryan, 2002c). The one-dimensional, idealised images of Irish femininity embedded in post-independence nationalist rhetoric not only simplified the multifaceted nature of actual women's experiences, they also masked the differences that exist between women. Moreover, such idealised images underestimate women's active agency and the diverse ways in which they cope with or react against their particular situations.

During the period from the 1920s to the 1950s the Irish Free State had a lower marriage rate than any other country for which records exist. Throughout the 1930s, for example, 29 per cent of males and 24 per cent of females remained permanently single, with 74 per cent of men in the 25–34 age group being recorded as unmarried in 1936 alone (*Commission on Emigration*, 1955: 72). It was precisely because of the need to preserve the traditions of land ownership and inheritance that postponed marriage and high rates of celibacy had to be maintained. In his famous study of life in rural Ireland Conrad Arensberg highlighted the apparent paradox of a 'social system centring so strongly round marriage and the family', while simultaneously condemning 'a large proportion of its members to celibacy and long-preserved virginity' (Arensberg, 1937: 102). There is growing evidence to suggest that the pressures to be celibate, coupled with taboos surrounding courtship, forced many unmarried women to conceal their pregnancies and abandon their unwanted babies in Ireland during this period (Ryan, 1996). Writing in the early 1950s, Mary Frances Keating claimed that 'illegitimate births are frequently concealed, and young unmarried mothers are usually hurried out of the country with a 10 pound note and the parental injunction not to show their faces at home again' (Keating, 1954: 175). Ten years later, Jackson traced an explicit link between unwanted pregnancies, emigration and attitudes to female sexuality. Since a young woman was only marriageable if she was of sound moral character, those who became pregnant outside of wedlock threatened the good name and honour of their entire family and were therefore confronted with a very limited set of choices:

Emigration may in this way provide an answer for the pregnant girl who can be sent to England to have her baby without anyone knowing the real reason for her departure. She can then return when all is over without an apparent blemish on her character, her child having been adopted. It is this social pattern which may explain the callousness deplored by English social workers attempting to gain the parents' assistance in cases of girls who are pregnant, and explains the unwillingness of some Irish unwed mothers in England to have anything to do with their illegitimate children. (Jackson, 1963: 33)

This analysis prompts one to ask why Irish men were under no pressure from their family, their community or their church to accept responsibility for children conceived outside wedlock, and why it was that women were forced to carry all the blame. The answer lies in part in the fact that, as emblems of national honour, Irish women were expected to protect their own honour and virtue much more than their male counterparts (Valiulis, 1995: 128). Nira Yuval-Davis argues that 'women's membership in their national and ethnic collectivities is of a double nature. On the one hand, women, like men, are members of the collectivity. On the other hand, there are always specific rules and regulations which relate to women as women' (Yuval-Davis, 1997: 37). She points out that this is especially significant when we consider the implications of 'the ways women are constructed as biological reproducers of "the nation"' (Yuval-Davis, 1997: 37). Women are held entirely accountable for their sexual behaviour and it is they alone, therefore, who are penalised for any sexual 'deviance'. So if a woman is deemed to behave in a sexually inappropriate way, both she and her child may be excluded from the community. Thus, female sexual behaviour marks the boundaries between inclusion and exclusion from national collectivities.

In line with Yuval-Davis, Martin has argued that Irish women's bodies have long been used to determine 'the moral, political and physical boundaries of the Republic', and that the 'X case' in particular raised anxieties about the integrity of these borders – and bodies – to new levels (Martin, 2000: 66). Furthermore, she maintains that the 1992 debates about abortion were framed by concerns about the rupturing of national borders caused by transnational deterritori-alisation and subsequent threats to Irish sovereignty, tradition and identity, symbolised by the 1992 Maastricht Treaty. In a context of increasing European integration, therefore, 'the death of Miss X's baby was somehow equivalent to the death of the Irish nation', and the deterritorialisation of the state led in turn 'to a violent, coercive and intrusive re-territorialization of feminine bodies by the Irish nation' (Martin, 2000: 75, 83).[3] The underlying assumption of Martin's argument appears to be that prior to the 1990s, Irish national boundaries had seemed more secure and clearly defined. However, as my work on the nation-building process of the 1920s and 1930s has shown, the nation's borders were always viewed as fragile, uncertain and vulnerable to outside influences (Ryan, 2002c: 43–56). Of course, the deterritorialisation of the female body has long been part of Catholic and conservative nationalist repertoire. But to focus solely on this discourse ignores far more complex, dynamic and heterogeneous realities.

So while drawing upon Yuval-Davis's theorisation of women's biological reproduction of the nation, I suggest that women's reproductive choices and decision-making were not always nation-bounded, but were also defined in relation to sites beyond the national space, especially Britain. This was clearly demonstrated during the 'X case' furore and the referenda that followed, when women's right to travel became a matter of central importance. Suddenly, the secret, silent, invisible and taken-for-granted escape route to Britain became a topic of public discussion and debate. Now that travel outside of Ireland to avail of abortion services in Britain was under threat, and a young woman had been prevented by the state from crossing the national boundaries, the full impact of curtailing access to what one might call 'the British solution' became apparent. The then leader of the Labour Party, Dick Spring, publicly expressed his regret that the young rape victim had become 'a prisoner of the state', and government embarrassment forced it to encourage the girl's family to seek an immediate appeal against the High Court ruling, which proved successful (L. Smyth, 1998: 68).[4]

Thus, I suggest that Irish reproductive policies and practices have long been defined in relation to Britain. While official state policies and Catholic teachings on contraception, adoption and abortion have propounded a pro-natalism based on family values and married motherhood, the option of escape to Britain has formed an important backdrop to the practical operation of these policies. Individual women, with or without family support, and sometimes with the forceful encouragement of their families, have used Britain to evade Ireland's uncompromising and unworkable laws. In this way migration, be it temporary or long-term, has effectively shaped the reproductive possibilities of Irish women by functioning as a safety valve. And surely it is no coincidence that the policy in relation to abortion was only really confronted head-on when the possibility of travel to Britain was suddenly denied. In other words, when the official legal policy was actually enforced, its unworkability became apparent and steps were quickly taken to affirm women's right to travel, thereby circumventing state law. It is highly significant, therefore, that in the November 1992 abortion referendum the Irish electorate voted by a large majority *in favour* of both the right to travel and the right to information, but overwhelmingly *against* limited abortion in Ireland (Connolly, 2002; A. Smyth, 1992). It seems that Irish voters shared the view that Ireland's problems were best dealt with by exporting them.

MIGRATION AND UNWANTED PREGNANCY, 1930–50: A CASE STUDY

In December 1936 the *Irish Independent* published a series of twelve lengthy articles on Irish female emigrants by Gertrude Gaffney, one of the best-known woman journalists of the decade. The series reported the findings of her detailed study of young women migrants in Liverpool and London whom Gaffney had interviewed earlier that year. As well as talking to these women about their experiences, she also met nuns, priests and charity and hostel personnel who worked with these emigrants. The series drew attention to the various problems and misfortunes experienced by young Irish women who arrived in Britain without a job, accommodation or family support. Although she claimed that the majority of such women did well in Britain by getting decent jobs and good wages, she also noted that there was a 'rapidly growing' minority of 'unlucky ones' who 'fall by the wayside' (Gaffney, 1936a: 6).

Gaffney's series reflected many of the contemporary concerns being expressed by 'rescue' organisations in Britain. Throughout the 1930s Catholic charities voiced their worries about the large numbers of young Irish women who were arriving in British cities, and the Catholic Women's League (CWL) magazine repeatedly highlighted their vulnerable plight. Concern for the 'moral welfare' of these women led the League to liaise with Catholic groups in Ireland, such as the Legion of Mary, in order to provide information and advice to young women before they left. The CWL also issued regular bulletins on the work being done by Catholic Mother and Baby Homes in Britain. For example, it reported that in London's

Westminster diocese, over 800 pregnant unmarried Catholic women were helped between 1935 and 1937, most of whom 'had come to London to work and were separated from their families; it was quite the exception to get a girl who was living at home'.[5] The women were described as 'mostly honest and likeable'; indeed, the average unmarried mother was characterised as 'a decent girl well worth helping', especially when it was her first pregnancy, and she deserved to make 'a fresh start'.[6] According to the League, the Catholic Homes aimed to provide these women with a secure and calm environment before and after delivery, after which the women returned to jobs in domestic service, usually within three months.

Although this particular report did not state how many of these young women were Irish, 'pregnant Irish girls' were frequently referred to in other CWL bulletins. Although many babies were adopted, there does not appear to have been an automatic adoption policy. In fact, several League reports stressed the importance of keeping baby and mother together. This was done for a number of reasons, one of which was to do with the scarcity of good Catholic adopters, which led many to argue that babies would be better off staying with their mothers than being adopted by non-Catholics. Thus, the CWL repeatedly urged households employing a domestic servant to find it in their hearts to let her bring her baby with her. Other justifications for encouraging young women to keep their babies had a morally pejorative edge to them. One rescue worker claimed that the type of girl who got into trouble was usually a little 'subnormal' – 'not mentally defective but in certain matters rather below average. She did not take anything very seriously, [...] she was impulsive and suggestible; had a poor sense of values'. Separating her from the baby, therefore, would frustrate her maternal feelings, whereas keeping and supporting the baby would give her a sense of responsibility and ensure that she was less likely to stray from the moral path and get pregnant again.

The recognition that few domestic servants were in a position to keep their babies led the Catholic Homes to place the children in foster care so that the mothers could return to work while continuing to pay for their upkeep and visit them regularly. The belief was that this would engender a sense of responsibility, even if the women were not in a position to be full-time mothers. It was acknowledged, however, that this ideal did not always work in practice, as some women gradually grew more distant from their babies. In March 1938 the Birmingham Archdiocesan Branch of the Rescue and Protection

Society reported a fairly typical story of a 'girl from Cork' whose baby had been born and baptised and then placed with a foster mother, while the girl 'returned to her situation' in domestic service.[7] Of course, the most practical way for mothers to keep their babies was by legitimating their relationship to the fathers, and the Catholic Homes appear to have played a role in encouraging young couples to marry. For example, the Woodville Maternity Home in Birmingham reported that 'marriages had been happily arranged with two girls leaving the Home, through the untiring efforts of the Matron'.[8]

During the 1930s the goal of these English Catholic charities appears to have been largely one of reform rather than punishment (Garrett, 2000: 30). The 'girls' were viewed as morally weak and highly suggestible, and as such needed to develop a sense of responsibility for their own moral development and for the welfare of their babies. The belief was that through education and the guiding influence of the Catholic church they could be reformed and prepared for future marriage and legitimate motherhood. This approach stands in marked contrast to the prevailing views of the Catholic church in Ireland at this time, where unmarried mothers were treated as perpetual penitents to be incarcerated and punished indefinitely in the infamous Magdalene laundries.[9] Given this choice, it is hardly surprising that pregnant unmarried women wanted to have their babies in England rather than in Ireland. However, Gaffney in her article series pointed out that some English charities attempted to send women and their babies back to Ireland, but that often they were either unwilling or unable to return. She cited several nuns, priests and social workers who spoke out against the uncharitable attitude towards unmarried mothers in Ireland, a criticism borne out by the fact that Irish parents rarely agreed to take their daughters home after they became pregnant. In fact, some parents had forced their daughters to emigrate to England once their pregnancy was known. Sometimes families further exacerbated the problem by agreeing to take the young women back but refusing to accept their babies, thus encouraging the practice of baby abandonment. An elderly nun told Gaffney that she had encountered many incidents where unmarried mothers were treated like 'outlaws' in Ireland, and quoted one social worker as saying: 'These girls are the scapegoats of a tradition of puritanism that will not admit that things are as they are.' She concludes that the general opinion of English charity workers was that these women were 'more sinned against than sinning' (Gaffney, 1936b: 7).

Once again, it is important to understand this phenomenon of 'exporting' unwanted Irish babies within the context of the official Irish government policy of the time. Despite growing demands for the introduction of legal adoption in the 1930s and 1940s, Eamon de Valera's Fianna Fáil government was reluctant to introduce any such policy, given the vehement opposition of the politically influential Archbishop of Dublin, John Charles McQuaid. However, there is evidence to suggest that some members of the Catholic hierarchy, and some voices inside the Oireachtas, were more open to the idea of legalising adoption, but they were repeatedly overruled. The law was eventually changed in 1952, as a result of the tireless efforts of pro-adoption lobby groups and the fact that the Catholic hierarchy finally gave their assent to the legislation (Keating, 2003). Meanwhile, throughout this period, while the rights and wrongs of adoption were proving so contentious in Ireland, hundreds if not thousands of Irish women were dealing with their unwanted pregnancies and 'illegitimate' babies by taking the boat to Britain.

Throughout my own research into Irish migrants in London I have been repeatedly struck by the ways in which unwanted pregnancy recurs as a narrative theme. In the oral history project I carried out at London Metropolitan University in 2000–1 I interviewed twelve Irish women who had emigrated during the interwar period (Ryan, 2002b). Unlike the younger women I interviewed for my more recent research, none of these women spoke about unwanted pregnancy in personal terms, but often told me stories about the experiences of friends and relatives. One, for example, who was too ill to be interviewed, narrated her story in a long and detailed letter, most of which was about her sister. This woman, 'Sheila', migrated to England but then heard news from home that her younger sister was 'in trouble'. She returned to find that her sister, who was in her mid-teens, had had a baby and was now in a Magdalene laundry. Against her family's wishes, Sheila went to visit her and made arrangements to bring her to London. Another of my respondents, 'Gertie', told me that her sister became pregnant as a result of an affair with a young man in Dublin, at which point he abandoned her and she was quickly dispatched to an aunt in Manchester where she lived for the rest of her life.[10] Yet another, 'Annie', worked in a London hotel in the 1940s and lived on the premises like most of her colleagues. While she herself had little free time, one of her Irish pals had a boyfriend and left the hotel so that she could spend more time with him. When Annie went to visit the girl in a bedsit a few months later, she discovered a dead baby concealed in a wardrobe. When I asked her how she reacted, Annie told me that she left immediately and never contacted the girl again. Annie's reluctance to discuss the matter further suggested that she may not have intended to tell this story at all had it not surfaced in the flow of remembering. Other oral history researchers have noted how respondents can sometimes reveal more then they intend during interviews, their distress arising as much from the involuntary nature of the disclosure as from the memory itself (Mouton and Pohlandt-McCormick, 1999). For me, however, Annie's revelation is highly illuminating. As I have argued elsewhere, concealment, infanticide and abandonment were common methods of dealing with unwanted pregnancy in 1920s and 1930s Ireland, and Annie's story suggests that they may well have been practised by pregnant Irish girls in England also (Ryan, 1996, 2003). Sadly but perhaps inevitably, not all Irish women in England availed of the services of Catholic Rescue Homes.

Moving to the 1950s context, Garrett's work reveals that the acronym PFI, meaning 'pregnant from Ireland', was part of the everyday vocabulary of English social workers dealing with unmarried mothers at this time. He has found that the registered cases of the English Catholic Rescue Society indicate that of the 800 expectant mothers referred to the agency, 61 per cent originated in the Irish Republic (Garrett, 2000: 27). Mechanisms were put in place to repatriate these young women and links were made with Catholic adoption agencies and Mother and Baby Homes in Ireland. However, repatriation proved problematic for several reasons. Not only was it expensive and sometimes impracticable, the women themselves often refused to return to an Irish institution run by nuns where they would be stigmatised as sinners.

Garrett also argues that the children of these Irish women, many of whom were given up for adoption, form part of Ireland's 'hidden diaspora', and concludes that both these mothers and their babies have been deemed to be 'outside history'. While their exclusion may be attributable to the secret nature of these pregnancies, Garrett draws on the work of feminist historians Maria Luddy and Cliona Murphy to indict the male-centred, patriarchal nature of Irish historiography, which regards issues surrounding reproduction, unwanted pregnancy, infanticide, abortion, adoption and child abandonment as unworthy of serious research. I would like to go further, however, and suggest that another reason why these topics have not been discussed seriously within Irish academia is because they have all been very successfully exported to Britain. The export of unwanted babies, whether for adoption in the 1950s or abortion in the 1990s, is mirrored in the metaphorical expunging of these babies and their mothers not only from Irish historiography, but also from the consciousness of the nation.

Yuval-Davis has also discussed this forced exclusion of some 'undesirable' babies from the national consciousness: 'The inclusion of a new baby in a national collectivity is far from being only a biological issue [...]. Social as well as legal conventions are of crucial importance here' (Yuval-Davis, 1997: 18). What is particularly interesting about the Irish case is that these babies were not simply excluded from membership of the national consciousness, they were also physically excluded from the national territory. The refusal to allow pregnant mothers to remain 'at home' – whether in the family or in the local community – coupled with the refusal to take their babies back from Britain, resulted in the permanent exclusion of these 'illegitimate' children from Irish society. Such acts of repudiation represent the ultimate denial of these children's existence and their excision from any notion of an Irish community. Thus, without an Irish parent, an Irish name, an Irish accent or any acknowledged connection to Ireland, these children were denied access to a full sense of identity.

CONCLUSION

In this chapter I have focused on the ways in which long-term and temporary migration to Britain has played a defining role in the often unspoken politics of reproduction in Ireland, both historically and in the contemporary era. As I have tried to show, migration is seldom a straightforward matter of relocating from one country to another; rather, it involves a complex and continual process of movement back and forth across territorial boundaries and between national spaces. My primary argument has been that unwanted pregnancy in Ireland has long involved a complex negotiation of national boundaries by individual women, their families, the state, the Catholic church and the judiciary. Far from being nation-bounded, it is my contention that the reproductive policies of successive governments have relied heavily on the possibility of exporting unwanted pregnancies, thereby creating a hidden Irish diaspora, the origins of which can be traced back to the 1930s at the very least. Thus, while Irish women have traditionally been depicted as idealised domestic guarantors of national boundaries in nationalist rhetoric and symbolism, the reality has always been more complex and even contradictory for actual women who find themselves pregnant with an unwanted child.

The 1992 'X case' is highly significant in this regard because it legally confined one young rape victim within the national boundaries and denied her the right to travel, as Turner's *Irish Times* cartoon so vividly portrayed. By implementing the law so uncompromisingly in this landmark case, the judiciary demonstrated the unworkability and impracticality of any attempt to impose a nation-bounded policy on Irish women. The case also demonstrated that Irish official policy on unwanted pregnancy could only work, and had ever only worked, because women availed of services outside the state. However, as the personal testimonies of the Irish women cited above suggest, freedom to travel does not necessarily imply freedom to choose. For this reason, it has not been my intention to celebrate Irish women's right to travel as inherently empowering, though for some women that has clearly been the case. Rather, we must remember that despite the apparent ease and affordability of travel between Ireland and Britain, private abortions are expensive and the reality is that many less well-off women have to borrow from moneylenders at exorbitant rates of interest.

The authors of a recent report on Irish abortion-seekers in Britain argue that while there has been a growth in research into the experiences of the Irish in Britain, there continues to be a general reluctance to discuss Irish women's reproductive health and their reproductive choices, which leads them to conclude: 'the eloquence of that silence is telling' (Hayes *et al.*, 2003: 3). This observation takes me back to my opening claim about the important role Irish Studies can play in illuminating hidden aspects of the migrant histories that link Ireland and Britain, and the unacknowledged interconnections that bind the peoples and cultures of the two islands. In cutting across traditional disciplinary boundaries, Irish Studies enables researchers to draw upon diverse theories, concepts and sources, and as such can provide those of us studying the silences and concealments of Ireland's diaspora with a vital framework within which to broaden and strengthen our analysis of previously inadmissible issues. If, as seems clear, the daily reality of the Irish abortion trail to Britain is to be the subject of further scholarly investigation, then it is imperative that such research be both informed by and grounded in an inter-disciplinary Irish Studies approach.

NOTES

1. These figures are based only on those women who gave an Irish address and thus may well underestimate the total numbers of Irish women who had abortions in British clinics. See the website http://www.ifpa. ie/abortion/iabst.html

2. Information cited on the Irish Family Planning Association website, www. ifpa.ie

3. The relationship between the European Courts and the Irish judiciary is particularly complex on the issue of abortion, however, and Irish governments have worked to minimise the impact of EU rulings on Irish abortion legislation. See A. Smyth (1992) and Fletcher (2000).

4. Within ten days of the original ruling, the Supreme Court overturned the High Court decision and allowed the pregnant girl to travel to Britain where she had an abortion.

5. *The Catholic Women's League Magazine*, November 1937, p. 4.

6. *The Catholic Women's League Magazine*, November 1937, p. 4.

7. *The Catholic Women's League Magazine*, March 1938, p. 14.

8. *The Catholic Women's League Magazine,* March 1930, p. 11.

9. For a very moving personal account of life in one of these Magdalene laundries in the 1950s, see Goulding (1998).

10. These stories are very similar to those related to Sharon Lambert by older Irish migrant women in Lancashire. Like Gertie, Lambert's interviewee, Lily, tells how her unmarried pregnant sister was dispatched to England by her family because of the shame the pregnancy would cause back home. See Lambert (2003).

10
Beating the Bounds:
Mapping an Irish Mediascape

Lance Pettitt

What we need today is not a theory of a new age, but rather a new theory of an age whose broad contours were laid down some while ago, and whose consequences we have yet fully to ascertain. (Thompson, 1995: 9)

This chapter considers two questions about the relations between the past and the present. Firstly, how might we set out to write a cultural history of Ireland's media? Secondly, sensing that we are on the cusp of change, having recently crossed the threshold into a new century, what precisely are the difficulties in defining and analysing the nature of an Irish mediascape? The study of media institutions, texts and audiences in and about Ireland is a relatively new sub-field that has emerged piecemeal from diverse disciplinary origins, a second-generation of scholarship within what has come to be called Irish Studies. Its emergence can perhaps best be dated from a 1984 special issue of the journal *The Crane Bag* devoted to media and popular culture.[1] Path-breaking monographs like *Cinema and Ireland* and *Irish Television Drama* (both published in 1987) soon followed, and while a growing body of work has appeared on cinema and television since then, Irish media studies remains an unevenly developed sub-field with comparatively few analyses of radio, the news press, advertising and popular visual culture, let alone audiences, readerships and new media forms. So while we need to sustain and promote research in specific media and allow for studies that adopt a more traditional disciplinary approach to a singular topic,[2] we also need to see the merit of an integrative, synoptic approach to mapping an Irish mediascape, since this will allow us to examine more clearly Ireland's problematic relationship with modernity and the processes of media convergence that characterise late capitalism.

What we should aspire to in media history, therefore, is the provision of 'a more contingent view of ebb and flow, opening and closure, advances in some areas and reverses in others', in the knowledge that '[t]he contextualisation of media history dissolves linear narratives – whether of progress or regress' (Curran, 2002: 51). In what follows, the institutional development of media studies in Ireland is reviewed, different modes of Irish cultural history are examined and Appadurai's (1996) theory of a global cultural economy – in particular his concept of 'mediascape' – is applied to the Irish case. Since the body of writing about the Irish media, its relationship to society and its cultural role are bound up with wider debates about the nature of Irish modernity, Appadurai's essays on the global cultural dimensions of 'modernity at large' provide an apposite framework within which to consider both states on the island of Ireland, particularly the Republic.[3] Put simply if expansively, an Irish mediascape comprises the press, radio, cinema, television, audio-visual services and products and technologies of the new media (digital, satellite, internet) both within Ireland and without, as well as in the spaces in between. Just as this scape's geo-political scope is elastic, so too are its temporal parameters, which embrace emergent histories of media in the nineteenth century as well as the defining forms of the twentieth. This protean scape also projects a future history into the twenty-first century, providing a perspective from which to examine the continuities, breaks and trans-formations that might constitute a new Irish media history. Further, the plethora of audio-visual images produced within a mediascape are crucially conceived in disjunctive relation to other scapes, notably the dynamic dimensions of people, finances, technologies and ideologies that shift over time and space.

In subsequent sections this chapter will critically review selected studies that have focused on the media in Ireland and identify four broad approaches, each with their characteristic emphases and disciplinary origins, ranging from the sociological and the historical to the literary-critical. They are: (a) a political economy/policy approach (Corcoran, 2004; Horgan, 2001); (b) an audience-centred approach (Kelly and O'Connor, 1997); (c) a cultural/critical theory approach (Barton, 2004; McLoone, 2000; O'Brien, 2004; Pettitt, 2000); and (d) an auto/biographical studies approach (Doorley, 2002; Quinn, 2001; Robbins 2004). Studies of the media typically adopt one or more of these modes of enquiry. Several fall into the third category, products of disciplinary tensions between more traditional historical approaches and newer theoretical analyses, many of which are framed within or against postcolonial and poststructuralist critical discourses. While there are overlaps between (a) and (d), least work has been done within the social science spectrum of approaches to media audiences in Ireland. This corpus of work – books, journals, reviews – not only constitutes part of Ireland's mediascape as the material product of a publishing industry that is an adjunct to other kinds of media, but also forms part of a discursive meta-narrative of that mediascape, reflexively informing how the media works, shapes and re-presents itself.

Such epistemological reflexivity is one of the conditions of modernity identified by Giddens who, speaking of sociological knowledge, argues that 'notions coined in the meta-languages of the social sciences routinely re-enter the universe of actions they were initially formulated to describe or account for' (Giddens, 1990: 15–16).[4] It must be acknowledged, however, that the difficulties of theorising a longer-term view of the media in Ireland are similar to those encountered by cultural historians in other fields, many of whom understand that their practice involves 'the analysis of the process of representation – that is, of the production of the classifications and exclusions that constitute the social and conceptual configurations proper to one time or one place' (Chartier, 1988: 13). With this in mind, I shall turn to the institutional development of what became 'media studies' and the attendant debates about how to conduct cultural history in Ireland.

MEDIA STUDIES AND CULTURAL HISTORY

Among the fundamental problems in mapping an Irish mediascape are what Appadurai terms the 'fractal' and 'polythetic' aspects of the political economies of culture. These terms refer to the shared characteristics and multiple interactions that exist between the macro economies and the state structures of Ireland and the UK, as well as the links between both polities in Ireland and their relationship to the EU, the USA and various multinational bodies. Within late capitalism, the higher education sectors of the developed world have become participants in globalisation and consumer values that challenge the 'innocence' of a cosmopolitan intellectual exchange of an earlier stage of modernity. These factors, combined with population growth and political policies to widen access to university learning, have led to the expansion of higher education institutions in the Republic and Northern Ireland. As this expansion has evolved, media and cultural studies programmes have emerged to take their place alongside traditional disciplines in the arts and social sciences. Among the reasons for this are a more consumer-led higher education sector, government recognition of the employment potential of 'cultural industries' and the perceived need to equip people with media literacy skills. Thus, as Irish film (and to a lesser extent television) began to attract scholarly attention from the mid-1980s onwards, media studies became a legitimate subject of academic study at most third-level institutions. The first chair in the subject was held by the sociologist-turned-filmmaker, Desmond Bell, in 1989 at the then New University of Ulster. Other professorial appointments followed, including John Horgan, Farrell Corcoran and Roddy Flynn at Dublin City University; Luke Gibbons, who holds chairs at both DCU and the University of Notre Dame; and John Hill, who held a chair at Ulster before moving to Royal Holloway, University of London in 2004.[5]

In addition to this academy-located research, there is a thin lineage of practical, archive-based scholarship in Irish cinema from Liam O'Leary (1910–92) and Robert Monks,[6] through to Sunniva O'Flynn and Eugene Finn, all of whom have either trained in or worked in Britain. Each has made significant contributions to the preservation and cataloguing of Ireland's historic collections in Dublin, as well as working on the Irish materials in the National Film Archive at the British Film Institute and the Northern Ireland Film Commission's digital archive in Belfast. Television has been institutionally less well served in Ireland, though significant individuals at RTÉ have included Barbara Durack, Brian Lynch and John MacMahon in the station's print archives and, among younger archivists, Joan Murphy (McLoone and MacMahon, 1984). North of the border, Ulster Television remains a wholly commercial organisation, but BBC Northern Ireland holds an historic broadcast archive, housed at the Ulster Folk and Transport Museum in Cultrá.[7] In 2003 the Corporation announced that selected areas of its holdings would form part of an online 'creative archive', thereby signalling a change from 'closed' programme-making based on audio-visual collections to a more open system using new technologies of preservation, capture and remediation for commercial use, a move that may also benefit academic scholarship. The creation of accessible electronic media archives in Ireland is not merely the result of technological innovation or commercial pressure to profit from audio-visual capital; it is also a feature of the maturity of 'old' media and the realisation that the conditions that have sustained their pre-eminence are threatened by change. What better response to this challenge than by demonstrating the national value of such material and, in the case of BBC Northern Ireland, its potential to contribute to a better understanding of the historical causes of social and political conflict.

From this brief survey of the discursive realm of media studies in Ireland it can be seen that by the late 1990s a growing intellectual, educational and commercial niche market existed for publications on media topics at home and abroad, serving both an indigenous and a diasporic readership. More recently, media research at postgraduate and post-doctoral levels in both parts of Ireland has gained support from newly established funding bodies, notably the UK Arts and Humanities Research Council (AHRC) and the Irish Research Council for the Humanities and Social Sciences (IRCHSS). Private donations have also helped support new initiatives, such as the John Huston Centre for Film at NUI Galway and Atlantic Philanthropic Enterprises' endowment of media studies at the University of Ulster. Indeed, in the wake of the Good Friday Agreement, the work at Ulster is uniquely part of both a larger AHRC-funded research project on the history of British film and television research and a cross-border research initiative with Trinity College Dublin. Yet despite these different forms of institutional development, and a growing body of Irish film and media specialists, there is little consensus or indeed evidence of sustained reflection on what constitutes 'Irish media studies'.[8] If the historical emergence of Irish Studies as an interdisciplinary field in the 1960s can be likened to a shotgun wedding between literature and history, its teenage offspring may be said to have mixed with the wrong sort, indulged in critical theory and taken too many media studies courses at summer school in the 1970s and 1980s. This second-generation progeny has produced in turn a variegated family of sub-fields centring on areas such as gender, sexuality and diaspora, which creatively interact with media studies, and which are often taught and discussed a long way from Ireland.

Alongside these developments, academic research on the media in Ireland has shadowed and interacted with debates that have been central to media and cultural studies in general since their emergence in the academies of Britain, Europe and America. Perhaps the most pertinent areas to identify here are the relationship between society and culture and the role of the communications media within particular national cultures. Classic liberalism, in contrast to Appadurai, posits a homologous relationship between society and culture and assumes a linear model of development in which the media is regarded as an integral, modernising vehicle that accompanies and reflects the kinds of socio-economic changes usually associated with notions of Western modernity, national independence and 'progress'. Alternative models, deriving ideas from Marxist and post-Marxist analyses, stress instead the contested nature of social orders within Western nation-states and regard the mass communications media as more or less endorsing the ideological imperatives of capitalism, industrialised production and various forms of state power. Post-Marxist thinkers such as Gramsci outlined a theory of politicised criticism that duly recognised the key role that the cultural realm played in the articulation of power within liberal democracies. In Britain, Gramsci-influenced critics such as Stuart Hall, Raymond Williams and Tony Bennett sparked off a generation of scholarship that pursued ways of conceptualising the media/society relationship as a contested site where different kinds of social and political power (not just class) were fought over in and through media organisations and audiences, but which did not assume that the state had a monopoly over power at all times.

In the context of Ireland, where the nature and status of the state has been a pressing point of conflict at critical moments in the twentieth century, conceptualisations of the media have been notably mixed. In addition to left-wing instrumentalist accounts such as Liz Curtis's *Ireland: The Propaganda War* (1984), we have broadly liberal studies such as Terence Brown's pioneering *Ireland: A Social and Cultural History*, first published in 1981, which exemplifies the cultural/critical mode of enquiry outlined above. Offering itself as a 'preliminary mapping of the territory' (Brown, 2004: xii), the book, which was recently revised and updated, acknowledges the significance of the media within the cultural realm but restricts itself to high culture, the arts and intellectual currents, although it makes passing reference to radio, television and cinema. Coming later in the decade, but in fact based substantially on material first published in the late 1970s and early 1980s, Richard Kearney's *Transitions: Narratives in Modern Irish Culture* (1988) surveys the twentieth century in a thematic rather than chronological manner, offering a different perspective from within the cultural/critical mode. Kearney's thesis centres on a perceived crisis in Irish culture produced by a series of transitional tensions stemming from the attempt to narrate 'the problematic relationship between tradition and modernity' as it is experienced in Ireland (Kearney, 1988: 10). Presenting itself as an interdisciplinary study and written with postmodernist verve, the book argues that 'there is no unitary master narrative of Irish cultural history, but a plurality of transitions between different perspectives' (Kearney, 1988: 16). Thus, analyses of Yeats, Joyce and Beckett are set alongside readings of the formalist experimental cinema of Pat Murphy and Neil Jordan, in a deconstructive attempt to interrogate the boundaries between high and popular culture. Instead of being ancillary, in Kearney's view the media and modernist literature work in tandem as the best expression of the cultural torque that prevailed in 1980s Ireland.

But perhaps the outstanding example of contemporary cultural criticism in recent years, one that demonstrates adroitness across a range of popular media and cultural artefacts, is Luke Gibbons's *Transformations in Irish Culture* (1996). By arguing that 'media representations, and cultural forces in general, act as transformative forces in society, rather than as "reflections" or mimetic forms at one remove from reality', Gibbons explicitly rejects a liberal interpretation of the relationship between media and society (Gibbons, 1996: xii). Such liberal notions of cultural history have been under severe scrutiny since poststructuralist ideas impacted on conventional history writing, the revisionist/nationalist debate within Irish historiography being just one inflection of this (Ashplant and Smyth, 2001: 35–43; Dunne, 1992). While much of this debate has taken place within academia, Irish professional historians have also been notably prominent in responding to cinematic representations of history, Neil Jordan's *Michael Collins* (1996) being a case in point. The film provoked clashes among historians, media pundits and 'ordinary' members of the public over Collins's historical achievement and legacy, the controversy gaining added piquancy from the delicately poised political negotiations over the future of Northern Ireland that were taking place at the time of its release.

It seems clear, then, that Irish cultural history retains its capacity to produce both popular, 'unrevised' versions of the past as well as liberal accounts 'untainted' by the cultural and media theory practised in the academy. A revealing example of the latter type of history is Brian Fallon's acerbic *An Age of Innocence: Irish Culture 1930–1960* (1998). This work fundamentally re-evaluates the view that de Valera's Ireland was culturally isolationist and provincial, thereby offering an important corrective to the prevailing critical consensus about the period. Fallon's critique, however, is premised on a curiously reactionary, untheorised notion of the relationship between the media and socio-cultural change. Broadly speaking, his notion of 'culture' encompasses literature, music, language, architecture and painting, with limited room for the press and only passing mention of broadcasting and cinema. And while he acknowledges the significance of cinema and radio as alternative, non-official forms of 'popular taste', he is nonetheless highly dismissive of such cultural values in the larger historical sweep. Fallon's position is made more explicit in his nostalgia for what he sees as a more variegated and interesting past compared to the present. So while he acknowledges the economic, technological and educational advances of the post-1960 period, and the positive effects of Ireland's heightened political status within the EU, his deep-seated distrust of the popular is explicit in his fulmination against the 'losses', including the 'abandonment of many previously cherished national and cultural aspirations, galloping Americanisation (often naively and misleadingly termed "internationalism") and – above all – a virtual capitulation to the Pop Culture, to consumerism and the omnipresent Fast Food values' (Fallon, 1998: 29).

Such comments from a liberal arts commentator make Fallon sound like an arch-traditionalist, not least in the way he critiques broad 'targets' that are foreign, modern, ephemeral and, above all, culturally pernicious. So although he is right to contest the conventional reading of Ireland's mid-twentieth-century cultural history, in so doing he condemns modernity *tout court*. Read in the context of Kearney, Gibbons and other analysts of Irish media in the 1990s, *An Age of Innocence* exemplifies Curran's earlier point about the non-linearity of media history: neo-liberal, conservative forms of the cultural/critical mode coexist in a complex fashion with more sophisticated approaches that theorise and do greater justice to the role of cultural mechanics in an Irish mediascape. As Thompson aptly observes, 'if we wish to understand the cultural transformations associated with the rise of modern societies, then we must give a central role to the development of communication media and their impact' (Thompson, 1995: 268).

MAPPING IRISH MODERNITIES

Until comparatively recently, Ireland, North and South, was popularly imagined as a 'backwater' in comparison to Britain and 'Europe'. Mired in history, religion and traditionalism, the country was typically seen as the antithesis of 'modernity'. This perception has changed greatly during the last decade or so as Ireland, in the guise of the Celtic Tiger, assumed a prominent economic, social and cultural position (relative to its size) in the twenty-first century. Indeed, by successfully marketing itself in global terms, Ireland could be said to have become the acme of modernity or, as some have claimed, postmodernity. A more cautious view, however, would question the nature of the country's relationship to modernity, noting that it has been problematic for historical reasons. Such a view would also note that obsessively ditching tradition and valorising newness over obsolescence tells us as much about the process by which states (or newly hegemonic elites within them) claim the economic and cultural power to attribute value as it does about any intrinsic qualities of 'modernisation' itself. However, given that the media is intimately related to the dynamic of modernity, it is important to map the co-ordinates of Irish modernity in order to see why it has been such a contested term in the cultural debates that have taken place in each generation of what is still a relatively young independent state.

Alan Swingewood (1998) distinguishes three ways in which modernity has been used as a term of analysis. The first is as a sociological–historical category associated with the Enlightenment, rationality, science and 'progress'. Modernity here is typically linked to the economic, political and social processes collectively known as 'modernisation'. This is most closely associated with European modernity and its cultural values – democracy, justice, secularism – which are taken as 'universal' core values that evolve smoothly over time if allowed. The second analytical usage of the concept is in a more literary–aesthetic sense (often referred to as 'modernism') to describe artistic responses to the accelerated pace and increasingly fragmented nature of modern urban society that emerged in expansionist, imperial Europe and in the industrialised regions of the USA and Russia in the late nineteenth and early twentieth centuries. This phenomenon is typically associated with the new and exhilarating creative possibilities of urban life and with modernisation in its social forms, as well as with new modes of technology (the press, cinema and broadcasting) and industrialised production.

However, modernity is also often linked to the debilitating anomie of modern life, to the atomisation of society, the dehumanising effects of industrialisation, the rise of bureaucracy. Critics such as Zygmunt Bauman, Paul Gilroy and Homi Bhabha have also noted that Enlightenment values underpinned imperial conquests and unjust regimes, and that whatever modernity's cultural achievements, it conceals a dark underside of enforced human displacement (slaves, war refugees, economic migrants) and mass destruction (the Holocaust and H-Bomb) that complicates and calls into question a singular, homogeneous, overarching narrative of Western 'progress'. Swingewood's third formulation – what might be termed a 'critical modernity' – represents a constructive response to this ambivalence and contestation, being concerned with modernity's transformative potential and emphasising human agency, collective action and the capacity to be actively reflexive (Swingewood, 1998: 140).

How, then, do such ideas about modernity relate to Ireland's cultural history and more particularly to the nature of its mediascape? There is no simple answer, as critics are divided in their interpretations of how Ireland may be located within these different conceptualisations of modernity. The bulk of commentary written since the late 1980s conforms to the literary-critical mode of cultural history within which we earlier contextualised the development of media studies, though with different emphases. Conor McCarthy, for example, argues that 'modernisation theory has succeeded in monopolising the field of the modern imagination in Ireland', and usefully shows how the 'rational modernity' of many intellectuals in the Republic coincided at key moments in the 1950s and 1980s with the state's economic and social policies, and later became the broadly accepted neo-liberal logic of the so-called Celtic Tiger (McCarthy, 2000: 21). In the process, he restates discontents earlier voiced by Gibbons (1988) and Bell (1988) in their corrosive critiques of revisionist history, built around analyses of state-funded advertising campaigns for industrial development and debates about communications policy. Both critics questioned enthusiastic claims for Ireland's modernity, noting the telling absences of the socially and politically progressive developments associated with the phenomenon in other countries. Bell's point – which was subsequently popularised for different, celebratory ends by Fintan O'Toole in *The Ex-Isle of Erin* (1996) – was that the Irish state's pursuit of international capital to 'modernise' a laggard economy after decades of high unemployment and emigration gave the lie to the extent and nature of its own so-called modernisation. While his call for a 'modernist avant garde project' now seems misdirected, and his prognostication that 'the Irish economy may have great difficulty evolving into an information-led "post-industrial society" precisely because it has never fully achieved the status of an industrial economy' has been proved wrong, he was nevertheless correct to pin-point the 'chronic crisis of imagination about the mass media' in Ireland at the time (Bell, 1988: 227–9).

Gibbons, meanwhile, acknowledged that Ireland's leap-frogging modernisation apparently broke the post-Fordian rules of industrial development, but he contested the idea that this 'catching up' of a backward state produced unequivocal socio-economic and cultural benefits (Gibbons, 1988: 218). Indeed, his interpretation of Irish cultural history rests on the central idea that instead of experiencing modernity later than most other European countries and the USA, 'Irish culture experienced modernity before its time' (Gibbons, 1996: 6). According to this view, Irish people's involvement in nineteenth-century British global imperialism and American modernisation meant that they were not only integral to the dominant economic and political dynamics of Western modernity, but also that cultural production within Ireland enacted the traumatic social transformations produced by such upheavals, leading him to the suggestive assertion that Ireland had become 'a First World country, but with a Third World memory' (Gibbons, 1998: 27). Along with Kirby and Cronin, Gibbons has developed this argument further in a recent polemical critique of the ideology underpinning the Celtic Tiger's economic success in the years 1994–2001 (Kirby *et al.*, 2002). Here it is argued that the state's neo-liberal economic orthodoxy necessitated the 'reinvention' of Ireland for global consumption in the form of inward investment and mass tourism. Such reinvention was also necessary for the creation of new kinds of 'social partnership' between government, employers and trade unions, to the detriment of Ireland's low-income earners and in some cases the materially better off. The authors' conception of a critical modernity in relation to Ireland echoes that of Swingewood, therefore, in that it has 'a self-aware and self-critical continuity with those traditions and movements in Irish life which have contested or continue to contest the monopoly of power and resources' (Kirby *et al.*, 2002: 206).

Gibbons is one of several critics who have variously applied postcolonial and postmodern approaches to produce more heterodox readings of Irish modernities, thereby building a bridge to a third generation of Irish Studies scholarship that has both broadened its insular framework and productively dislocated it. Joe Cleary is one of those who has refined the general thrust of Gibbons's thesis by arguing that 'although Ireland belonged to the same geo-cultural locale, the same orbit of capital as the major European powers, it was integrated into that orbit of capital in a very different way to its main European neighbours', producing a cultural legacy that he terms 'the experience of incongruity' (Cleary, 2003: 95). Cleary's is a Marxist application of postcolonial theory, situating Ireland's longer history of involvement within early and late forms of capitalism in an Atlantic economic structure that emerged between European continental colonialism and the Americas since the sixteenth century.

Echoing Appadurai, his dislocated reading of Irish cultural history argues that 'it is the disjunctive way in which these metropolitan influences are articulated in a socio-economic context different to those in which they originally emerged that constitutes the real interest of the Irish situation' (Cleary, 2003: 103).

This reading has affinities with previous analyses that questioned the temporal and geo-spatial terms within which both parts of Ireland have traditionally been framed. David Lloyd, for example, sees the states as 'neither modern nor traditional, developed nor backward', but rather occupying 'a space that is uncapturable by any such conceptual couple. The non-modern is a name for such a set of spaces that emerge out of kilter with modernity but none the less in a dynamic relation to it' (Lloyd, 1999: 2). Clearly, critics like Gibbons and Lloyd are concerned to wrest back from revisionism the idea that nationalism is outmoded, a hurdle to social advancement and cultural plurality. Gibbons in particular has consistently argued that those aspects of the Irish past that are often overlooked by contemporary historians – the traditional, the uncanny, the oral tradition – are the constituent elements of an important critical modernity, and as such are vital resources for cultural resistance to both liberal post-nationalism and a vacuous postmodernity celebrated in much of contemporary Ireland (Gibbons, 1996: 4).[9]

Colin Graham, however, takes Lloyd to task and cautions against theorising the subaltern as a repository of authentic forms of national–popular resistance on which dissident critics may draw to justify their support for a cultural politics underpinned by notions of the nation. Drawing on poststructuralist thought, he goes on to observe that Irish cultural criticism appears to be locked into a dynamic, almost gyring process characterised by 'a noise of argument and a silence around the foundations of those arguments' (Graham, 2001: 55). Graham interprets the moment of the Celtic Tiger as an instance of ambivalence within late capitalism that is dependent upon the relationship between rapacious capital and existing political forms, both of which are epitomised and enabled by twenty-first-century technologies: 'If global capital creates the cultural effects of modernisation but functionally needs the nation-state as part of the mechanism, then the symbiosis between the two is less anomalous, and the accommodation of the new technologies within the Celtic Tiger economy, for example, less of a surprise' (Graham, 2001: 26–7). Graham's cultural criticism works out of a literary context, but does so more effectively than Lloyd's, as when he makes the point that the idea of 'Ireland' has been theorised, overdetermined and 'written' as literary text. Like Gibbons, he astutely recognises the need to focus on popular culture, not least the ephemeral and marginal cultural representations of 'Ireland' that 'find their often uncatalogued place both easily within and challengingly beyond the epistemologies which proclaim a certain ability to describe and define Ireland' (Graham, 2001: 155, 167). Taken as a whole, Graham's analysis is by far the most challenging and persuasive application of Gramscian theory about the nature of hegemony and the subaltern to the Irish experience of modernity.

In this section we have seen how contested ideas of modernity have been a recurring feature of critical debate about Ireland's cultural history. This contest has implications for our understanding of how as part of that history an Irish mediascape has been shaped to the changing contours of both the physical terrain and what Appadurai terms the mental 'ideoscape' of the nation and its relationship to modernity. The heterogeneous instability of the national formation was compromised even before formal, if partial, political independence was achieved in 1922. Ireland's media history may therefore be said to bear traces of the kind of ambivalent, alternative modernity of transatlantic Western culture suggested by Bauman (1990: 1–15). Beyond the bounds of nation, an Irish mediascape occupies a liminal, largely Anglophone culture that has been deterritorialised by broadcasting, cinema, satellite and internet technologies, producing a global traffic and a series of definitive, if uneven, material exchanges. So while Gibbons and others see the concept of the nation as a resource for emancipation in what they term 'critical modernity', critics like Cleary and Graham emphasise the importance of understanding the enduring role of the nation-state in their analysis of global capitalism.

BEATING THE BOUNDARIES OF AN IRISH MEDIASCAPE?

A generation ago Gearóid Ó Tuathaigh observed that media structures in Ireland were very 'open', but wryly commented that 'while [the] media forms are easy to list, the provenance of the media in Ireland is a more complex matter' (Ó Tuathaigh, 1984: 97). Since then, the advent of digital technologies and the internet have made the matter more complex still, questioning established boundaries between media and forcing criticism to beat new bounds. Ó Tuathaigh doubted the capacity of heavily penetrated media cultures like Ireland's to exercise meaningful freedom of choice or engage in the 'voluntary borrowing' that produces healthy innovation (Ó Tuathaigh, 1984: 107–8). Appadurai's observation – made a decade later in a South Asian context – that an emerging global cultural system 'is filled with ironies and resistances, sometimes camouflaged as passivity and a bottomless appetite [...] for things Western' (Appadurai, 1996: 29) is a useful resource for countering Ó Tuathaigh's embattled scepticism. Questions of media ownership and access, and understanding how the contours of the mediascape are shaped, remain crucial to a critically reflexive media culture and to media practice and pedagogy in Ireland.[10] Further, the way to gain a greater sense of critical self-definition is to reflect on how different media forms have developed historically and the frames of reference that have been used to analyse them. So while radio and cinema may be considered 'separate' media technologies, they also coexist diachronically and are connected in myriad ways with the news press, television and theatrical and literary production.[11]

Book-length studies published since 2000 have begun to investigate the diverse ways in which disparate trends and forces – globalisation, technological convergence, media cross-ownership and interactivity – form part of a critique of late modernity as it has emerged in Ireland. For example, Martin McLoone's *Irish Film* and my own *Screening Ireland*, both published in 2000, base their arguments and analyses on a body of relatively closely matched, carefully contextualised film texts. Both provide a summary and critique of the cultural debates discussed above, McLoone memorably claiming that 'Ireland now inhabits a cultural space somewhere between its nationalist past, its European future and its American imagination' (McLoone, 2000: 7). But while the books share similar theoretical bases and interpret cinema and television as both products and interrogators of the forces of modernity in which Ireland is enmeshed, they differ in style, emphasis and choice of material. Whereas *Screening Ireland* features a chronological and generic arrangement of material that attempts to survey cinema and television in tandem as they coexist in the cultural experience, McLoone's text remains sharply focused on film. Moreover, he contests aspects of the postcolonial paradigm adopted by cultural critics, noting that 'the process of reimagining Irish national identity to accommodate the kinds of difference outlined above [gendered, sexual, racial, political] has reconfigured nationalism' (McLoone, 2000: 110). His text is also notable for its critical application of 'Third Cinema' theory to Irish film in the

1970s and 1980s, offering a clear lineage for the emergence of a contemporary cinema. *Screening Ireland*, on the other hand, draws on different aspects of contemporary cultural theory in its analysis of Irish television, as it seeks to elucidate how popular programmes engage with the problematic globalised modernity characteristic of Irish media culture at the turn of the millennium.

Ruth Barton's *Irish National Cinema* (2004) combines a historical reading of the practices of cinema-going with a thematic analysis of a selection of key films to produce an exploded sense of Irish national cinema in which familiar or 'classic' titles sit alongside lesser-known material, including some newly archived amateur films not available to earlier critics. She uses gender analysis particularly well to produce new readings and reconfigurations, and dexterously works in references to popular television culture throughout, though her bald claim that 'cinema has now replaced Catholicism as a validating belief system' stretches credulity (Barton, 2004: 189). Barton argues the need for 'a greater interest in Irish cinema culture', from 'the popular coverage [...] in fan magazines [...] to the academic literature that has analysed them [...], but equally the spaces in which they have been viewed' (Barton, 2004: 10–11). In short, she recognises the need to locate both the cultural practice of cinema-going and the critical analysis of film within the wider Irish mediascape. Like *Irish Film* and *Screening Ireland*, her book highlights the crucial significance of Ireland's diaspora for the development of cinema at home, both in terms of imagination and cultural production. Concluding with an analysis of Jim Sheridan's *In America* (2003), she selects an image from the film to make a telling point about the nature of cinema in Ireland: 'it is a home movie [...] that foreign finance, in this case American, has allowed him to make and exhibit to a worldwide audience, an analogy if you like, for the evolution of Irish national cinema' (Barton, 2004: 190).

While all three of these authors frequently refer to viewers, their deployment of the term 'reception' is largely confined to the citation of viewing statistics for radio and television, cinema attendance figures and newspaper reviews. Indeed, as was noted earlier, there have been very few academic studies of Irish media audiences based on recognised qualitative research methods such as focus-group interviews with film-goers, radio listeners, television viewers, magazine readers and internet users.[12] One notable exception is *Media Audiences in Ireland* (1997), edited by sociologists Mary Kelly and Barbara O'Connor. Elements of audience interview and cognition are also integral to parts of David Miller's book about propaganda and the media in Northern Ireland, *Don't Mention the War* (1994), and to Eoin Devereux's study of RTÉ's representation of poverty on television, *Devils and Angels* (1998). Since the mid-1980s, work on media audiences and practitioners has established a body of ethnographic literature, methodological discussion and interdisciplinary debate. In some instances such work can shade into the functional requirements of public relations, advertising and commercial imperatives to 'deliver data' about TV audience ratings or readership surveys. Within academia, however, these social science antecedents have encouraged further research on the ways in which individuals and key groups in Irish society (differentiated by generation, gender, geography and class) apprehend, experience and 'use' different kinds of media texts for cognitive mapping and identity formation in an increasingly complex and fluid mediascape (McGuigan, 1999: 74–5).

Since the late 1970s, critics whose main role has been to interpret a corpus of film texts that constitutes an edifice collectively termed 'a cinema' have taken increasing cognisance of the importance of production policy and funding regimes for Irish film and television. *Cinema and Ireland* (1987) not only had scholarly impetus and method; its publication at the same time as the closure of the Irish Film Board, after only seven years' formal existence, gave it a crucial interventional impact in political debates about funding policy. Subsequent studies by Roddy Flynn (2002), John Hill and others (Hill *et al.*, 1994) have further advanced the political economy/policy approach to film and media. Work within this area is centrally linked to questions of media ownership, production and forms of control, with the most thorough and historically wide-ranging study to date being John Horgan's *Irish Media* (2001). Horgan outlines the key changes within the mainstream media environment over an extended period, giving quantitative detail about ownership change and such like. He also examines the relationships between policy-making, technological uptake and the political economy of the different media industries, detailing how these forces interact competitively across the Irish border and between Ireland and Britain. The book's strength lies in its integrated approach – Horgan's analysis of the press, radio and television is particularly good – while also paying due attention to the recent 'pluriformity' of the Irish mediascape and the impact of newer media. However, the argument that 'the media inform social and political change as well as reflecting it' falls short of the 'transformative' analysis put forward by critics such as Gibbons. Further, we get little understanding of the types of agency operating within organisations and no analysis of media texts. We need to understand that political economic aspects of media are shaped by policies that are generated from deep within institutional structures, which are themselves subject to historical pressures and changes, to examine the dynamic interaction between such institutions and newer commercial organisations, and to take account of the legislative agendas of particular government ministers.

Something approaching this multilayered analysis is achieved by Farrell Corcoran's *RTÉ and the Globalisation of Irish Television* (2004), a highly focused study of an eight-year period (1995–2003) in RTÉ's recent development. It is both an academic examination of the oldest public service media institution in the Republic and an executive manager's institutional analysis of the debates, debacles and decision-making processes surrounding communications policy in contemporary Ireland. Its analysis is informed by a clear understanding of the current trends in the global economics of television production and the embattled politics involved at an organisational level for a small public service broadcaster. Corcoran effectively scrutinises the complexity of interests within and between different government departments, examines the external lobbying groups and commercial interests that influence decision-making in RTÉ, and evaluates how policy is shaped and implemented. The book also clearly articulates the values that underpin journalism and its role in enlivening public debate and enhancing the quality of peoples' lives. Because of the author's dual position as university professor and senior executive, the book is marked by a dialectical tension: it is both a diary and a dissertation in which he reflects on recent events with some acuity, thereby contributing to what he calls the 'national conversation' at the heart of the media in Ireland. Corcoran believes that 'RTÉ is the most important producer and custodian of collective memory in the country', and reminds us that while the Irish mediascape is becoming increasingly deterritorialised and time-altered, it is still experienced by individuals who are socially and culturally situated on an island of four million people, which has a 'pluriform' but small media economy and a tight-knit group of professional practitioners (Corcoran, 2004: 17).[13] While this smallness of scale is problematic in political economic terms, it remains central to any understanding of the nature of Ireland's mediascape.

From one perspective, the 'national conversation' facilitated by the press, television and – perhaps even more importantly – radio has been seen as being led by media professionals, many of whom have socio-economic and kinship ties to political and business elites.[14] An audience-centred approach, on the other hand, registers a fundamental shift of recognition in relation to the sovereignty of 'ordinary' consumers-as-audiences. But there is, I would argue, another productive mode of enquiry related to the small scale of the Irish media, namely, the auto/biographical. By now we have a body of popular memoirs by two generations of Irish media practitioners including journalists, producers, presenters and technicians. In one sense, this corpus constitutes one of the oldest elements of what I earlier termed the Irish mediascape's meta-narrative: personal accounts by media professionals of their memories of working in a particular medium at a specific historical moment.[15] Works such as Kieron Hickey's *Short Story: Irish cinema 1945–58* (1986), for example, indicated that film could be used in a creative, non-fictional fashion to tell its own history, while the recent films of Des Bell exploit the possibilities of creatively re-presenting media archive material to tell history differently (Bell, 2004). Typically, the auto/biographical mode of media history narrates through home-movie and video-diary essays various kinds of personal, local and unofficial histories, the stuff of anecdote and imagination, which collectively constitutes an 'improper' history of memory (Radstone, 2000). More innovative kinds of cultural history would recognise the problematic validity of such material and devise fresh methods of enquiry from which to produce new kinds of media history. Both RTÉ and BBC Northern Ireland have, with varying degrees of success, recently begun to produce a body of reflexive media histories based on the personal accounts of media professionals and 'ordinary' viewers alike, as evidenced by *Home Movie Nights* and *Eighty Listening Years* (2004).[16] These kinds of projects have come about partly through the availability of new technologies, but also because of the widespread recognition that the experiences they chronicle have historical significance, a view heightened by the sense that one media 'age' is about to be eclipsed by another. Ultimately, it is by drawing on diverse disciplinary methods and fusing them into different interdisciplinary frameworks that we may better undertake 'the contextualised interpretation of symbolic forms' (Thompson, 1995: 8) of a new mediascape within a broader cultural history of Ireland.

CONCLUSIONS

To 'beat the bounds', then, is not merely to explore fresh terrain and establish new knowledge; it is also an injunction to exceed disciplinary boundaries in productive ways. In exploring the idea that 'history is turning to [critical] practices that give meaning to the world in plural and often contradictory ways' (Chartier, 1988: 14), we can observe that Irish media history is best characterised as a complex dynamic composed of successive conformities and countervailing forms of dissent. This dynamic, the outcome of a dialectical relationship between society, politics and culture, has been shaped by powerful political and economic forces – capitalism, colonialism, nationalism – both within and without the island of Ireland in its historical passage from pre-modern polity to European democracy. The significance of projecting an Irish cultural history within a debate about modernity, therefore, lies in the need to understand a particular transatlantic experience of a post-imperial European modernisation process.[17] Offered as a critique of late capitalism as it has emerged in Ireland, a new cultural history would consist of an amalgam of different interpretative readings of the structures and practices, texts and performances, social actors and economic imperatives that constitute a significant part of its media culture. Such a history would also show how the realm of the cultural in which the Irish mediascape is situated has been crucial in testing the boundaries and indeed the core notion of national culture in its various manifestations. By accenting the local and the subaltern contexts of Ireland's changing mediascape, as well as its global and international dimensions, we can better gauge how forces of conformity and dissent have both underpinned and undermined received ideas of national cultural histories, and how they might sustain connections with comparable mediascapes elsewhere.

NOTES

1.   1984 was a particularly rich year for books on the Irish media. It saw the publications of Rex Cathcart's history of the BBC in Northern Ireland, Liz Curtis's searing indictment of British media coverage of the North, John McMahon and Martin McLoone's *Irish Television and Society*, and Brian Farrell's edited collection of the RTÉ Thomas Davis Lectures, *Communications and Community in Ireland*. Significant earlier titles include O Laoghaire's *Invitation to Film* (1945), Gorham's *Forty Years of Irish Broadcasting* (1967) and Doolan and Quinn's *Sit Down and Be Counted*

(1969). For a snapshot outline of the development of scholarship and institutions in this sub-field, see Pettitt (2001).

2. An example is the 'Broadcasting and Irish Society' series edited by Richard Pine published by the Four Courts Press, Dublin. Titles so far include *2RN and the Origins of Irish Radio* (Pine, 2002) and *Broadcasting in Irish* (Watson, 2003).

3. In addition to its phenomenal economic growth between 1994 and 2001, the Republic attained the status of the world's most globalised country early in the twentieth-first century, according to the US journal *Foreign Policy*, which compiles a globalisation index based on a variety of indicators such as economic integration, technological connectivity, political engagement and travel. See www.foreignpolicy.com

4. It should also be noted that studies of the media are to some extent dependent on the practical knowledge – activated on a daily basis by media practitioners – of organisations with an underdeveloped historical sense of themselves: witness RTÉ's wiping of videotape archives in the 1980s.

5. Interestingly, two recent professorial appointments – Bell at Queen's University Belfast and McLoone at Ulster – are both from Derry and were members of the Media Association of Ireland in the 1980s, a Dublin-based group of scholars, educationalists and media professionals that organised periodic seminar series and published occasional pamphlets. McLoone also served as Education Officer at the Irish Film Institute in the 1980s.

6. A former camera operator, Monks is now a semi-retired archivist of the O'Leary Archive at the National Library of Ireland.

7. The organisation's paper archive forms part of the BBC's Written Archives at Caversham in Berkshire.

8. North American-based academics who have made significant contributions to Irish media studies include Slide (1988), Savage (1996), McIlroy (1998) and McKillop (1999).

9. Michel Peillon and Eamonn Slater's edited collection introduces a selection of essays premised on the notion that Irish culture exemplifies the characteristics of 'late modernity' rather than postmodernity, citing commodification, globalisation, visualisation, aestheticisation, pluralism, social fragmentation and reflexivity as key components (Peillon and Slater, 1998: 3–6).

10. Witness, for instance, the panel debate and audience discussion at the 'Keeping It Real' conference on Irish film and television in April 2002 at University College Dublin.

11. One of the few innovative publishing ventures to tackle the relationship between literature and cinema in Ireland is the 'Ireland into Film' series, inaugurated by the Cork University Press in 2001. Edited by Keith Hopper and Grainne Humphreys, the series examines notable examples of fiction-to-film adaptation in the Irish canon. The Liffey Press's 'Contemporary Irish Writers and Filmmakers' series, which was launched in 2004 under the editorship of Eugene O'Brien, occupies similar ground, though it is more auteurist in approach, featuring titles on Jim Sheridan, Neil Jordan and Roddy Doyle.

12. One of the explanations for the dearth of research on audiences is that properly constructed, rigorously designed projects can be more time-consuming and therefore more costly in research terms than purely theoretical work. The most sustained and most fruitful work to date has focused on understanding the sometimes complex 'industry' regimes of constraint and opportunity involved in media production.

13. Corcoran's study includes a rebuttal of filmmaker and fellow RTÉ Authority member Bob Quinn's *Maverick* (2001), in which he discusses his campaign against advertising during RTÉ's children's programming.

14. See Kenny (1994), which sets out the classic liberal argument for understanding the Irish media as a 'fourth estate'.

15. On pirate radio in Ireland, see Mulryan (1988); on cinema, see Doorley (2002) and Robbins (2004); on the press, see O'Toole (1992).

16. *Eighty Listening Years* was an eight-part radio history, made to mark the BBC's anniversary in Northern Ireland, which drew on archive sound and contemporary interview material.

17. Cleary (2003: 104) insists that we remember that 'the ways in which specific national configurations are always the product of dislocating intersections between local and global processes that are not simply random but part of the internally contradictory structure of the modern capitalist world system'.

11
Placing Geography in Irish Studies: Symbolic Landscapes of Spectacle and Memory

Yvonne Whelan and Liam Harte

The word 'geography' probably brings painful memories to most people. [...] It conjures up the dullest subject of their school days: the long uninteresting lists of bays and rivers and mountains; the sing-song repetition of 'France, Paris, on the Seine; Germany, Berlin, on the Spree; Ireland, Dublin, on the Liffey'. (*Irish Times*, 15 May 1937)

Geography is suddenly sexy – although many of us are not exactly sure why. (Nally, 2004: 132)

The cultural turn of the late 1980s had great ramifications for the practice of social and cultural geography. Freshly invigorated by postmodern and poststructuralist ideas, geographers set about challenging traditional approaches and methodologies within the discipline and the neglect of geographical perspectives in other fields. The critical human geography that began to take shape announced the interpretive significance of space and the arrival of 'a new animating polemic on the theoretical and political agenda, one which rings with significantly different ways of seeing time and space together, the interplay of history and geography' (Soja, 1989: 11). As space became a resurgent analytic, geographers began to revise received views of the cultural landscape, a concept that lies at the heart of much geographical enquiry. Instead of seeing landscapes as sites of settlement, they sought 'to recover layers of meaning lying beyond (or "beneath") those surface remains and relict features' (Gregory, 1994: 145). The work of Denis Cosgrove and James Duncan was especially influential in this regard. In *Social Formation and Symbolic Landscape* Cosgrove conceptualised landscape as 'an ideologically-charged and very complex cultural product' and demonstrated a reflexive, sympathetic approach to the nuances and tensions evident in the processes of landscape creation (Cosgrove, 1984: 11). Duncan, meanwhile, was instrumental in positing a view of landscape as 'one of the central elements in a cultural system, for as an ordered assemblage of objects, a text, it acts as a signifying system through which a social system is communicated, reproduced, experienced and explored' (Duncan, 1990: 184).

These broader disciplinary developments had significant implications for the trajectories of cultural and historical geography within Ireland, the roots of which can be traced back to 1945, the year in which E. Estyn Evans was appointed to the first chair of Geography at Queen's University Belfast. Evans was the first of a number of influential British scholars who took up positions in Irish universities in the postwar years, seeing the country's emerging geography departments as springboards in their early careers (Buchanan *et al.*, 1971). Evans's work was largely based on fieldwork and focused on traditional rural settlement patterns and house-types along the north-western Atlantic fringe of Ireland, while his colleague Tom Jones Hughes's research explored nineteenth-century documentary sources and the mediation of social power through landholding practices (Simms, 2000: 228–9). Not surprisingly, much of the geography produced in Ireland under the aegis of these scholars was heavily biased towards the historical and tended to focus on the unique aspects of Ireland's landscape and history. The immense legacy of these and other pioneering geographers of their day shaped a whole generation of scholars and was further transmitted through their many doctoral students who continued to foster approaches rooted in rigorous archival and field-based research.

The 1980s cultural turn, however, marked the start of a new era for Irish geography, albeit a somewhat muted one compared with con-temporaneous developments in British cultural geography. The fresh approaches to landscape study spawned innovative research in both rural and urban domains and took cultural and historical geographers down a number of productive new paths. As Anngret Simms explains, one of the key conceptual developments that enabled and enlivened much of this research was the theorisation of landscape as a multi-faceted symbolic text to be interrogated and decoded: 'The intention is to understand the iconography of the landscape for what it can tell us about the politically, economically and culturally dominant group in society [...] settlement is both medium and message, site and symbol, terrain and text' (Simms, 2000: 237). A body of work has subsequently evolved that approaches urban, rural, historical and contemporary spaces as emblematic sites of representation and as dynamic symbolic constituents of socio-cultural and political systems. Much of this research is sensitive to the symbolism and ideological significance of the built form in the construction, mobilisation and representation of identity. An early work that heralded this changing approach was Graham and Proudfoot's *An Historical Geography of Ireland* (1993), which challenged the insularity of received interpretive frameworks and sought to reconceptualise Irish historical geography from new theoretical perspectives. The blurring of the boundaries between historical and cultural geography further strengthened the theoretical rigour of this sub-field and foregrounded the spatial dimensions of the negotiation of social and communal identities in Ireland. This has produced more nuanced readings of Irish cultural landscapes and sites of heritage that focus attention on the politics of space and interrogate singular, clear-cut schemes of Irishness (Graham, 1997; W. J. Smyth, 1997). A number of key themes have thus emerged pertaining to the theorisation of cultural landscapes in the context of dissolving meta-narratives.

One distinct strand of research on the iconographic meanings embedded in Ireland's cultural landscapes has repeatedly underlined the significance of sites of memory in different political and geographical contexts. Graham's work on contested landscape representations among Northern Irish Protestants, for example, has been important in advancing the notion of the representative landscape, defined as 'an encapsulation of a people's image of itself, a collage, based upon the particularity of territory and a shared past which helps define communal identity' (Graham, 1994: 258). Representative landscapes have also been a feature of Catherine Nash's work on the gendered dimensions of literary and artistic configurations of place. For example, her analysis of the construction of the west of Ireland as an iconic landscape purposefully blends literary criticism and spatial interpretation to expose the multiplicity of meanings that gives the west its symbolic power (Nash, 1993; 1997). Nuala Johnson's research on the commemoration of World War I in post-partition Ireland further illuminates the emblematic power of landscape by foregrounding the constitutive role of space in the poetics and politics of remembrance. Building on her earlier work on the commemoration of the 1798 rebellion and nationalist memorials in Dublin, Johnson explores 'the "civil war" of identity and memory' that underpinned the public remembrance of Ireland's war dead and the casualties of the Easter Rising, arguing that what took place was 'a dialogue between remembering and forgetting, between providing moral legitimacy and denying it' (Johnson, 2003: 170, 168). Her emphasis on the dialogical aspects of memory and identity is echoed in Yvonne Whelan's work on the spatial politics of Dublin's cultural landscape before and after independence. *Reinventing Modern Dublin* examines how the cityscape became a highly contested site in which competing ideologies found symbolic representation in the city's monuments, street names and architecture. The book also considers the contemporary iconography of a city where issues of collective memory, cultural heritage and commemoration still cause controversy, as evidenced by the debates surrounding the construction of the Dublin Spire in 2003 (Whelan, 2003).

The application of postcolonial theory within historical geography has also yielded a number of nuanced analyses that contest monolithic notions of identity and dismantle historical dualities. John Morrissey's work on the early modern period, which envisages the barony of Kilnamanagh in Tipperary as a lens through which to examine the multiple historical geographies of a colonised contact zone, is but one example of this research strand (Morrissey, 2003, 2005). Another is provided by Gerry Kearns's exploration of the contested nature of women's exclusion from public space in early twentieth-century Dublin (Kearns, 2004). The spatial politics of the Irish overseas have also assumed fresh significance in recent geographical scholarship with a postcolonial inflection. For example, William Jenkins's research on Irish Protestant immigrants in late Victorian Toronto attends to the social and spatial processes that determined their negotiation of the dualities of Irishness and Britishness, whereas Mervyn Busteed's work on Irish migrant identities in nineteenth-century Manchester usefully explicates the performative nature of hegemonic power and subaltern resistance through an analysis of broadside ballads and nationalist parades (Busteed, 1998, 2005; Jenkins, 2003). Bronwen Walter, meanwhile, has done much to tease out the gendered dimensions of Irish diaspora space, and has recently turned her attention to the genealogical 'entanglements' that bind native and newcomer within the national space of England (Walter, 2001, 2005).

As this brief overview suggests, cultural and historical geography research in and about Ireland is in a vibrantly healthy state. Increasingly internationalised and no longer solely wedded to archival and field-based research, much of this 'new' geography, as we have seen, privileges social space as an arena in which power is mediated, represented and resisted, and it is in this area that the interpenetration of postmodern geography and Irish Studies has been most productive. For long a blind spot within Irish Studies, geography's heightened theoretical engagement with the modalities of social space has coincided with and to some extent fuelled the emergence of space as an analytical category within Irish cultural criticism. This trend has been particularly evident among scholars working with literary texts, as a perusal of the pages of *Irish Studies Review*, for example, will confirm. This is not to say that Irish Studies has suddenly become spatialised, or that Irish time has been erased by Irish space. Rather, there appears to be a growing appreciation of the need to attend to the interplay of the synchronous and the diachronous in the formation and articulation of Irish identities, a trend epitomised by Gerry Smyth's *Space and the Irish Cultural Imagination* (2001), the most sustained examination to date of the ideological underpinnings of the spatial practices that permeate Irish culture.

Inspired by Smyth's approach and prompted by Graham's contention that 'social power cannot be conceived without a geographical context; its exercise shapes space which in turn shapes social power' (Graham, 1997: xi), we want to reflect further here on the dynamic relationship between space, time, memory and ideology, with a view to showing how a spatially informed approach, grounded in a conception of landscape as a discursive site in which cultures are continually reproduced and contested, can productively expand historical interpretations of processional and commemorative practices within and without Ireland. To this end, we propose to examine three case-study examples that highlight different aspects of the constitutive role of landscapes, both real and symbolic, in the contestation of power and the representation of history in different periods and contexts.

Our first example focuses on the politics of spectacular display during Queen Victoria's visit to Dublin in 1900. We explore the material manifestations of empire on the streets of turn-of-the century Dublin, as well as the spatially anchored attempts to subvert and resist imperial power. In our second example we probe further the relationship between landscape, memory and history by reviewing some of the memorial spaces created in response to the Northern Ireland Troubles. Whereas unofficial local memorials tend to mirror the wider political divisions, thereby fulfilling a range of territorial and sectarian functions, official commemorative initiatives, exemplified here by the 1998 Bloomfield report, seek to use memorialisation to enable post-conflict resolution. For all their palliative rhetoric, however, such official initiatives are marked by tensions that bear witness to the troubling nature of remembrance in a politically contested society. This interplay between landscape, memory and historical trauma is further explored in our final case-study example, which focuses on the material geographies of Irish diasporic communities, with particular reference to Famine commemoration in North America.

LANDSCAPE, SPECTACLE AND PROCESSIONAL SPACE

'Did you see me little flags,' Rashers asked. [...]
'Red, white and blue,' Rashers said, 'the colours of loyalty.'
'My husband doesn't hold with England,' Mrs. Bartley said.
'That's been catered for,' Rashers explained, showing her a sample, 'the green ribbon is for Ireland.'
'It doesn't match up, somehow.'
'It never did, ma'am,' Rashers said. 'Isn't that what all the bloody commotion is about for the last seven hundred years?' (Plunkett, 1969: 18)

In interrogating the 'real geographies' of colonialism and postcolonialism, parades and public performances have become important tools of geographical enquiry. Endowed with meaning on many levels, public parades not only serve as rituals of remembrance, but are also choreographed expressions of state power, as studies of the politics of ritual and spectacle in different international contexts have attested (Goheen, 1990, 1993; Jarman and Bryan, 1998). Particularly noteworthy in this regard is Kong and Yeoh's analysis of state-sponsored National Day parades in Singapore which, they argue, achieve their effects by 'combining the architectural spectacularity of the past and the animated spectacularity of the moment':

As national ritual, National Day parades draw selectively from historically sedimented symbolic capital in the landscape; at the same time, since landscape is a constantly growing repository of collective memory, new uses [...] inscribe new meanings which go some way in obscuring older significances. (Kong and Yeoh, 1997: 220)

Such spatially engaged readings of symbolic landscapes are rich in suggestive potential for fresh studies of the Irish parading tradition, most of which tend to focus on the historical significance of loyalist and nationalist parades in the North and the role of St Patrick's Day parades in the articulation of Irish diasporic identity (Cronin and Adair, 2002; T. G. Fraser, 2000). An alternative, spatial reading of

Irish processional practice is offered by Busteed in his study of two sympathy parades organised in response to the execution of the Manchester 'martyrs' in 1867, which he interprets as expressions of subaltern resistance that appropriated local and national cultural motifs and public spaces (Busteed, 2005). Such studies demonstrate how as landscape metaphors, parades have a manifold impact that is mediated aurally and visually, materially and militarily. There are, therefore, a range of aspects to be considered when reading processional practice spatially, including the space that is the parade route, the role of the military, the forms of theatrical display, and the role of decorations, lighting, fireworks and music. With these elements in mind, we want to examine the spectacular aspects of Queen Victoria's visit to Dublin in April 1900 from a spatial perspective, paying particular attention to the ways in which political dominance was spatially produced and contested.

The 90-year period from 1821 to 1911 witnessed a total of nine Irish visits by British monarchs, each of which occasioned a considerable measure of fanfare and ceremonial ritual: King George IV in 1821; Queen Victoria in 1849, 1853, 1861 and 1900; King Edward VII in 1903, 1904 and 1907; and King George V in 1911. The pomp and pageantry surrounding these visits bore witness to the politicisation of public space through the transformation of the urban landscape. On each occasion the state authorities manipulated invented ritual and landscape spectacle in order to underline the enduring importance of the monarchy to Irish culture and identity and undermine the growing threat of separatist nationalism. The spectacular elements of these visits – the street decorations, the erection of temporary structures, the soundscape created by military bands, the fireworks, the symbolic welcoming of the monarch, the royal procession – combined to create a 'web of signification' (Ley and Olds, 1988) that was skilfully spun by the state to assert its hegemonic authority. Not all of these elements were unchanging, however; particular noteworthy for our purposes are the varying ways in which the authorities exploited the sedimented symbolic capital in Dublin's cultural landscape in response to a shifting Irish political landscape.

Queen Victoria's 1900 visit brings some key aspects of this strategic appropriation of urban space into sharp focus. For this visit, the royal procession from Kingstown to the Viceregal Lodge in the Phoenix Park was carefully orchestrated in a manner that reinforces the view that 'the choice of the landscape in which to stage a spectacle is not a matter of indifference, for some sites have more significance that others. [...] Parades do not simply occupy central space, but also move through space as a means of diffusing the effects of the spectacle' (Kuper, 1972: 421). To begin with, the procession passed through Dublin's more affluent southern suburbs, where many of the street names were already redolent of the city's imperial status. When the royal cortège arrived at Leeson Street bridge, the Queen was formally welcomed and presented with the city keys and civic sword, as had happened on previous visits. What was new on this occasion was the erection of a mock medieval castle gate in place of the more traditional triumphal arch. Designed by Thomas Drew, this painted wooden structure, 70 feet in height, was presented as a replica of medieval Baggotrath Castle (Fig. 11.1), the site where, in August 1649, Royalist forces were defeated by the Roundheads, thus enabling Cromwell's entry into Dublin. This impressive showpiece was no mere decorative pastiche, therefore, but a calculated attempt to exploit the residual symbolic capital in Dublin's cultural landscape by invoking the memory of a time when Irish and Royalist forces stood together as allies.

Figure 11.1   The mock medieval gate, modelled on Baggotrath Castle, erected on Leeson Street bridge for the 1900 visit of Queen Victoria

After the presentation of the address of welcome, the royal cortège entered the city boundary and passed along Merrion Square to College Green, where it received a resounding welcome from the assembled students and fellows of Trinity College. An *Irish Times* reporter succinctly underlined the suitability of this part of the city as the setting for a dramatisation of imperial power and noted the use of evanescent display as a means of interpellating the local populace:

The scene in College Green was one that will linger long and pleasantly in the memory of all who were fortunate enough to witness it. College Green, the heart of the city, and which has from time immemorial been the central point of all processions and pageants occurring within the civic bounds, was yesterday the great central rallying point in the triumphal progress of the Queen. [...] The immense open space, the magnificent architectural surroundings – Trinity College, the Bank of Ireland, and the other splendid buildings – all helped to enhance the picturesque character of the scene. (*Irish Times*, 5 April 1900)

The procession then moved north via Dame Street and Parliament Street where it crossed the river Liffey and made its way along the quays to the Phoenix Park, bypassing completely the largely slum-ridden and poverty-stricken north inner city.

Unlike other truly imperial cities, where such choreographed spectacles usually proceeded smoothly, turn-of-the-century Dublin was caught in a schizophrenic position, which these royal events crystallised anew. While the unionist press delighted in the city's adornment, nationalist commentators were quick to register local objections to the royal visit, many of which centred on the orchestrated politicisation of social space. For example, an *Irish People* commentator protested that the 'gaudy' 'foreign' colours 'do not suggest an Irish welcome. They only indicate that wealthy Dublin Unionists have [...] given the Southern side of Dublin the appearance of an English city for the time being.' Combining anti-imperial animus with socialist critique, the writer went on to complain that every Union flag is

an outward and visible token of the degradation of the capital – a symbol of the still dominant power of the English ascendancy. [...] Under all the banners and floral devices and glaring illuminations, was still poor old humdrum Dublin, with its 200,000 dwellers in squalid tenements, its ruined trade, its teeming workhouses, its hopeless poverty – the once-proud capital of a free nation degraded to the level of the biggest city of a decaying and fettered province. (*Irish People*, 7 April 1900)

Capitalising on such dissent, militant nationalists actively contested the politicisation of public space by organising a counter-demonstration in the form of a torchlight procession on the night of the royal party's arrival in Ireland. This oppositional activism reached its height some weeks later when, on 1 July, an 'Irish patriotic children's treat' was staged by Maud Gonne and Inghinidhe na hÉireann (Daughters of Ireland) as a calculated counterweight to the two 'children's treats' hosted by the Queen during her visit. This pointedly counter-hegemonic gesture proved to be the most celebrated anti-royalist event of the year (Condon, 2000: 173). Just as public space had earlier been manipulated by the state to reinforce Irish imperial loyalties, nationalists used space and spectacle to articulate Ireland's resistance to empire, thereby exemplifying the argument that 'the mimicry of the post-colonial subject is [...] always potentially destabilizing to colonial discourse, and locates an area of considerable political and cultural uncertainty in the structure of imperial dominance' (Ashcroft *et al.*, 2002: 142).

This brief reading of Queen Victoria's 1900 visit seeks to augment traditional historical accounts by drawing attention to the material role of landscape, social space and spectacular display in the mediation of state power. As evanescent spectacles, such state occasions sought to leave an indelible mark upon the popular consciousness by exploiting both the enchanting power of grand display and the latent symbolic capital of the cultural landscape. They also drew the ire of subaltern groups who themselves used social space to stage symbolic gestures of resistance. As Ireland inched closer to Home Rule, nationalist opposition to royal tours hardened, so that while each monarch's visit to Dublin succeeded in generating widespread fervour, they were less successful in cultivating long-term imperial loyalty. In fact, the British state's efforts to invent ritual and create landscape spectacle as a means of asserting its hegemonic authority increasingly served to expose the very fault-lines it sought to conceal. By effectively galvanising nationalist groups into oppositional activity, therefore, these spectacular events confirm the view that 'while ideology is dominant, it is also contradictory, fragmentary and inconsistent and does not necessarily or inevitably blindfold the "interpellated" subject to a perception of its operations' (Ashcroft *et al.*, 2002: 222).

LANDSCAPE, TRAUMA AND COMMEMORATIVE SPACE

When all this is over [...] they'll probably want to make a memorial. I hope they do something original. They should build it around the sky. [...] Cate's voice trailed away, and she continued to stare out of the window. She imagined a room, a perfectly square room. Three of its walls, unbroken by windows, would be covered by neat rows of names, over three thousand of them; and the fourth wall would be nothing but window. The whole structure would be built where the horizon was low, and the sky huge. It would be a place which afforded dignity to memory, where you could bring your anger, as well as your grief. (Madden, 1996: 149)

Having considered the role of spectacular display and symbolic landscape in the contest for power in turn-of-the-century Dublin, we wish to turn now to the competition for monumental public space that attends the representation of shared historical trauma in the present, with reference to the commemoration of two distinct categories of victims: those (thousands) killed during the Troubles in Northern Ireland and those (hundreds of thousands) who perished as a result of the mid-nineteenth-century Irish Famine. In his essay 'Monument and trauma: varieties of remembrance' Joep Leerssen usefully distinguishes between two modes of collective commemoration. One he terms 'society remembrancing', which is state-sanctioned, officially instituted and ideologically conservative; the other, 'community remembrancing', is 'sub-elite and demotic' and as such does not always solidify into monumental forms. The latter commemorative mode, moreover, typically evinces a subaltern view of history termed 'traumatic' remembrancing, which seeks to register that which society remembrancing omits (Leerssen, 2001: 215, 221). Although he suggests that the boundaries between these two types of remembrance are blurring, we wish to retain them as separate categories for the purposes of our discussion of sites of Troubles commemoration in the North, for which they have a clear relevance, as Leerssen himself indicates.

Urban and rural landscapes across the North are marked by a large number of unofficial memorials erected by republican organisations, chiefly Sinn Féin and the Irish Republican Army (IRA), and by the more fragmented loyalist paramilitary groups, notably the Ulster Defence Association (UDA) and Ulster Volunteer Force (UVF). These examples of 'community remembrancing', which include memorials, statues, plaques and wall murals, serve as subversive icons of identity that transform 'neutral' spaces into ideologically charged sites of symbolic struggle. As improvised, piecemeal memorials, they represent strategic displays of resistance through remembrance. For republicans, events such as Derry's 'Bloody Sunday' and the 1981 IRA hunger strike are woven into the iconography of the landscape, whereas loyalists frequently draw on the imagery and rhetoric of the Battle of the Somme in order to align their recent dead with those of World War I (Graham and Shirlow, 2002). Both paramilitary groupings find political wall murals to be a particularly potent and relatively inexpensive means of staging strategic forms of remembrance. As Jarman notes, 'over the past twenty years mural painting has developed into one of the most dynamic means of cultural and symbolic expression in the North of Ireland' (Jarman, 2001: 6). Although more ephemeral than monuments, murals effectively claim space at a community level and often mobilise local populations in support of particular political initiatives. Thus, 'they are not just a backdrop to politics, but a dynamic part of the political process' (Rolston, 2003: 14). While such unofficial memorial landscapes sustain and legitimate a bank of shared memories, they are also invariably sectarian spaces that serve to divide rather than unite by marking territorial boundaries and shaping situated identities in contradistinction to the ethnic other. Further, as sites of 'remembrance resistance', monuments, murals and even graffiti represent internal divisions *between* and *within* communities. Thus, the recent splintering of loyalism has been marked by attempts on the part of the UVF and the Ulster Freedom Fighters (UFF) to control and claim social space on the Shankill Road, where intracommunal animosities can be read via the iconography of adjacent gable walls.

In recent years, more permanent monumental sites of remembrance have evolved, with various groups funding and commissioning statues and other figurative memorials, a trend that is captured in microcosm by the commemorative landscape of the city of Derry. In the republican Bogside area, for example, artists have created a trail of gable wall murals that graphically recreates key events of the Troubles (Kelly, 2001). These murals frame the commemorative centrepiece, a memorial cross at 'Free Derry' corner, erected in 1974 in memory of the victims of 'Bloody Sunday'. Close by, a granite monument built in 2001 to commemorate the twenty-fifth anniversary of the Maze hunger strike lists the names of each of those who took part, together with plaques honouring hunger strikers who died in the 1920s (Fig. 11.2). This commemorative tableau is completed by a ten-foot-high statue of a paramilitary fighter that was unveiled in March 2000 at the graves of two 1981 hunger strikers in Creggan cemetery. Those who commissioned the monument saw it as 'a fitting tribute to members of the Irish National Liberation Army and Irish Republican

Socialist Party from counties Derry and Tyrone who gave their lives during the latest phase of the war against the British establishment in Ireland'.[1]

Figure 11.2 Hunger Strike Memorial, Bogside, Derry

Alongside and in opposition to these non-official memorial statements, there have also been a number of official attempts to commemorate victims of the Troubles. These 'consultative remembrance initiatives' have at their core a desire to utilise memory in a palliative manner, as a means of engendering social healing in a still deeply divided community. The most extensive formal process for dealing with the past was initiated in November 1997 with the establishment by Westminster of a commission, under the chairmanship of Sir Kenneth Bloomfield, to 'examine the feasibility of providing greater recognition for those who have become victims in the last thirty years as a consequence of events in Northern Ireland, recognising that those events have also had appalling repercussions for many people not living in Northern Ireland' (Bloomfield, 1998: 8). Bloomfield was asked to 'have particular regard to the possibility of establishing a new memorial reflecting both the sorrows of the past and hope for a stable future', and to consult with various organisations concerned with the welfare of the bereaved and disabled, as well as with community groups, churches and political parties (Bloomfield, 1998: 8). A particular point of concern was whether or not a permanent memorial dedicated to all victims of the Troubles should be erected, the chairman being keen 'to test the issue of whether people would prefer memorials in their own locality rather than some single project for the whole of Northern Ireland' (Bloomfield, 1998: 18). An exhaustive consultation exercise thus got underway involving political and church leaders, as well as a wide range of statutory, voluntary and community-based organisations. Many members of the general public also contacted the commission to offer comments and suggestions. The resultant report, *We Will Remember Them*, was published in April 1998.

The Bloomfield report made a number of recommendations regarding the kinds of practical assistance that ought to be provided to victims of the Northern conflict. It also made much of the uses of memory and remembrance as part of the post-conflict healing process. Alongside proposals for a Troubles archive and a new public holiday to be called 'Memorial and Reconciliation Day', the report recommended the creation of a public memorial that would recognise victims' suffering. Several forms were proposed, among them 'an arch; an obelisk or plinth; a building dedicated to contemplation or specific religious use; a museum; an archive; a multi-media presentation of the events remembered and the lessons to be learned from them' (Bloomfield, 1998: 46). Although a minority of the groups consulted were antipathetic to 'any action by way of remembrance either now or in foreseeable circumstances', the chairman insisted that a monument was necessary. In doing so, he conceptualised remembrance not only in restorative terms, but also as a means of communicating a future-oriented political message: 'we truly need to remember those who have suffered, to grieve at the side of this communal grave, to reflect upon the truth of what occurred and to move forward from there. Above all, we have to persuade our children how costly and counter-productive it would be to pursue the animosities of the past' (Bloomfield, 1998: 23).[2]

Having considered a range of initiatives, Bloomfield described his preferred memorial in terms that echo Deirdre Madden's novelistic vision, cited above. Set in 'a peaceful location, amidst beautifully-landscaped gardens', the proposed memorial would take the form of

a building which would be a striking work of modern architecture, and embodying within itself appropriate works of art contributed by communities or countries outside Northern Ireland in memory of those of their citizens who have suffered; this building to be dedicated to purposes of rest and reflection, care and counselling, and an appropriate archive of the troubles. (Bloomfield, 1998: 47)

This ecumenical commemorative space, like Madden's fictional light-filled room, seeks to harness the unifying, remedial power of symbolic landscapes in a society that has been otherwise riven by a divisive sectarian iconography. As such, the Bloomfield report encodes a distinctly different ideology of remembrance from that inscribed by the North's modes of 'community remembrancing'. Whereas republican memorials use remembrance as a means of enacting political resistance by 'keeping memory alive', as it were, the British state, through its appointed arbiter, seeks to promote a form of remembrance that is at once restorative and instructive and that, crucially, relies on an ideology of victim effacement as the preferred means of enabling post-conflict resolution.

This ideology is exemplified by Bloomfield's recommendation that any officially sanctioned Troubles memorial should take the form of an abstract, depersonalised monument rather than a figurative, individuated one. What is particularly telling in this context is the fact that the proposed monument would deviate not only from paramilitary memorials and their customary rolls of honour, but also from British war memorials, the 'high diction' (Fussell, 1975: 21) of which the report's title echoes. In a rationale that significantly undermines the promise of that title, Bloomfield argues:

In the current circumstances of Northern Ireland, any attempt to incorporate a catalogue of the names of victims in a central memorial would be certain to provide endless controversy and expose a subsequent memorial to a real danger of becoming a target for protest and demonstration; for the paint thrower or the crude slogan. (Bloomfield, 1998: 47)

This rationale reveals a fundamental tension at the heart of state-sanctioned Troubles commemoration: the difficulty, even the impossibility, of reconciling, in monumental form, the need to remember with the imperative to forget. There is, it seems, no safe commemorative space in which the North's incendiary past may be 'decommissioned' and a form of inclusive memory found. Communal memory is too unstable to be defused memorially; history's potency is marked by a monumental *absence*. If, as Luke Gibbons claims, monuments 'do not embody memory but efface it, absolving the citizen of the burden of remembering by relocating it in static form' (Gibbons, 1996: 145), then the failure to map out new kinds of commemorative social space in post-conflict Northern Ireland suggests an opposite thesis: memory cannot be made to yield to static effacement in the absence of political closure. The Northern Irish past, it would seem, is not yet ready to be preserved as an objective reality that will yield to symbolic embodiment, but is instead subject to continual contestation and recasting in the present.

But what of the commemoration of traumatic social and political events that are more distant from their historical location, both temporally and spatially? What ethical, aesthetic and political considerations attend the memorial mediation of transgenerationally transmitted trauma? What kinds of historical awareness do such memorials embody? In posing such questions, we have in mind the material role of landscape and social space in the construction and consumption of North American memorials to the Irish Famine, of which there are several notable recent examples. How do such monuments resolve the tension between the need to remain 'true' to the reality of past trauma and the desire to give visual embodiment to popular memories of the horror and its manifold effects? If, as has been claimed, diaspora 'destroys the naïve invocation of common memory as the basis of particularity by drawing attention to the dynamics of commemoration' (Gilroy, 1997: 328), what kind of memory is being 'remembered' at this distance in time, and by whom?

In recent years the material geographies of the Irish overseas have assumed greater prominence in Irish academic scholarship, in concert with the increased visibility of the diaspora in Irish cultural life in general, a phenomenon usually attributed to Mary Robinson's sustained emphasis on this theme during her presidential term in the 1990s. Long before this, however, memory and its manifestation in monuments, street iconography and public processions proved to be an important identity resource throughout many sites of the Irish diaspora. For such migrant communities, the desire to re-imagine spaces of the homeland engendered a variety of commemorative practices whereby collective memory was distilled into visual icons such as the Celtic cross or round tower, which were made to stand in for complex histories, thereby symbolically underpinning shared narratives of identity. Further, in building monuments to historical figures and events, the activities of Irish communities abroad parallel those of elite groups who 'justify their existence and order their actions in terms of a collection of stories, ceremonies, insignia, formalities, and appurtenances that they have either inherited or, in more revolutionary situations, invented' (Geertz, 1983: 124). Such comments have particular relevance for readings of the commemorative practices of Irish Americans, especially those who trace their ancestry to the three-quarters of a million Irish people who made their way to the United States during and after the Great Hunger. For this constituency, the Famine has long since assumed the status of a founding mythology or 'charter myth' which inscribes a potent communal memory, 'a creation story that both explains our presence in the new land and connects us to the old via a powerful sense of grievance' (O'Neill, 2001: 118).

The sesquicentenary of the Famine in the mid-1990s marked the onset of a concerted effort by many Irish Americans to commemorate the plight of their ancestors, chiefly but not exclusively in monumental form.[3] As Famine memorials were added to a number of cityscapes, notably Boston, Buffalo, Philadelphia and New York, commentators were quick to note the way in which the Famine Irish were co-opted into the narrative of the American dream. At many of these commemorative sites, the past is scripted as a triumphant journey from penury to socio-economic success, typically through the depiction of family groups departing Ireland in various states of emaciation and despair, only to arrive in America with hearts full of purposeful hope (Edkins, 2003: 118; Kelleher, 2002: 268). So while the bronze figures of the Great Hunger Memorial of Westchester County in upstate New York are gaunt and haggard, they nevertheless 'stand straight and tall, a sign of their strength, determination and hope amid poverty and desolation'.[4] Similarly, the Boston memorial, unveiled in 1998, juxtaposes one wretched family group escaping certain death in Ireland with another arriving in America, seemingly energised by new-found hope and determination (Kelleher, 2002: 265). The theme of triumph in the face of adversity is even more explicitly engraved in the centrepiece of the Philadelphia Famine memorial at Penn's Landing, a large bronze sculpture representing 35 life-sized figures that was unveiled in October 2003. Designed by Glenna Goodacre, who sculpted the Vietnam Women's Memorial in Washington, it depicts 'the cruel starvation which claimed one million Irish lives between 1845 to 1850; the harrowing journey to America taken by a million more; and the indomitable spirit of those who arrived safely and resolved to face the challenges of life in a new world'.[5]

But if the majority of these memorials signify 'a time of forgetting – or at least forgetting the rawness of trauma' (Edkins, 2003: 122) in favour of a celebration of an immigrant group's fortitude and triumph, the most recent Famine monument embodies a more complex response to, and representation of, social catastrophe. The Irish Hunger Memorial, designed by New York sculptor Brian Tolle (see Figs. 11.3, 11.4) was unveiled in July 2003 in Lower Manhattan by President Mary McAleese, in what she described as 'the memory-shadow of that tragic absence that is the Twin Towers of the World Trade Center'.[6] Its origins go back to March 2000, when New York governor George E. Pataki launched a competition for a memorial that would 'serve as a reminder to millions of New Yorkers and Americans who proudly trace their heritage to Ireland of those who were forced to emigrate during one of the most heart-breaking tragedies in the history of the world'.[7] When Tolle's design was chosen as the winner, a site was prepared in Battery Park City overlooking the Hudson River, in view of the Statue of Liberty and Ellis Island. Here, the centrepiece of the memorial was installed: a derelict stone cottage set in a quarter-acre of farmland, transplanted from Attymass in County Mayo and reconstructed atop a raised and tilted concrete base, which comprises the second element of the memorial.[8] This naturalistic plot was planted with Mayo vegetation and strewn with 32 fieldstones, one from each Irish county, and a single carved pilgrim stone. One entry to the base of the memorial takes the viewer through a passageway that is redolent of a neolithic burial mound, the walls of which are lined with glass-covered strands of text that deliberately mingle Famine facts, statistics about world hunger and obesity today, and quotations from literature and song.

Described by Tolle himself as 'a landscape supported by language' (Kaizen, 2001), the memorial at once invokes and interrogates the metaphysics of home and memory that haunts the migrant imaginary. On one, obvious level, the work derives its symbolic power from its literal physicality. In place of sculpted art we have actual ruins, the past evoked through the palpable realness of a patch of transplanted Mayo earth. Historical specificity underwrites this material fragment; hunger 'is not naturalized or aestheticized here but contextualized historically and politically' (Lydenberg, 2003: 131). Not only does every stone proclaim its authenticity, every detail on this cantilevered slope works to fortify the memorial's fragmentary link to the historical event it commemorates. The quarter-acre plot replicates the maximum area farmers could hold in order to qualify for British government aid

Figure 11.3 Irish Hunger Memorial, Battery Park City, New York

Figure 11.4 Internal view of the Irish Hunger Memorial

in the 1840s, while the cottage's roofless state registers the destructive impact of Famine evictions.[9] Such concern for historical accuracy echoes the transformation of actual sites of Nazi destruction into Holocaust memorials in the aftermath of World War II. Such sites, it is argued, 'tend to collapse the distinction between themselves and what they evoke. In the rhetoric of their ruins, these memorial sites seem not merely to gesture towards past events but to suggest themselves as fragments of events, inviting us to mistake the debris of history for history itself' (Young, 1993: 120–1).

While the Hunger Memorial could be said to draw part of its emotional power from an analogous consecration of the material trace of calamity, it derives even greater rhetorical authority from its exploitation of the symbolic iconography of the thatched stone cottage, which has been an integral part of the Irish national imaginary since the late nineteenth-century Literary Revival. Divested of its associations with poverty and emigration, the idealised stone cottage has been appropriated as a symbol of essentialist Irishness by many artists, writers and politicians, from Paul Henry to Eamon de Valera (Kennedy, 1993). As a signifier of restorative pastoral, this image exerts a particularly potent hold over the Irish-American imagination, its iconic appeal intensified by the glow of emigrant nostalgia. The romance of this archetype is effectively evoked in Brian Moore's *The Lonely Passion of Judith Hearne* (1955) through the character of James Madden, who takes refuge from the depredations of his menial life in New York in

the dream. The dream of all Donegal men when they first came across the water. The dream that some day the pile will be made, the little piece of land back home will be bought and the last years spent there in peace and comfort. [...] For them, for Madden, the dream was there for warming over with beer or bourbon. The little place went Hollywood in the mind. The fields grew green, the cottage was always milk-white, the technicoloured corn was for ever stooked, ready for harvest. (Moore, 1988: 47)

It is precisely this form of fetishised remembering that the Hunger Memorial contests as part of its overall demythologising strategy. What at first appears to be a commemorative sculpture that trades in nostalgic essentialism turns out on closer inspection to be a work that interrogates sentiment and stereotype, but does so without irony, in a way that allows the visitor to experience pathos, grief, even rage. In memorialising this iconic fragment of the 'homeland', the work challenges the migrant viewer to enter into a dialogue with themselves and their pasts, indeed with memory itself. Commenting on his non-figurative aesthetic, Tolle explained: 'I've tried to create situations where the viewer becomes part of the subject matter. I'm not interested in situations where there's an empathetic other. When you're dealing with history, it's too easy to say, "This is about them, then." It's about the experience you're having right now. It's about *you*' (Kaizen, 2001, original emphasis). Viewers, therefore, 'cannot simply delight in the landscape as idealized icon' (Lydenberg, 2003: 131); rather, they are invited to contemplate both the necessity of remembrance and the irretrievability of the past, to meditate on both history itself and their own relationship to that history.

The viewer is also compelled to consider the role of landscapes, both real and symbolic, in diasporic cultures of memory. This disembodied landscape has not been transplanted, Tolle insists, but 'suspended between here and there. Not just between Ireland and the US, but also between past and present' (Kaizen, 2001). He continues:

The Irish community in this country is a group distinct from the people who remained; they share a common heritage but they've evolved into two different people. One group continues to experience the landscape on a daily basis, actually using and changing the landscape, building new buildings, new roads. And the other group left at a moment that's frozen in their mind because that's the event: their departure. It's a collective memory. It's an *idea* of place that's suspended between these two worlds: it exists as an imaginary thing here and it exists as a reality there. To bring these two things together is the challenge. (Kaizen, 2001, original emphasis)

The emphasis here on interstitiality and in-betweenness undermines the association of monuments with static, unyielding emplacement and frustrates the desire to fix a singular memory or meaning on the memorial. As such, the Irish Hunger Memorial assumes the character of a self-reflexive anti- or counter-memorial that challenges the very idea of monumentality. Mutability and fluidity are woven into the work's material and symbolic fabric, from its non-linear, updateable text panels, which allow for multiple readings of the Famine and its relationship to contemporary food crises, to its precarious tilt, which from one angle appears 'ship-shaped, the prow pointing toward the Hudson' (Schama, 2002: 58). Tolle also relishes the appropriateness of the memorial's susceptibility to physical change in the Manhattan climate, in ways that cannot be foreseen. Viewed in this perspective, this memorial to living, evolving memory has the potential to become an ever-changing memorial text, the very antithesis of a traditional public monument.

CONCLUSION

In exploring the role of material and symbolic landscapes in the mediation and contestation of power, history and memory at particular sites in Ireland and its diaspora, this chapter has sought to highlight the merits of an analytical approach that attends to matters of space and spectacle as well as to temporal concerns. In doing so, we concur with those who contend that space 'is more than a container in which historical narratives of memory are placed' (Johnson, 2003: 171), and with those who claim that 'the materiality of landscape does not simply provide a passive backcloth for the enactment of spectacle but its architecture and aesthetics are designed to invade the private realm and invite visual consumption of inscribed meanings' (Kong and Yeoh, 1997: 220). We believe that a spatially aware approach to the cultivation of landscapes of social memory – whether transient in the case of processions and parades, or permanent in the case of memorials – can illuminate hidden dimensions of the struggle to stabilise the ever evolving meanings of the past in the present. Spatial readings can also enhance our understanding of how the ideologies inscribed by spaces of public spectacle and commemoration shape not only *what* we remember, but also *how* we remember. Thus, the contest for public space can ultimately be read as an ongoing struggle for spatialised power, a symbolic battle for the very ground upon which communal and national identities are forged.

NOTES

1. http://www.angelfire.com/space/derryirsp/monument.htm
2. The emphasis here on the need to draw a line under the past and separate it from the present and future calls to mind David Lloyd's critique of the 'therapeutic' discourse of recent Irish Famine commemoration, which, he argues, supports 'a distinctly developmental narrative: if we could leave our dead and their suffering behind and overcome our melancholy, we could at last shake off the burden of the past and enter modernity as fully formed subjects' (Lloyd, 2002: 221).
3. Controversially, the Famine became a subject on New York State's High School Human Rights Curriculum in 2002, being taught alongside units on the Holocaust and American slavery.
4. http://www.cny.org/archive/ft/ft070501.htm

5. http://www.irishmemorial.org. The Philadelphia memorial is somewhat unusual in that, by explicitly invoking an interstitial zone – the passage from Ireland to America, during which many Famine refugees died – it works to bridge the disjunction between point of departure and point of destination (Kelleher, 2002: 268).
6. Cited by Jane Holtz Kay in 'Hunger for Memorials: New York's Monument to the Irish Famine', http://www.janeholtzkay.com/Articles/hunger.html
7. http://www.ny.gov/governor/press/01/march15_2_01.htm
8. Mayo was among the counties hardest hit by the Famine. It experienced one of the highest death rates overall and had the second-highest level of evictions between 1849 and 1854 (Litton, 1994: 98, 130). The cottage, which was donated to the project by the Slack family, was built in the 1820s and continuously occupied until the 1960s.
9. At least one visitor has found the memorial ahistorical, however. Archaeologist Stephen Brighton noted that the replica cottage is in fact twice the size of a typical Mayo homestead in the 1840s. See Jane Holtz Kay, 'Hunger for Memorials'.

12
Listening to the Future:
Music and Irish Studies

Gerry Smyth

For twenty-five centuries, Western knowledge has tried to look upon the world. It has failed to understand that the world is not for the beholding. It is for hearing. It is not legible, but audible.

Our science has always desired to monitor, measure, abstract, and castrate meaning, forgetting that life is full of noise and that death alone is silent: work noise, noise of man, and noise of beast. Noise bought, sold, or prohibited. Nothing essential happens in the absence of noise.

Today, our sight has dimmed; it no longer sees our future, having constructed a present made of abstraction, nonsense, and silence. Now we must learn to judge a society more by its sounds, by its art, and by its festivals, than by its statistics. By listening to noise, we can better understand where the folly of men and their calculations is leading us, and what hopes it is still possible to have. (Attali, 1985: 1)

MUSIC AND IRISH STUDIES

I think it is fair to say that music has not loomed large in the legend of Irish Studies.[1] When I say 'Irish Studies' I don't mean the long-established and widely dispersed 'study' of diverse Irish cultural produce – the consumption, discussion, appreciation and review of Irish culture that, like the poor, has always been with us. I mean, rather, the specialised academic field that began to emerge as a discrete intellectual and institutional concern during the 1970s, and which, as I understand the matter, forms the focus of the present collection. Irish Studies has in fact tended to be dominated by a range of literary-critical and historical discourses, which have in turn mediated a number of theories, issues and agenda with which those involved in the field are more or less familiar by this stage. These include, for example, the representation (in all senses) of women, the legitimacy of colonialism and postcolonialism as paradigms for the analysis of Irish culture, and the political provenance of revisionism. Music, to restate, has not fared particularly well under this dispensation.[2] Of course, the same is true of a good many other areas: issues such as disability, immigration, repatriation, institutional crime (to name just some) all await fuller development. But the inattention suffered by music in contemporary academic discourse is particularly surprising when one considers Ireland's age-old reputation as a highly musical society. Music was an immensely important aspect of first-millennium, medieval and early modern Irish culture, and was indeed recognised as such by commentators of various persuasion. A significant moment occurred when the Welsh-Norman cleric Giraldus Cambrensis reluctantly acknowledged the prowess of the natives, writing: 'It is only in the case of musical instruments that I find any commendable diligence in the people. They seem to me to be incomparably more skilled in these than any other people that I have seen' (Cambrensis, 1982: 103).

The systematic association of Irishness with musicality, however, began in earnest during the first Celtic Revival of the eighteenth century when figures such as Joseph Cooper Walker and Charlotte Brooke sought to vindicate an ancient Irish culture in support of a politically valid modern nation (Smyth, 1998: 64–71). Music was fully politicised shortly thereafter with the debates that emerged around the antiquarian practices of Edward Bunting and the romantic adaptations of Thomas Moore (Smith, 2000; White, 1998: 36–52). During the eighteenth and nineteenth centuries, all sides in the colonial debate made tactical use of some supposed special Irish feeling for music. For sympathetic English ideologues such as Matthew Arnold, it was a cultural concession. Arnold granted the Celts an advanced cultural sensibility – relative to the Saxons and Latinate Normans with whom they shared the Atlantic archipelago – but at the cost of an ability to function effectively in 'the real world' (Smyth, 1996). Moreover, Arnold's racism was underpinned by the scholarly and scientific discourses in which he couched his analysis; the stereotypes in which he trafficked – poetic but flighty Celts, practical but dull Saxons, strenuous but insolent Latins – are still the currency in which significant numbers of people (some of them disturbingly powerful) trade. One of the most enduring ideas laid down by Arnold's influential analysis was that of 'the musical Irish' with their wistful, feckless attitude towards the mystery of life (or at least the mystery of life under British rule). This idea has in turn given rise to the remarkably long-lived, Janus-faced stereotype that pits elegiac Paddy Sad (think misty mountains, low whistles and slow airs) against festive Paddy Mad (think smoky pubs and diddley-eye tunes) in a constant battle for the 'meaning' of Irishness.[3]

For the Anglo-Irish, as I've suggested, music offered a respectable means of *being* Irish that didn't threaten the 'Anglo' part of their composite identity. A classic example, in a musical context, of the schizophrenic Anglo-Irish condition may be observed in Samuel Ferguson's 1834 review of a book entitled *Irish Minstrelsy*, which had been published by James Hardiman in 1831 (Ferguson, 1834; Smyth, 1998: 64–8). Although proceeding from an extremely partial understanding of what music is, 'music' nonetheless becomes the platform upon which Ferguson attempts to construe a viable Anglo-Irish role within the narrative of Irish cultural, and thus political, history. In a move that curiously anticipates certain developments in twentieth-century critical theory, Ferguson opts for a kind of ironic maturity with regard to contemporary colonial relations. He cannot countenance an innate 'essential' identity in the cultural produce (including the music) of Gaelic civilisation, since this would exclude himself and the Anglo-Irish fraction he represents, but he is willing to make strategic use of such a concept in order to resist any totalising imperial narrative that might attempt to integrate all forms of regional otherness into a single corporate 'Britishness'. All this made for an extremely complex critical politics in which the Anglo-Irish subject is never precisely sure of who are his allies and who his enemies. A collateral effect in this instance was that music became a vital clue as to the wider cultural and political fate of the various colonial communities vying for control of the national nomenclature. Thus it has remained down to the present.

As for the Irish themselves, music was a compensation for being born into a politically vanquished race – a comfort when they wished to remember and a distraction when they wished to forget. Collectors such as George Petrie and P. W. Joyce found time among all their other activities to build on Bunting's pioneering work; these researchers began to establish the idea of an indigenous music that, like the language, the customs and the literary and architectural remains, was in dire need of preservation (Joyce, 1909; Petrie, 2002). It was also during the nineteenth century, however, that music began to perform the important socio-political functions in Irish life, both at home and among the diaspora, with which we are still coming to terms today. Music was both a private, affective action and a public, social ritual whereby the subject could 'act out' his or her Irish identity, fired by the belief that each individual musical act – be it a composition, a performance or simply listening to a piece of music – was in some way part of an ancient, ongoing tradition that confirmed and, with each new act, reconfirmed the validity of both the individual and the nation.

Irishness and musicality remained locked together following the political revolution of the early twentieth century. With the growth in recording and playback technology in the years after 1922, 'Irish music' was capable of being disseminated to great numbers of people in a variety of new media, although with the proliferation of performance contexts came an increase in the uncertainty regarding the precise nature of the phenomenon. Of the three main musical streams running through twentieth-century Ireland, the art tradition has had the least exposure, while at the same time being the most troubled over its own status – indeed, its own possibility. And while there can be no doubting the validity of this tradition in terms of audience, certainly, but also in institutional and educational terms, its failure to produce a major composer of international standing presents the art community with some pressing questions as to the role of that particular form of music in the culture at large.

The revival of so-called 'traditional' Irish music had already been underway for a number of years when it came into creative collision with the international urban folk movement, spearheaded by a young Jewish-American singer-songwriter named Robert Zimmerman, during the 1960s. The result – when modified still further by diasporic 'Irish' styles that had been developing along their own independent lines in major emigrant centres such as London and New York – made for an enormously vibrant scene producing some of the most evocative 'Irish' music of the modern era. Again, however, the questions proliferate. Just how 'traditional' *is* traditional music? How did it get to have the form – the sounds, the rhythms, the gestures – it does? Can you remove it from its apparently 'natural' setting (the house, the pub, the village hall) and expect it to survive? And, crucially, how far can the music evolve before it becomes something else? Such questions have an academic purchase, certainly, but they also trouble the music-making practices of 'traditional' Irish musicians the world over every time they pick up an instrument, step on to a stage, or walk into a recording studio.

Ireland has also always produced music scenes of various size and composition devoted to one or other of the twentieth century's popular styles. The 'showbands' that began to emerge during the 1950s represented a recurring trend towards the adaptation and modification of international popular music for local conditions. The spirit of the showbands survives in the highly successful tradition of Irish pop music, although it is likely that the major factor influencing the emergence of acts such as Boyzone, B*Witched and Westlife during the 1990s was the greater cultural confidence that accompanied Irish economic recovery. Meanwhile, the rock music that began to emerge during the 1960s as a self-styled 'authentic' response to the perceived 'artificiality' of the showbands has also produced a number of telling engagements with modern Irish identity. Some rock artists have embraced their Irishness and attempted to articulate it in a rock idiom; others have rejected it outright, immersing themselves instead in the trappings of international rock discourse. A very few have searched for some form of accommodation between the different impulses bearing upon their musical consciences, between what Noel McLaughlin and Martin McLoone in a discussion of Van Morrison and the 'hybridity' of Irish rock music characterise as 'transcendence and rootedness'. Some of the artists who have explored this tension include The Pogues, Sinéad O'Connor and U2, although, as McLaughlin and McLoone maintain, it is Morrison,

more than any other Irish (or British) rock musician, [who] has maintained a strong sense of his roots while at the same time exploring – and extending considerably – the international rock idiom. His art is an art of the periphery, soaking up the influences of the centre, adapting them to its own designs and then offering them back to the centre in a wholly unique form. (McLaughlin and McLoone, 2000: 184)

The question of how a range of 'alternative' practices such as the art tradition and various 'foreign' popular styles (not to mention an 'adulterated' traditional music) fare in the story of modern Irish music is fraught with the many difficulties born of belief, conviction and downright prejudice. If music became an important measure of Irish identity at some point during the nineteenth century, then, by a reciprocal manoeuvre, and as part of the much wider project of cultural nationalism, Irishness soon became a measure of music. The effect was to bring a socio-political agenda to bear upon musicological discourse. What exactly were the criteria according to which musical Irishness was to be considered? How 'Irish' is that tune, that instrument, that arrangement, that performance, that sound?[4] What systems – institutional and otherwise – exist for demarcating the gradations of musical identity (*non-Irish, Irish, Irisher, Irishest*) and, when these gradations have been established, what measures are in place to reward the worthy and sanction the culpable? I would like to suggest that, in ways that have as yet not even begun to be considered, musicians as diverse as Brian Boydell and Bono, the Bothy Band and Brendan Bowyer, are all locked together in a critical matrix in which the stakes are the meaning and limits of a modern Irish identity.

The main points I wish to make at this stage are that music and Ireland have existed symbiotically for as far back as we can reckon, and that the relationship between the practice and the identity has become more and more self-consciously politicised as time has passed. As I shall go on to suggest towards the end of this chapter, the concept of Irish musicality may be *much* more significant than we imagine; but even an initial glance exposes the untenability of a modern scholarly field that marginalises to the point of ignorance one of the most important and powerful cultural manifestations of its object.

MUSIC AND CRITICISM

Of course, people continue to study, analyse and criticise Irish music in a wide range of institutional contexts and discursive languages. Most of the higher educational institutions across the island possess dedicated music departments, which offer opportunities to study various aspects of the art tradition, including performance, composition, education, history and theory. There is also the Irish World Music Centre, founded in 1994 under the direction of Mícheál Ó Súilleabháin who, as a charismatic (and controversial) composer, performer and facilitator, provides the public persona of modern Irish traditional music. There are besides a multitude of official and semi-official societies, associations and boards dedicated to various aspects of Irish musical practice. Such institutions are energetic and committed, providing spaces in which scholars, performers and interested amateurs can explore various aspects of the country's rich musical heritage. While some, for example, are engaged in recovering a 'lost' Irish art repertoire, others conduct in-depth analyses of traditional melodic structure or the geo-social development of folk composition.

Such work is undoubtedly useful and necessary. Disciplinary 'hard yards' are always made by scholars working closely within relatively minor aspects of their field, counting, classifying, categorising. At the same time, it is clear that none of the principal music traditions in Ireland – art, folk or rock – have managed to develop coherent theoretical responses to the Irish cultural condition as defined and engaged by the 'new' Irish Studies. Besides the up-to-the-minute journalism that is its principal modus operandi, Irish rock music produced only two general book-length studies before 2005, both characterised by a high degree of journalistic speculation and a more or less complete absence of any wider critical engagement (Clayton-Lea and Taylor, 1992; Prendergast, 1987). In 1988 and 1994, two other journalists, Eamon Dunphy and John Waters, produced books about U2 that attempted to place the band and its music against the background of a developing Ireland (Dunphy, 1988; Waters, 1994). Whereas the first was hampered by a limited knowledge of the rock tradition, the second was compromised by a fast-and-loose attitude towards highly sensitive critical and cultural theories. The country's premier popular music magazine, *Hot Press*, continues to carry the flag for intelligent rock journalism, and to integrate its music coverage into a wider socio-political agenda. Extended responses from the contemporary Irish Studies community to the phenomenon of Irish rock music are thin on the ground, however, as indeed they are to traditional and folk music (Keohane, 1997; McLaughlin and McLoone, 2000; Rolston, 2001; G. Smyth, 1992, 2005). This is not to deny that commentary and analysis proliferate with regard to Irish traditional music, much of it of a high scholarly standard. By and large, however, such responses tend to be couched in the specific disciplinary languages under whose auspices they operate. Some scholars, including Mícheál Ó Súilleabháin himself, have attempted to bring new theoretical methods to bear upon Irish traditional music; but the fact is that the gulf between ethnomusicology, which has historically dominated the scholarly analysis of Irish traditional music, and mainstream Irish Studies, with its peculiar array of historical and cultural concerns, has yet to be bridged.

To date, the one major attempt to create such a bridge proved flawed. I am referring to *The Keeper's Recital: Music and Cultural History in Ireland, 1770–1970* (1998) by Harry White, Professor of Music at University College Dublin. White has been a champion of Irish music studies for a number of years and has published widely on matters relating to the subject. *The Keeper's Recital* was the sixth title in the 'Critical Conditions' series, published by Cork University Press for Field Day under the general editorship of Seamus Deane. The series contains titles by some of the most influential scholars in Irish Studies, including Terry Eagleton, David Lloyd, Joep Leerssen, Kevin

Whelan and Luke Gibbons. With such impeccable credentials, the auspices were good for a reckoning between this well-established cultural practice and a relatively new critical discourse. *The Keeper's Recital* was welcome insofar as it helped to reveal the extent to which Ireland's critical establishment had marginalised music as a component of the island's cultural history. Problems arose, however, with White's conceptualisation of cultural discourse in general, and musical discourse in particular. The central thesis of the book is that, unlike comparable European countries such as Poland and Finland, modern Ireland has failed to produce a sympathetic or coherent art music. A number of reasons are adduced for this. One is the spurious precedence given to what the author terms the 'ethnic' tradition in Irish anti-colonial politics. This began (as noted above) with the antiquarians of the first Celtic Revival during the 1780s, but has continued to thrive well into the supposedly 'postcolonial' period. For White, the continuing, indeed growing, infatuation with Irish traditional music is indicative not of the country's inherent musicality, but of its naïveté in accepting and perpetuating just such an essentialist (colonialist) fantasy. He argues that the popularity of ethnic music has been achieved at the cost of 'serious' musical culture, including the key areas of education, performance and, most damagingly, composition.

A related problem is that the energies required to negotiate a creative interface between ethnic and classical aesthetics were channelled into other cultural forms – most famously and most successfully, literature. Music as metaphor has been crucial to all the major Irish cultural initiatives over the past two centuries (as we shall consider in more depth below), but this has paradoxically led to a situation in which music as a creative mediation of Irish socio-political identity has been denied. White's catalogue of failures ends with Seán Ó Riada, a classically trained musician who, after composing a number of promising serial works in the 1950s, abandoned the disintegrating European tradition to form Ceoltóirí Cualann, a band of virtuoso musicians – later reformed as The Chieftains – with whom he revitalised traditional music in Ireland during the 1960s. Ó Riada's influence on all aspects of contemporary Irish music has in fact been seminal. In ways that have yet to be adequately addressed, his troubled vision informs progressive purveyors of the ethnic tradition such as Kila and Donal Lunny, as well as opportunistic engagements typified by bands such as The Corrs, and all points in between. But again, this is indicative for White of the cycle of failure in Irish music, as official neglect and artistic complacency feed into each other to deny Irish culture its right to a sympathetic art music.

The Keeper's Recital is in fact concerned not so much with Irish music *per se* as with issues of *reception* in Irish cultural history, and the ways in which music has been recruited for more or less openly political ends in the modern period. The question of reception is of course central to any adequate cultural history. However, when a musicological dimension does peep through from time to time, it is invariably infused with a high modernist sensibility – part Adorno, part BBC Radio 3 – which leaves the reader in no doubt as to the culpability of the ethnic tradition in respect of the island's cultural health. Where is the Irish Chopin, the Irish Sibelius, the Irish Smetana – composers who believed they were expressing some essential element of their respective national characters in musical form? One senses White's bemusement and disappointment at the continued attraction of simple ethnic melody when set against a mature, creative engagement with the polyphonic complexities of the European tradition and its history of harmony, counterpoint and serialism. The possibilities (emerging more from a cultural studies perspective) that the ethnic tradition might be anything more than a foil for art music, or that the former comprises a set of highly complex cultural negotiations, do not appear to have been seriously entertained.

If Professor White's circumscribed engagement with 'culture' bespeaks a certain theoretical innocence, so too does his model of Irish history, which seems to be informed by an all-encompassing dialectic of colonial (Anglo-Irish) and ethnic (Gaelic) impulses, what he refers to as 'the bewildering condition of two mutually inhospitable systems of language, polity and civilisation' (White, 1998: 4). This 'bewildering condition' determines the author's analysis of Irish music, from the competing claims of antiquarianism and romanticism in Thomas Moore's *Irish Melodies* through to Ó Riada's inability to discover 'a durable aesthetic' or 'an authentic mode of Irish composition' (White, 1998: 138). This nostalgia for the 'durable' and the 'authentic' is touching but hardly tenable. It is as if the 'postal' revolution in intellectual discourse and the ensuing critical emphases on hybridity and liminality never happened. Indeed, the most ardent structuralist would blush at the weight of interpretation placed upon a single binary, that of Anglo-Irish domination and Irish cultural nationalism. This analysis is even more questionable in a country whose history is characterised to such an extent by partiality, inconsistency and opportunism. One suspects also that such a simplistic model would not meet with the approval of Seamus Deane who, besides being the general editor of the series, emerges as one of White's major critical authorities, meriting 14 separate citations in the main body of the text and many more in the lengthy annotations. Having worked for over 20 years to justify the history and legitimacy of Irish nationalist resistance from within a grander narrative of complex, progressive pluralism, it is doubtful if he would be happy to find himself recruited for such a limited critical vision.

MUSIC AND LITERATURE

What, then, would a fully integrated discourse of Irish music criticism look like? Well, one crucial element with which it would have to come to terms is broached by White during the course of his study: the degree to which Irish creative energy has traditionally been siphoned off, so to speak, by artists working in the written medium. We all know the roll call of 'great Irish writers', but most non-specialists would be hard pressed to name half a dozen Irish composers from the last two centuries. The same is true of the fine arts. In some senses, Irish cultural history has been warped by its literary riches; the price of our unrivalled pantheon of writers may be the lack of a more balanced artistic tradition in which each of the arts, with their particular ways of articulating human experience, is enabled to develop. Yet one curious aspect of the peculiar manner in which Irish artistic activity has evolved during the modern era is the propensity of imaginative writers to write *about* music. Music continues to crop up from time to time as a consideration in the analysis of literary figures such as Joyce and Beckett. Indeed, 'musical Joyce' is now a recognised sub-specialist field, especially in the United States, where academic territorialisation can be a pretty brutal business (Bauerle, 1993; Weaver, 1998). One of the things that has emerged from the study of music in Joyce and Beckett, however, is the realisation that these writers were far from unique in their musical concerns, and that the modern Western literary tradition has in fact been obsessed with music, or more precisely, with calculating the essential properties of music in relation to literature, and with the question of what occurs when the former is represented through the medium of the latter (Aronson, 1980). Generally speaking, literature since the time of Rousseau has suffered something of an inferiority complex in relation to music; because their chosen medium represents a double alienation from reality (firstly through verbalisation, secondly through writing), many writers have coveted, and attempted to ape, the properties of a cultural practice they perceived to be both beautiful and truthful in a way that mere writing never could be.[5]

Literature's concern with music has proved something of an embarrassment for its attendant critical discourses, which after all have both an intellectual and a material investment in the institution of literature. Since its inception in the eighteenth century, modern literary criticism has been anxious enough about its object of study (writing) *and* about its own relationship with that object, without having to worry about incursions from alien disciplines (Smyth, 1998: 35–53). Some Joyce critics, as indicated above, are aspirationally inter-disciplinary, attempting to explore the ways in which writing and music interrogate each other in the great man's work. Irish Studies, however, by and large continues to locate itself and the work carried out under its auspices within established disciplinary boundaries. In this context, we may observe that the dearth of musical analysis in the field reflects a long-established trend within cultural criticism, in which music has tended to be marginalised in favour of 'properly' literary or 'properly' historical analysis, however these are defined, and the routes have been mapped many times.

Everywhere we look in Irish writing we find music and musical imagery, not only in the high modernist work of writers such as Joyce and Beckett, but throughout the canon. As an example, let us take *Star of the Sea* (2002) by Joseph O'Connor, a writer who has always been interested in music as a theme. His debut novel *Cowboys and Indians* (1991) features an Irish exile in London trying to make it big with a rock band, and the journalism collected in *The Secret World of the Irish Male* (1994) contains a great many musical references. *Star of the Sea*, which became something of a 'reading group' classic in the UK following its endorsement by day-time television chat show hosts, Richard and Judy, continues this trend. The action of the novel is set on a Famine ship sailing from Ireland to New York in 1847. One of the principal characters has at a particular point in his past composed an anti-recruiting ballad based upon an incident described at an early stage in the story. The narrative details the creative process in great depth, describing first of all the 'real' events behind the song and the immediate circumstances leading to its composition. We are then shown the creative process itself in some depth, focalised through the main character: how the song evolves in response to aesthetic and institutional circumstances, how it relates to the 'real' incident, and how certain images and locutions are invoked, rejected or improved.

O'Connor's introduction of the dynamics of folk composition is in keeping with the carnivalesque nature of the text as a whole, which incorporates a variety of narrative discourses, including visual representation, during its course. There is another level on which this particular narrative detail functions, however. Although anti-recruiting ballads abound within the Irish folk tradition, the variation described in *Star of the Sea* is clearly based on a well-known version entitled 'Arthur McBride', a song definitively covered by Andy Irvine and Paul Brady on their eponymous 1976 album, which remains in many ways a benchmark for the fusion of a number of different Irish musical sensibilities (traditional, folk, pop and rock). Indeed, *The Purple Album*, as it is sometimes known, marks the culmination of a decade of agonising over the relations between 'real' Irish music and the great variety of styles and genres with which it was – sometimes happily, sometimes uneasily – linked. O'Connor's invocation of 'Arthur McBride' in the context of his novel, therefore, sets in motion a string of ironic resonances concerning, among other things, the relations between writing and music, between past and present, and between authenticity and adaptability – issues that go to the heart of the Irish cultural historical condition.

Let's take another, rather better known example of Irish writers' engagement with musical themes. Roddy Doyle's *The Commitments* has been many things to many people since it first appeared in 1987. Most commentators appear to agree, however, that the major theme of both book (and film) is the hybrid status of late twentieth-century Irish identity, the latter term apprehended with reference to some or other hierarchy involving the constituent discourses of gender, race, class and age. Such critical concerns have by and large emerged from the perspectives of postcolonialist and/or postmodernist literary theory, in both of which the category of identity is revealed to be strung out between centripetal (unified and localising) and centrifugal (dispersed and globalising) discourses (Booker, 1997; Donnelly, 2000; Taylor, 1998). However, no analysis of either the novel itself or of the film adaptation by Alan Parker (for which Doyle co-wrote the screenplay) has, so far as I know, engaged with what seems to me to be the text's most obvious frame of reference: the dynamics of local popular music-making. This is strange; after all, before it 'represents' anything else at a greater or lesser symbolic level, both the literary and the filmic narratives focus quite clearly on the formation, recruitment, early success and precipitant demise of a group of local musicians playing a form of popular music to local Dublin audiences. Most critical attention has focused on Jimmy's exorbitant claim that '[the] Irish are the niggers of Europe', rather than his immediately preceding statement that '[your] music should be abou' where you're from an' the sort o' people yeh come from' (Doyle, 1992: 13). Here, I suggest, is a rather obvious elephant in the room, roaring for attention from those preoccupied with some supposedly 'real' or 'primary' critical agenda.

The marginalisation of this aspect of the narrative is even less acceptable in light of the fact that there exists an extensive critical literature dedicated to explicating the dynamics of local music-making. True, this literature is located at some remove from contemporary Irish cultural criticism and its established array of interests and methodologies; but as someone steeped in those interests and methodologies, it has been interesting for me to learn that analyses of local music-making (emerging from the institutional-intellectual field of popular music studies) tend to be concerned with issues of socialisation, authenticity, identity and so on – concerned, that is, with many of the very issues that animate Irish Studies and its focus on the 'troubled' status of modern Irish identity. The kind of analysis of *The Commitments* I'm suggesting, therefore, could proceed by comparing and contrasting the experiences and practices of Doyle's fictional band with some of the experiences and practices described in three classic accounts of local music-making: *On Becoming a Rock Musician* (1980) by the American sociologist H. Stith Bennett, Ruth Finnegan's anthropological study *The Hidden Musicians* (1989), and Sara Cohen's *Rock Culture in Liverpool* (1991). All three offer extended ethnographic accounts of the beginning phase of the local musician's career, the same phase experienced by The Commitments during the course of Doyle's narrative. It is my impression that *The Commitments* warrants an analysis focused on this, its most obvious theme, local music-making. I also believe that such an analysis will lead us back to many of the concerns identified as central to modern Irish Studies.

MUSIC AND NOISE

Thus far I have commented on: (a) the ubiquity of musical discourse throughout Irish cultural history; (b) the failure of modern Irish Studies and modern music studies in Ireland to achieve a meaningful interface; and (c) the basis of a criticism that would be alert to both the presence and the function of music within Irish literary texts. All these issues come into focus in the work of the French theorist and philosopher Jacques Attali who, as the quotation that prefaces this chapter shows, wished to place 'noise' at the centre of human history and, more radically, *at the centre of human thought about human history*. The goal of his celebrated study, *Noise: The Political Economy of Music*, is 'not only to theorize *about* music, but to theorize *through* music' (Attali, 1985: 4). Noise is everywhere, he avers, the most fundamental sign of human activity and – when it is organised into formal practices we are disposed to call 'music' – the attempt to order the natural world in response to our fears and desires. 'Listening to music is listening to all noise,' Attali claims, 'realizing that its appropriation and control is a reflection of power, that it is essentially political' (Attali, 1985: 6).

Attali tracks the history of the 'appropriation and control' of noise over three phases or 'zones':

In one of these zones, it seems that music is used and produced in the ritual in an attempt to make people *forget* the general violence; in another, it is employed to make people *believe* in the harmony of the world, that there is order in exchange and legitimacy in commercial power; and finally, there is one in which it serves to *silence*, by mass-producing a deafening, syncretic kind of music, and censoring all other human noises.

Make people Forget, make them Believe, Silence them. In all three cases, music is a tool of power. (Attali, 1985: 19, original emphasis)

These zones are examined at length in brilliant chapters on 'Sacrificing', 'Representation' and 'Repetition', the latter being the dominant form of noise organisation during the era of capitalism. The suggestiveness of this model for a new history of Ireland cannot be overestimated. An Attalian analysis of twentieth-century Ireland would encourage us to become alert to the many and various ways in which 'noise' has been organised in the developing forces that share the island: noise industrial, technological, sectarian, sporting, and so on ad infinitum. At a more fundamental level, however, such an analysis could help us to trace how a state-sponsored quest for a 'representational' noise was gradually overcome in the latter half of the century by systems (both aesthetic and institutional) of 'repetition' that represent the logic of the community at this particular stage of its economico-political development. 'Janis Joplin, Bob Dylan, and Jimi Hendrix say more about the liberatory dream of the 1960s than any theory of crisis,' writes Attali (1985: 6). Just so; in which case I would suggest that Westlife, Michael Flatley and the Irish Tenors say more about the state of Ireland in the 1990s – a time and place, lest we forget, in which Irish music attained successful brand status, to the great satisfaction of the government and the regulatory institutions it sponsors[6] – than any political or economic theory ever could.

Attali also theorises 'the seeds of a new noise', a different way of making music in which 'in embryonic form, beyond repetition, lies freedom: more than a new music, a fourth kind of musical practice. It heralds the arrival of new social relations. Music is becoming *composition*' (Attali, 1985: 133, original emphasis). By this latter term Attali means a form of music that 'calls into question the distinction between worker and consumer, between doing and destroying [...] to compose is to take pleasure in the instruments, the tools of communication, in use-time and exchange-time as lived and no longer as stockpiled' (Attali, 1985: 135). 'Composition', then, is associated with any form of music used – however temporarily, in however fragmented or unstable a context – beyond the confining power of sacrifice, representation or repetition. Attali's theory of 'composition', formulated during the early 1970s, anticipated the advent of the digital revolution in music-making which, based on technological and other socio-cultural developments, has changed forever not only the ways in which 'music' can be made, but also the ways in which it functions to create meaning in a variety of social, political and cultural contexts. 'Composition' is no doubt a utopian notion, but I would suggest that it is precisely such a form of noise that modern Ireland, with its relentless 'stockpiling' of just about everything material and immaterial, could benefit from at this particular stage in its history.

Above all, what the attempt to 'theorize through music' leads Attali to is a recognition of music's predictive power, the fact that music 'is prophesy. Its styles and economic organization are ahead of the rest of society because it explores, much faster than material reality can, the entire range of possibilities in a given code' (Attali, 1985: 12). Which is to say: music, defined now as the political organisation of noise, has throughout history constituted both the clearest exercise of power and at the same time the most available locus of resistance to, and subversion of, established discourses of power. Therein lies the source of its political importance: 'Music, the quintessential mass activity, like the crowd, is simultaneously a threat and a necessary source of legitimacy; trying to channel it is a risk that every system of power must run' (Attali, 1985: 14). We ignore music at our peril, therefore, for at the same time as it affords us the most accurate impression of *how things are*, it offers us the most enabling impressions of *how things might be*.

MUSIC AND ...

In an historical formation in which it figures so prominently as an index of identity, it becomes imperative to understand music's role in the formation of discourses of power and dissent. By *listening* to contemporary Irish society – rather than looking at it or reducing it to one or another series of statistical abstractions – we shall come not only to a stronger sense of where we have come from and where we are, but also, in the political struggles that are conducted over the relations between music, noise and silence, of where we might be going. If some noises can tell us a lot about the former, others – predictably less well known and more difficult to discern – can alert us to the latter, providing us with echoes of our future and of the struggles that lie in wait. Of course I am not suggesting that we all become music specialists overnight. But Irish Studies cannot afford to remain ignorant of the role and function of noise within its object practices. For those with ears to hear, the isle is indeed full of noises, as is the global diasporic culture that claims affiliation with the homeland. But while we are encouraged to consider some of these as Shakespearean 'sweet airs, that give delight and hurt not' – in other words, as music – many others carry all the pejorative weight of the word – ('STOP THAT *NOISE!*') – and are as a consequence marginalised or condemned in a variety of moral, legal and political discourses. Trying to discover the difference between these two concepts – the processes whereby the one is formally or institutionally separated from the other, and the means by which such processes are resisted – presents the Irish Studies community with one of its most pressing, as well as potentially rewarding, tasks. I began this essay with Attali's indictment of traditional forms of knowledge and his repositioning of noise at the centre of human experience. I end with his bold call for us to begin listening seriously to the world:

Can we make the connections? Can we hear the crisis of society in the crisis of music? Can we understand music through its relations with money? [...] The noises of society are in advance of its images and material conflicts. Our music foretells our future. Let us lend it an ear. (Attali, 1985: 11)

NOTES

1. A portion of this chapter first appeared in the introduction to a special edition of the *Irish Studies Review* (April 2004) on the subject of music in contemporary Ireland.

2. For example, a survey of music-related items in the *Irish Studies Review* (the leading Irish Studies journal in Great Britain) since its inception in 1992 shows that whereas developing subjects such as sport and film have made significant strides, music has produced only three main articles and fewer than ten reviews.

3. These stereotypes are usefully encapsulated in James Cameron's film *Titanic* (1997), in which festive dance music below decks (Paddy Mad) is set off against a plaintive whistle melody to accompany the love story above decks (Paddy Sad).

4. Martin Stokes suggests that 'music is socially meaningful not entirely but largely because it provides means by which people recognise identities and places, and the boundaries which separate them' (Stokes, 1994: 5). He goes on to discuss the way in which certain instruments such as the bouzouki have been welcomed within Irish traditional music circles, while others such as the guitar are still regarded with suspicion.

5. On Rousseau's contradictory formulation of the relations between thought, speech, music and writing, see Jacques Derrida's *Of Grammatology* (1967).

6. See Bertie Ahern's speech at the formal launch of IMRO, Conrad Hotel (2 March 1998), reproduced at <http://www.imro.ie/speeches.html>.

13
Beyond Sectarianism: Sport and Irish Culture

Mike Cronin

Ireland has a long and rich sporting heritage. Whether in Gaelic games, soccer, rugby, golf, horse or dog racing, the Irish have regularly produced champions and heroes who have captivated the public imagination. Since the evolution of modern organised sport in the late nineteenth century right up to its saturation of the mass media in the twenty-first, the Irish have shown themselves to be passionate about, and in many cases obsessed by, sport. In essence, sport is about those who watch and those who play. It is about passion, belief, occasional joy, frequent heartbreak and, all too commonly, standing on a lonely, rain-soaked terrace watching a dreadful match. But what do such experiences tell us about the Irish and their culture? How does sport differ from other popular cultural forms – literature, film, television, theatre – that have been embraced by Irish Studies? How has it been represented in such media? And how have scholars reacted to the conceptual and theoretical challenges of a subject that, while appearing to be a trivial part of popular culture, is enthusiastically embraced by so many Irish men and women?

In the early 1990s Adele Dalsimer and Vera Kreilkamp made a plea for a more imaginative and interdisciplinary approach to Irish Studies, 'one that would incorporate the iconography of popular as well as elite culture' (Dalsimer and Kreilkamp, 1993: 7). At the end of the decade, the editors of an *Éire-Ireland* special issue on visual culture argued that there was a need to 'illustrate the benefits of interdisciplinarity in recovering often-neglected areas of critical inquiry and scholarship for Irish Studies' (Kreilkamp and Curtin, 1998: 5). This chapter seeks to meet these challenges with respect to sport. Recent works have, perhaps by necessity, been dominated by an examination of the subject in its historical, political and sectarian contexts. But sport in Ireland has a much wider cultural resonance. Beyond the field of play, it features in art and theatre, provides inspiration for musicians, and is increasingly the subject of film and television drama. Sport is not simply an isolated recreational or competitive activity, then, but one that permeates the boundaries of various cultural media. So to understand its role in Irish culture and society fully one must examine sport within its representational contexts, rather than solely in its own terms. In the process, alternative ways of accessing the subject have to be employed to circumvent traditional political and sectarian-centred approaches.

It is my intention in this chapter to demonstrate how sport, as one of the most potent expressions of popular culture, has been appropriated and represented by different forms of artistic, literary and cultural production in contemporary Ireland. By analysing specific works of literature and music, I aim to illustrate how a reading of sport in its representational contexts can illuminate certain key aspects of that culture. What is most apparent is the way in which the use of sport as a vehicle for the interrogation of different themes within Irish Studies – especially those relating to masculinity and local, regional and national identities – can highlight apparently ephemeral, escapist and pleasurable matters of popular culture. Sport, indeed, appears almost purpose-made for the challenge of meeting the call for a version of Irish Studies that might 'integrate the experimental and draw upon a local, urban and national constituency as both subjects and agents of knowledge' (Sharkey, 1997b: 174). To meet Sharkey's challenge is to recognise that sport is a common feature of modern life and media, where athletes are celebrities and where the calendar is shaped by the different sporting seasons and punctuated by annual spectaculars such as the Grand National. This calendar, which is supplemented at regular intervals by global events such as the football World Cup and the Olympic Games, provides the rhythm to many people's lives and creates a synergy between communities and the construction of shared narratives of identity. By analysing how sport and major sporting events have been written and sung about in Ireland, this chapter seeks to demonstrate how this common feature of our lives has been harnessed to give voice to changing conceptions of identity – personal, regional, national and gendered.

As well as outlining a fresh way of exploring Irish Studies through sport and its associated texts, I will also suggest how sport functions as an agent of identity formation and argue that much of the recent critical literature in this area, especially that which deals with the phenomenon of football fandom, is not applicable to the Irish case. In opposition to the fandom thesis, which views followers as single-minded obsessives, prisoners of their passion, I regard sport in Ireland as an essentially evanescent or ephemeral pleasure. Whereas proponents of the fandom thesis posit sport (specifically soccer) as a central part of a supporter's identity, I argue, in line with international studies of sport by Pope (1997), Dyreson (1998) and Booth and Tatz (2000), that it is but one, albeit important, element in the construction and definition of Irish identities. That is to say, the participation of the national football team in the World Cup finals, or of a county side in an All-Ireland final, is an irregular event, an occasional thrill and transitory spectacle. The displays of emotion and excitement that accompany such occasions assist in the temporary articulation of national and local identities, but do not provide definition in themselves. When the game or tournament ends, other factors replace or supplement sport in sustaining and defining identities. The literature and songs under consideration here are exemplars of this evanescence insofar as they seek to document, recreate and recapture the temporary excitement and camaraderie generated by modern Irish sporting culture.

SPORT, POLITICS AND IRISH POPULAR CULTURE

During the 1980s and 1990s a group of writers and researchers, using established approaches and methodologies from sports sociology and history, produced the first scholarly studies of sport in Ireland and its function within society. The most important texts were Mandle's *The Gaelic Athletic Association and Irish Nationalist Politics* (1987), Sugden and Bairner's *Sport, Sectarianism and Society in Ireland* (1993) and my own *Sport and Nationalism in Ireland* (1999). While these works played a crucial role in opening out the field and encouraging researchers to engage with the nation's sporting past, they were primarily concerned with the politics of sport, and more often than not revolved around the omnipresence of sectarianism within particular sporting cultures. The fascination of Irish sport for those working on the topic was that it seemed atypical and anomalous; it did not follow the norms of sporting practice and organisation in Britain or the US because it was tainted by sectarianism. Thus, Mandle concentrated on the historic links between the Gaelic Athletic Association (GAA), the Irish Republican Brotherhood and the period of revolution in early twentieth-century Ireland; Sugden and Bairner rooted their study in an analysis of the power relationships that were apparent in the sectarian workings of sport in Northern Ireland; and my own analysis, although attempting to bridge these two books chronologically, was based on a consideration of sport in Ireland as a carrier and conductor of a predominantly politicised form of nationalism. This collective endeavour was very worthwhile in that it produced much valuable research, introduced new vehicles for understanding and studying Ireland, and advanced the scholarly status of sport within Irish Studies. The most notable measure of this advancement is the inclusion of a separate chapter on sport in Comerford's *Ireland: Inventing the Nation* (2003) and in Cleary and Connolly's *The Cambridge Companion to Modern Irish Culture* (2005). Although a common feature of British historiography (McKibbin, 1998), this is a unique departure in the historiography of 'mainstream' Irish survey texts, the most popular and well-respected of which almost totally ignore the historical and cultural significance of sport (Fallon, 1998; Keogh, 1994; Kiberd, 1995; Lee, 1989; Townshend, 1999).

However, this concentration on the political and sectarian aspects of Ireland's sporting heritage produced an element of scholarly self-justification, in that the more the politics of sport were deemed worthy of investigation, the greater the necessity to undertake additional work to demonstrate this. Nevertheless, there have been further valuable additions to the historiography of sport in Ireland since the late 1990s, though much still remains to be done.[1] There is a need, for example, for scholars to focus on the social and cultural history of particular sports such as rugby, golf, boxing and horse racing, which have been so important in Ireland for over two centuries. Studies of this kind would doubtless shed much light on the sporting ideology and behaviour of the Irish middle classes, which have largely been ignored by traditional scholarship, and usefully analyse topics such as gambling, private club culture and the apparent Britishness of the amateur and club values of Irish golf and rugby. In this way, the traditional bias towards predominantly working-class sports such as Gaelic games and soccer, which has led to the absence from history of the classes as opposed to the masses, might be corrected. If nothing else, it is important that future writers begin to recognise and examine the part played by solicitors, schoolmasters and businessmen in the evolution of Irish sporting culture.

If a certain class prejudice characterises the historiography of sport in Ireland, then gender bias is one of the defining features of cultural representations of sport. Traditionally, sport has been represented as the preserve of a mainly male following, as evidenced by the 'Cyclops' episode of Joyce's *Ulysses*, which explores the allegedly degenerative effects of sporting activity on the male psyche (Valente, 2000). While this male dominance has lately been challenged by the growth of women's participation in sport, Irish artists and cultural producers continue to be preoccupied by men's experience, representations of which have multiplied in recent years. For example, the tradition of depicting Gaelic games, famously embodied by Jack Yeats's portrait of the hurler, has developed to the extent that an entire exhibition, 'The Art of Hurling', was staged in Galway in 2001. There has also been increased attention on the historical, biographical and folkloric aspects of the GAA, from Art Ó Maolfabhail's work on the origins of hurling to recent biographies of legendary stars such as Jack Lynch and Páidí O Sé (Arnold, 2002; Ó Maolfabhail, 1973; Potts, 2001).

In film, sport has featured as both thematic focal point, as in Fergus Tighe's *The Clash of the Ash* (1987), and central subject, as in Jim Sheridan's *The Boxer* (1997). Irish documentary films have also regularly showcased sporting themes, from the seminal Gael-Linn film *Christy Ring* (1961) to the screening of a weekly sporting documentary, *Laochra Gael*, on the Irish-language channel TG4.[2] TG4 has also broadcast a fly-on-the-wall documentary series, *Underdogs*, which followed the creation and training of a team of unknown Gaelic footballers in 2003. This series coincided with a BBC2 Northern Ireland documentary series called *Gaelic Passions*, which presented a portrait of the close-knit community of Silverbridge in south Armagh through the activities of the local GAA club. Television dramas about sport have not been universally acclaimed, however. *On Home Ground* (2001), RTÉ's attempt to base an entire soap opera around a GAA club, came in for heavy criticism and was dismissed by some as a travesty.

Irish theatrical representations of sporting themes have had much greater success in recent years. For example, the 2003 Galway Arts Festival staged two impressive sports-based productions. *Hurl* centred on Ireland's first multi-ethnic hurling team to reach an All-Ireland final, whereas the Irish-language play *Scaoil leis an gCaid* focused on a Gaeltacht team's first visit to a county final.[3] This contemporary tradition of staging Irish sport can be traced to Paul Mercier's powerful soccer-based drama *Studs* (1986), which combined innovative stagecraft, demotic language and left-wing polemic in its dramatisation of the fortunes of a hapless Dublin working-class team. Eight years later, Marie Jones's *A Night in November* (1994) used the passions aroused by the 1993 World Cup qualifying game between Northern Ireland and the Republic to explore one Northern Protestant supporter's rejection of sectarianism. More recently, John

Breen's exuberant ensemble piece, *Alone It Stands* (1999), based on Munster's famous 1978 victory over the touring All Black rugby team, interspersed quick-fire comic action with shrewd observations on the class-based dimensions of Limerick rugby. Dramatic coverage of Irish sport has even extended to the internet in the form of a GAA soap opera based around the fictional villages of Knockmult and Gowlnacalley.[4]

But what does this multiplicity of recent artistic output dealing with Irish sport reveal? Why has sport become such a powerful theme within popular cultural representation? While there are no simple answers to such questions, Gerry Smyth offers one explanation in his study of contemporary Irish fiction. Writing about Roddy Doyle's *The Van* (1991), he suggests that 'in his exploration of soccer as a theme and symbol of Barrytown life, Doyle taps into a wider discourse in which sport is understood to play a major role in the functioning of post-industrial societies in the west' (Smyth, 1997: 75). Although Smyth does not identify what the role of sport actually is here, he does posit a clear link between the local and the global by identifying the way in which sporting activity functions as a form of mass-consumption entertainment in contemporary culture, one that is often subservient to the demands of television executives, schedulers and sponsors. Such media exposure, and the corresponding position of sport and sports stars at the heart of the fashion, advertising and fitness industries, only serves to reinforce the idea that sport has some intrinsic importance of its own. But what might that be?

Clearly, sport allows those who follow it to suspend or transcend their regular lives for the duration of a fixture, contest or tournament. On a deeper level, it enables many different people – the oft-quoted 'imagined community' – to come together either in person or through the media to support an individual, club, province or nation, and thereby invest their emotions in certain elite teams or athletes as carriers of shared identities. In the process, sport becomes a force for both exclusion and inclusion. It can unite a diverse cross-section of social groups – rural and urban, privileged and poor – while simultaneously excluding others on grounds of race, gender or politics. However, these processes of exclusion and inclusion can sometimes contradict each other as the boundaries of differentiation are not fixed, and are often dependent on the nature of the particular sport or setting. Thus, the terraces of a regular season fixture at Linfield's Windsor Park would be the dominant preserve of young, working-class loyalist males, whereas Croke Park on All-Ireland final day would, by the nature of the spectacle, draw a more diverse crowd, at least in terms of age and gender. Nevertheless, the social relationships engendered by the omnipresence of sport in popular culture can be instrumental in understanding a variety of cultural, political and ideological issues, a fact noted by Daniel Corkery as he watched a game of hurling with 30,000 other supporters in Thurles in the early decades of the twentieth century. Corkery, in passing, drew an analogy between of those hurling spectators and 'any of the great crowds that assemble of [sic] Saturday afternoons in England to witness Association football matches' (Corkery, 1931: 12). Both, he claimed, were typical of their nations. He makes no mention, since he has other ends in view, of the factors that set these sporting cultures apart. Such comparative insights have had to await the rise of sports science in our own time.

In Britain, the emergence of a critical discourse of fandom, which asserts that sport has a permanent function in people's lives, was a response to the near total disappearance of the hooligan dynamic from English soccer in the 1990s, a dynamic that has never applied to Irish sport. Sports sociologists and others, in an attempt to justify their existence and offer an analysis of the seismic shifts that were taking place in football culture, turned to the work of writers such as Robert Stebbins (1997) and his concept of 'serious leisure' as a way of understanding and contextualising the life of the English soccer supporter. The most concise analysis of soccer fandom, one that builds on Stebbins's work, is that by Ian Jones (2000). Essentially, he argues that being a fan is a long-term activity that requires perseverance and can even be thought of as an alternative 'career path'. It also requires a significant personal investment and the acquisition of specialist knowledge and skills through which fans develop individual self-esteem and collective norms and values. Despite the problematic nature of the emotional investment that fans make in their teams (which cannot always win), most of those studied by Jones believed that being a fan was a serious leisure activity. Jones's findings have been echoed in a series of case studies and arguments by other authors, notably Redhead (1997), Brown (1998), King (2000) and Farred (2002).[5] It is my belief, however, that the entire literature on fandom, while producing some highly worthwhile insights about the role and function of sport in society and its relationship to issues of race and gender, is a misguided exercise in self-justification. By positing fandom as a serious, all-consuming activity – 'the lengthiest emotional commitment we make' (Edge, 1999: 18) – such studies falsely privilege football fandom over other markers of identity. While it is true that many followers know every detail about their teams and invest emotionally and financially in them, their support is part of a much bigger whole, so that to posit fandom as the defining attribute of their identities skews the importance of sport in people's lives.

Studies of fandom also tend to ignore the fact that the hardcore supporter constitutes only one element of the sporting crowd. This point is especially important to bear in mind when considering the nature of sports spectatorship and team support in Ireland, where only a minority of followers would fall into the fandom category as it has been conceptualised in an English context. For example, only a few thousand Irish fans might travel to a football qualifier in Spain or Latvia, but tens of thousands will attend an international tournament, spiritually accompanied by the armchair spectators at home. Indeed, for most Irish football fans, enthusiastic support for the national team is a recent phenomenon and not a constant feature of their lives. Equally, many GAA followers' support for their county team is more passive than active. By this I mean that they are more likely to follow the team's fortunes via the media than by spending time on the terraces. Success is the spur: a provincial or national final has a much greater galvanising force than an early-season league match.

Thus, for most Irish people, team support is more ephemeral than permanent, a feature that fluctuates in accordance with the nature of the spectacle that beckons. True, matches are regularly recalled and analysed, but this only serves to reinforce the point that sport is a passing moment in life. The importance of such national and local specificities will, I hope, become clearer in the remainder of this chapter in which I propose to analyse how certain Irish writers and musicians use sport – specifically, the recent successes of the Republic of Ireland soccer team and the Galway Gaelic football team – as a lens through which to examine changing attitudes towards masculinity, class, emigration and identity. Each of the writers and musicians under discussion – Roddy Doyle, Dermot Bolger, Joseph O'Connor and The Folk Footballers – focus on the meanings of moments of transitory sporting excitement that motivate entire communities, not merely dedicated individuals. They show how sport functions both as a repository of communal values and as a sanctioned space for the public expression of deep personal feeling, especially between Irish men, many of whom associate public displays of emotion with a lack of masculine strength. In the process, they illuminate the shaping role of sport in the formation and articulation of Irish identities at a local, national and global level.

WRITING ABOUT SOCCER

Writing about sport has always been popular, whether in journalistic, biographical or novelistic form. The last decade, however, has witnessed a notable upsurge of interest, at least in Britain and Ireland, in factual, fictional and cinematic accounts of sporting prowess, achievement and obsession. Soccer has featured prominently in this phenomenon, from Nick Hornby's Arsenal-based memoir *Fever Pitch* (1993), one of the bestselling books of the 1990s, to the film *Bend it like Beckham* (2002), which centred on the struggles of a young British Asian woman to play football despite opposition from her traditionally minded parents. The film was notable for the way it challenged virtually every stereotype of soccer as a male, working-class game – a vision that was central to the success of Hornby's book – and so used sport to explore attitudes towards ethnicity and gender in contemporary British society. Soccer autobiographies have also featured prominently on bestseller lists in recent years. While some, such as David Beckham's *My World* (2000), are as much about the subject's celebrity status as his sporting talent, others, such as *Roy Keane: The Autobiography* (2002), shed much light on the inner workings of the modern game and the psychological make-up of one of its most controversial characters. The biographies of many less glamorous figures have also sold well, especially those written about successful journeymen players such as Tony Cascarino and Niall Quinn, both of whom were instrumental in the recent glory years of the Irish soccer team. These books, and a host of others by and about Gaelic footballers, hurlers, golfers and even greyhounds, serve a popular need to understand sporting icons and the attributes and attitudes that set them apart from the non-elite (O'Connor, 1985; Powell, 1990; Tanner, 2003).

The popularity of soccer in Ireland has undergone a similar renaissance during the last two decades or so. Although it has never been a leading spectator sport, the success of the Irish national football team since the mid-1980s has aroused much public interest and passion. In the late 1980s and early 1990s, with Jack Charlton as manager, the team took part in three major international championships for the first time in its history. In 1988 it qualified for the finals of the European championships in Germany. Two years later, the Republic made its first ever appearance in the finals of the World Cup and repeated this achievement in 1994. Participation in these major events had a huge impact in Ireland, and for the relevant weeks of competition the nation was gripped by soccer mania. Immediately, these sporting successes became the inspiration for a number of works of fiction, memoir and drama, three of which will be considered here: Dermot Bolger's play *In High Germany* (1990), the action of which takes place during the 1988 European championships; Roddy Doyle's aforementioned *The Van*, set in Dublin around the time of the 1990 World Cup; and the 1994 World Cup diary of Joseph O'Connor, originally written for the *Sunday Tribune* newspaper and subsequently published as the final chapter of *The Secret World of the Irish Male* (1994), a collection of his journalistic writings.

Bolger's *In High Germany* reveals a multitude of themes that are central to the connection between sport and the study of Irish (male) identities (Cronin 1999; Harte, 1997). The play is set on the platform of Altona railway station in Hamburg as the sole character, Eoin, an Irishman living in Germany, travels home to his pregnant German partner, having spent the previous fortnight with his schoolboy friends from Dublin, Mick and Shane, following the Irish soccer team's progress in the tournament. In his central monologue Eoin recounts his personal history, which includes memories of watching his father travel back and forth to England in search of work, his own experiences at school with Molloy, a teacher of traditional-ist nationalist views who frowned upon the soccer obsession of his young charges, and his journey to continental Europe to find work following the Irish economic recession of the 1970s. In the process of remembering, Eoin identifies some of the underlying patterns and defining tensions of late twentieth-century Irish life. He recalls an urbanised Dublin where soccer was the game of the streets and the working classes, the antithesis of the Gaelic games that were promoted by a seemingly distant, rural and still Gaelicised education system. He also registers the loss of nationalist idealism in the 1960s and the subsequent economic downturn that led to his own emigration, and which caused the unemployment and associated death of his father.

However, as Liam Harte has observed, Eoin is not wholly despondent at this train of events but rather recognises that, through the multi-ethnicities of the Irish soccer team, he is part of a transforming world in which a new transnational conception of Irishness is taking shape (Harte, 1997: 20). The tournament gives Eoin and his friends one last opportunity – an evanescent moment – to be together again as they once were, before dispersing and moving on to a new phase of their lives. Solace is found in the fact that their fellow supporters are in the same transitional state, since they come not only from Ireland, but also from 'Munich and Stuttgart, three coaches from London, lads from Berlin and Eindhoven, Cologne and the Hague' (Bolger, 1992: 84). Bolger's characters are not in a state of fandom; rather, they are following the team for its moment of temporary excitement, for the spectacle and the potential for enjoyment. For them, the team represents one version of Irish identity, but does not, in the context of fandom, define them exclusively.

The play is clearly of its time, being set in the years prior to the Celtic Tiger phenomenon and the economic boom that ended decades of net emigration. In this respect it differs from O'Connor's piece, which speaks to a more prosperous Irish society. *In High Germany* is particularly important, however, for its recognition of the social changes that took place during the 1960s and 1970s, and the link between soccer, class and urbanisation. It offers a positive assessment of the role of soccer as a catalyst for a new sense of nationalism, one that was more flexible and diasporic, less wedded to a socially and ideologically conservative conception of what it meant to be Irish. Through Eoin, Bolger portrays a group of men who are little different from those whom Doyle depicts in Barrytown, in that their city roots and love of soccer are strong. Much of this portrayal evidently stems from the playwright's own background and his sense of soccer in Ireland as an urban phenomenon that was given to its followers by men from similar backgrounds as themselves, working-class northside Dubliners such as Liam Brady, David O'Leary and Frank Stapleton. The 1980s ushered in a new era when such players were joined by 'foreigners' with English accents: the children of emigrants keen to declare their allegiance to Ireland. The team as a whole, therefore, increasingly came to replicate the experience of those who supported it: working-class, usually urban, sometimes transitory, often emigrants – but Irish nonetheless.

Bolger's play is primarily concerned with a consideration of the contemporary Irish condition, as seen through the eyes of an unillusioned male working-class migrant. At its heart are the close bonds that exist between Eoin and his friends, which are a product of a laddish culture that revolved around 'poker sessions and parties in bedsits, football in Fairview Park on Sunday mornings before the pubs opened, walking out the long roads to Phibsborough and Rathmines on Saturday nights with sixpacks and dope and a sense of belonging so ingrained we were never aware of it' (Bolger, 1992: 108). However, this rather stereotypical portrayal of Irish male relationships, which also permeates the works of Doyle and O'Connor, is complicated by Eoin's radical migrant perspective, which renders his former sense of belonging suddenly unreal and insubstantial, eclipsed by a new-found diasporic identification, which the Irish team embodies:

I raised my hands and applauded, having finally, in my last moments with Shane and Mick, found the only Ireland whose name I can sing, given to me by eleven men dressed in green. And the only Ireland I can pass on to the son who will carry my name in a foreign land. (Bolger, 1992: 107)

Here Bolger brilliantly exploits the essentially transient passion of a sporting occasion (albeit one marked by defeat) by making it serve as an emblem of Eoin's evanescent vision of national identity that seems to transcend territory and borders. What Eoin finds in the Irish soccer team is a vehicle that allows him to express and analyse his love for his friends and his country, while accepting the changing patterns of his life.

The themes of masculinity, identity and emigration raised by Bolger's largely positive depiction of the cultural significance and symbolism the Irish soccer team re-emerge in the works of Doyle and O'Connor. Doyle's *The Van* represents the final instalment of his Barrytown trilogy, completing the story of the Rabbitte family begun in *The Commitments* (1987) and continued in *The Snapper* (1990). In it, Jimmy Rabbitte and his friend Bimbo use their redundancy money to set up in business selling fast food from a van, trading as 'Bimbo's Burgers'. Essentially the novel is about the relationship between these two middle-aged men and their struggles with self-esteem as they try to come to terms with the loss of their traditional roles as breadwinners. Critics differ, however, about the novel's treatment of these themes and subjects. Carmine White regards *The Van* as Doyle's bleakest, seeing it as 'the story of a man who life has defeated, [which] marks the transition from Doyle's riotous and raucous novels to his more serious work' (White, 2001: 97). By contrast, Rüdiger Imhof argues that the question is 'whether what Doyle chooses to show can qualify as a serious-minded analysis of contemporary life in Dublin, especially because the social problems engaged with are almost completely drowned by plenty of laughs' (Imhof, 2002: 241).

Such comments exemplify the critical tendency to judge *The Van* in terms of its depiction of social conditions, to the exclusion of its treatment of sport. Imhof, indeed, is particularly curt in his dismissal of the passages that deal with World Cup euphoria. Although lasting barely 30 pages, this narrative strand brilliantly evokes the heady summer of 1990, precisely because it is full of laughter and therefore captures the unifying, fun aspects of being a football follower. As Ulrike Paschel argues, 'the great event in Barrytown is the soccer World Cup when the celebratory spirit reaches its climax [...]. Just like Christmas, it is a time for reconciliation, old animosities are forgotten when friend and foe are united in their support for the "Boys in Green"' (Paschel, 1998: 97). Sport indeed is a central element of Doyle's portrayal of the complexities and challenges of middle-aged working-class males. In the case of *The Van*, 'Irish working class manhood is revealed to be based upon an elaborate system of rituals and codes – alcohol, slagging, the crack and, *perhaps most importantly, sport*' (Smyth, 1997: 75, emphasis added). The Irish team's successes are not only emotionally stirring; they also offer the male characters an opportunity to bond, briefly unencumbered by their myriad social and financial problems, and to affirm their shared experiences through collective validation. Much of this expression is concerned with national identity and the arrival of the Irish on the world sporting stage, though sport also functions as the site of an emotional and often public demonstration of friendship between Jimmy, Bimbo and their mates.

We see an example of this in the description of the men's reactions to Ireland scoring the equaliser against England: 'Jimmy Sr grabbed Bimbo and nearly broke him in half with the hug he gave him. Bertie was up on one of the tables thumping his chest. Even Paddy, the crankiest fucker ever invented, was jumping up and down and shaking his arse like a Brazilian' (Doyle, 1991: 152). Such exuberance continues after the final whistle when Jimmy proceeds to hug everyone in the pub. Thus, the shared, carnivalesque mood that sport engenders enables the Barrytown men to participate in an important moment in the cultural and sporting history of the nation, the most important factor of which is their essential togetherness. For all the academic debates surrounding the validity of Anderson's concept of imagined communities, Doyle captures perfectly how the idea works in reality. And while the emotion attached to such a sporting event is fleeting and does not constitute any change in the structure or fabric of society, it is important in facilitating both the expression of shared communal values and the replacement or augmentation of larger social, economic and political considerations with feelings of evanescent pleasure.

The Ireland versus Romania match produces a new wave of communal celebration, and again allows for the expression of male feelings that are normally submerged and unexpressed. Indeed, it appears that it is only in the pressure-cooker atmosphere of a penalty shoot-out that men can reveal their true selves. For instance, the chaos after the game witnesses a reconciliation between Jimmy and his son, which culminates in the former telling the latter that he loves him. However, this declaration is still couched in male reticence: 'he could say it and no one could hear him, except young Jimmy, because of the singing and roaring and breaking of glasses' (Doyle, 1991: 182). Significantly, the football matches themselves are not described in any detail; it is the importance attached to them by the main characters, and the feelings that victory evokes, that are paramount. Doyle himself acknowledged the value of sport as a means of character illumination and interrogation when he said in interview that 'one of the things that welds people together is mutual affection and sentimental moments. For example, football. Looked at from the outside, people might wonder what's going on, but what seems like utter stupidity – grown men crying over a football match – can be very important' (Smyth, 1997: 110).

Three years after *The Van* appeared, Joseph O'Connor transferred the spirit of fictionalised characters embracing the excitement of the 1990 World Cup to actual supporters who travelled to the US to support the Irish team in the 1994 finals. Whereas Doyle's characters are locked into their familiar landscape of Dublin's northside, O'Connor's are journeying in the disorientating spaces of New York and Orlando. His World Cup diary, entitled 'The Road to God knows where', covers the period from his departure from Dublin Airport on 15 June until American Independence Day in Orlando, by which time the Irish team had been knocked out of the competition by the Dutch. Despite differences in genre, tone and sensibility, O'Connor's narrative has one striking similarity to that of Bolger and Doyle: the accent is on the sense of communality that exists and develops among a predominantly male group of Irish football supporters during an international tournament. In other words, it is the way in which personal relationships combine to produce a sense of national community through a shared sporting experience that is the primary focus of the work. The diaristic form reinforces the sense of evanescence that defines this experience and underlines the fact that O'Connor was not writing a piece that sought to illuminate a permanent condition but was rather trying to capture the immediacy of the moment.

'The Road to God knows where' revels in the excitement and passion of following the Irish team in America. While the group with which he travels comprises people from all over Ireland, their journeys through bars, hotels, tourist attractions and football stadiums bring them into contact with American-based friends and relatives who form part of the wider Irish diaspora. The diary is revealing in that it demonstrates the sheer enjoyment attached to this emotion-filled journey, and the unifying role that soccer plays in provoking public declarations of one's love for the team, its players and the nation. The sociological aspects of the 1994 Irish soccer experience have been well covered in the work of Richard Giulianotti (1996), but O'Connor articulates best what such journeys are about: people travelling together in a shared sporting cause, having fun, singing songs and communally expressing what they see as best about their Irish identities and personalities. These are not the poor, vulnerable Irish immigrants of the 1850s but rather the affluent, self-confident tourists of the 1990s, whose journey is characterised by temporary pleasure rather than economic necessity. True, the portrait O'Connor presents can be labelled stereotypical: supporters drink to excess, make puerile jokes and indulge in overtly laddish behaviour. But to dismiss the fans by means of politically correct judgments is to miss the point. The strength of the diary is that it gives us an unvarnished insight into the gendered nature of the camaraderie that develops among a group of working-class football supporters, released from the cares and constraints of home.

O'Connor's analysis of the 1994 World Cup experience differs from that of Bolger and Doyle in that there are no great emotional scenes mediated through sport that allow the supporters to reveal themselves in the way that Eoin and Jimmy Rabbitte do. The only expressions of deep feelings are those attached to concepts of national identity and the sense of communal belonging it entails. As narrator, O'Connor finds that his own sense of empathy and commonality with the supporters deepens after the team has been eliminated from the tournament, and he registers one notably poignant moment on the bus back to the hotel immediately after Ireland's final match. By now the fans are in a mood of subdued sadness, and most dejected of all is a ten-year-old boy who is sobbing because of Ireland's exit. In an attempt to placate the boy, his father tells him: '"Sure it's only a game, soldier [...] there'll be another day, don't worry"' (O'Connor, 1994: 244). This narrative moment encapsulates the evanescent nature of sport – at least in terms of performance and results – that marks it out as different from other cultural activities. Celebration gives way to the despondency of defeat, but the prospect of future triumphs is already forming. So while specific conclusions can be drawn from literary and dramatic representations of Ireland's recent participation in international football events, in sporting terms, defeat merely signifies the end of one particular narrative of competition.

Yet it is also true that sport continually allows supporters to revisit the scenes of their triumphs and frustrations, enables them to escape the 'real' world and express feelings they may well suppress at other times. In sport every season, match or tournament has a paradoxical quality to it. On the one hand, it represents a clean slate, a chance to renew the roller-coaster ride through a torrent of emotions and experiences; on the other, each new beginning becomes in time a memory that contributes to a sense of shared identity, one that can be added to the catalogue of past victories or defeats and that will ultimately be overlaid by the next victory or defeat. The writings of Bolger, Doyle and O'Connor effectively capture this essence of sport: the fact that it is both an ephemeral and an abiding presence in people's lives, a source of much transient pleasure, yet also a means of expressing and affirming deep-rooted communal identities. By the same token, their works illuminate the importance of certain sporting moments in Irish people's lives, without affording them disproportionate significance. Sport helps define Irish identity at specific times; it does not define the Irish in perpetuity.

SINGING ABOUT GAELIC FOOTBALL

The tradition of depicting sport in art and literature has a much longer pedigree than representing sport in music and song. Historically, most Irish sporting songs have emerged from the changing room or the terrace, composed and sung by supporters extolling famous victories and legendary players, often using traditional local airs and ballads.[6] Recent decades have witnessed the inevitable commercialisation of this genre, influenced in part by the British practice of adapting the lyrics of popular songs to mark the participation of club and national teams in the finals of major domestic and international competitions.[7] It is now customary to celebrate the provincial and national achievements of county football and hurling teams in song, though these tend to be recorded by local acts and as such have limited appeal. But when the Galway Gaelic football team reached – and eventually won – the 1998 All-Ireland final, this practice was given fresh impetus when The Folk Footballers, an offshoot of The Saw Doctors comprising Leo Moran and Pádraig Stevens, released an album entitled *Ten Songs About Gaelic*, later reissued as *The First Fifteen* (2001).[8] Before moving on to a textual analysis of these football-related songs, it is important to gloss the musicians themselves and the place from which they come, Tuam.

Tuam is a town of approximately 8,000 people, an archbishopric and an episcopal see. Traditionally a predominantly agricultural town, it developed industrially during the economic expansion of the 1960s, though like many western towns it continued to suffer high levels of emigration through to the 1990s. More recently, however, it has benefited from the EU and US investment that has underpinned the dramatic growth of Galway city, and now has the appearance of a relatively affluent and expanding satellite town. Tuam is also a heartland of Gaelic football and has produced many players who have appeared at county level. It has also assumed significance as the home of The Saw Doctors, who were formed there in 1988. Kieran Keohane summarises the essence of the group's musical and cultural appeal as follows:

The Saw Doctors are lads, or should I say, they play at being a pack of lads from small-town Ireland. They sing about the itchiness of FCA uniforms, the camaraderie and rivalry of inter-parish hurling and football matches [...], and they sing about the painful inevitability of emigration at the end of Irish teenage innocence. Their music is Irish country and western rock 'n roll [...]. But it plays a crude melody on Irish heartstrings none the less. (Keohane, 1997: 277)

Despite, or perhaps because of, their cultural specificity, The Saw Doctors have achieved a high degree of commercial success both at home and abroad, and are justly famous for their long-running tours of Britain and the US, where their songs resonate with the experiences of many in the Irish diaspora. As well as reflecting on the minutiae of everyday life in small-town Ireland, their lyrics contain a critical commentary on larger social issues such as religion, emigration and, significantly, sport. However, the group's music does not embrace all of the developments of Celtic Tiger Ireland. Their songs rarely address the social impact of the country's recent transformation into a globalised economy, for example, but instead celebrate the culture and value systems of a more traditional Ireland where many of Dublin's young professionals come from. This is essentially what The Saw Doctors' music is about: it eulogises a version of parochial Irish culture that is often sneered at by city sophisticates and by many in the Dublin-based national media. But this does not mean that it idealises an outmoded or dying culture in the way of nineteenth-century Gaelic revivalists. On the contrary, it celebrates what is distinctive and unique about non-metropolitan Ireland, and familiar to most.

Given the nature of The Saw Doctors and their background, it is perhaps not surprising that The Folk Footballers, who share much of the same heritage and context, should embrace Gaelic games so readily. Long before The Folk Footballers released *The First Fifteen*, The Saw Doctors' repertoire had featured several songs that dealt with the ways in which GAA culture provides people with a sense of shared identity and an annual, summer-long rhythm to their lives. Yet despite being Ireland's leading national sporting association, the GAA and its supporters are frequently criticised for their parochialism and lack of sophistication. Many are seen as culturally irredentist sporting separatists owing to their seeming unwillingness to share a refurbished Croke Park with rugby and soccer. By celebrating GAA culture in song, therefore, The Saw Doctors risk being regarded as apologists for this particular brand of Irishness, one that is frequently at odds with the voices of progressive liberalism. What this viewpoint ignores, however, is the extent to which the group's music gives authentic expression to the defining emotions and experiences of a large number of Irish people in a distinctive local idiom.

The songs on *The First Fifteen*, though not exclusively concerned with Gaelic football, can be read as the testimonies of men rooted in a deep affection for and affiliation to Galway football. More generally, the lyrics of Moran and Stevens articulate a cross-gender understanding of the appeal of sport, locality, history and folklore to the rural Irish as a whole. What is portrayed throughout is a local landscape peopled by passionate followers of a game that embodies both their Galwegian and their Irish identities. 'Galway C'mon C'mon' typifies this theme. This song, which deals with the magnetic appeal of Croke Park on All-Ireland Sunday, depicts supporters from all over the city and county uniting on an epic journey to Dublin in the hope of winning the Sam Maguire trophy, the capture of which symbolises the victory of the non-metropolitan west over the metropolitan east. The lyrics evoke a regional and communal sense of identity – 'Coming from the country, coming from the town / From Mike O'Regan's, coming from Browne's' – which is underpinned by the enumeration of earlier Galway victories: 'Coming from the 1934, '56 and '64'. Such sentiments serve to remind us that in sport, as in other forms of communal activity, the invocation of previous triumphs is central to the creation of a mythology of belonging. It locates contemporary players and supporters in a historical continuum and provides them with a measuring stick for their own sense of worth. Of course, this invocation of old glories is by no means unique. Many parish and county teams have songs that are familiar only to local audiences and which therefore tend towards exclusivity. The Folk Footballers' lyrics, however, although local in the sense that they are about Galway, articulate sentiments that are common to anyone familiar with the game and its history, and as such acquire a resonance that extends beyond the county boundary. Such sentiments are not consistent with fandom, however. Local awareness of previous victories and former stars is the product of a community-based folklore, knowledge that is absorbed through everyday experience and acted out at appropriate times of success, rather than ritualistically expressed on a weekly basis. It exists as the quiet backdrop to local lives rather than as the locus of self-definition.

'Heroes of the Hour' conjures up a similar sense of sporting occasion and tradition. Here too we have the hope-filled journey ('That day in September sun shone through the mist,/ I was going to the All-Ireland, silver money in my fist'); the recollection of listening to broadcasts of previous matches ('We used to listen in the kitchen to Mícheál O'Hehir,/ The wonder of the wireless as holy as prayer'); the familiar pre-match spectacle ('All the pomp and the pageant, the band from Artane,/ Was the sound of the summer, in sunshine and rain'). 'Maroon and White' takes this narrative a stage further by dramatising one supporter's dream of becoming a top-flight player. The lyrics capture the profound emotional appeal of having a specific county identity, and being a focal part of the traditions, rituals and symbolism of All-Ireland final day:

> I dreamt I'd wear the jersey, on All-Ireland final day,
> Stand out there in Croke Park, with a mighty part to play,
> We'd come out of the tunnel to a great big Galway roar,
> We'd have our picture taken, and head down to the goal.
> [....]

> And I dreamt I'd hold a medal so precious in my hand,
> With the people all around me and the ghosts up in the stands,
> And then on Monday evening when we bring the cup back home,
> The bonfires would be blazing all along the road.

What such songs articulate is the specifically local and communal nature of GAA identities, centred on the nexus of relationships that exist between village, parish and county. The sense of belonging that is afforded by these local affiliations is reinforced by the amateur status of Gaelic games, which fosters a close personal bond between players and supporters, unlike soccer, where a money-rich transfer market has largely destroyed the local ties between footballer and fan. As the persona in 'Heroes of the Hour' succinctly observes: 'they picked my first cousin – well this can't be missed'.

This link between the localism of the GAA and the volunteer culture that sustains it at both parish and national levels is central to The Folk Footballers' representation of Gaelic football. By recognising that 'Gaelic would perish if it wasn't for the parish,/ The mothers wash the jerseys, the fathers get the ball', *The First Fifteen* locates the GAA at the heart of rural community and posits a mutually sustaining relationship between club and parish, through which a shared sense of place is kept alive. Moreover, this relationship is shown to be a highly active one, in that the majority of Gaelic supporters participate in a parish club structure that directly links them to the county team and its players, who are thus familiar and known. This intimately personal dimension of GAA sporting identities distinguishes them from the kind engendered by soccer, where the passions aroused by the national team tend to be based on a more impersonal relationship between players and supporters. Soccer fans may well identify with and feel that they 'know' the players, but few have any active involvement in or access to the team structures within which they work. This, then, is one of the central ways in which The Folk Footballers' narratives of sporting identities differ from those of Bolger, Doyle and O'Connor. Whereas these writers depict Irish soccer culture as being a male-dominated mix of urban and diasporic identities, The Folk Footballers' songs embody a vision of Gaelic sporting identities that are deeply rooted in shared local traditions, parochial loyalties and personal memories. This sense of belonging is not necessarily about a singular, homogeneous nation-state identity but is rather composed of a complex network of intertwined allegiances to club, parish, county and province.

The band's musical style and idiom play a central role in communicating this multi-layered sense of belonging.[9] Broadly speaking, The Folk Footballers' style, and that of The Saw Doctors, can be defined as a distinctive mixture of Irish traditional modes, American country influences and rock 'n' roll rhythms, a musical cross-fertilisation that represents a reaction (unconscious or otherwise) against English cultural hegemony. By 'cementing social ties, bolstering self-esteem and [...] securing of mutual warmth and belonging amongst audiences', this hybrid musical style echoes and reinforces the identity-forming practices of sport (Llewellyn, 1998).[10] Although both sport and music represent a global currency, Simon Frith argues that rather than become avowedly global, music must embody authentic traces of communal histories if it wishes to avoid the pitfalls of nostalgia (Frith, 1996). This point is highly relevant to The Folk Footballers' representation of Gaelic games, since it illuminates the way their songs capture something that is culturally real and organic, and bear traces of authentic communal values, traditions and histories.[11] So while the GAA may be viewed in some quarters as anachronistic, for its many supporters The Folk Footballers' articulation of the values and meanings of Gaelic games has an authentic and contemporary resonance, and adds up to much more than mere nostalgic whimsy. As the celebratory songs on *The First Fifteen* make clear, the GAA continues to be a force for continuity in a changing world. They suggest, moreover – and this is at the very heart of any reading of the album – that no matter how much Ireland may change in the future, the GAA will remain a focal point for the expression of local rivalries and affinities, communal histories and traditions, and the sheer joy of winning the big prize.

CONCLUSION

Sport is a major part of Ireland's social and cultural life. For this reason, scholarly explorations of the subject need to consider it in its wider representational and ideological contexts rather than limit themselves to discussions of its organisational, political and sectarian dimensions, as has been the tradition. This chapter has attempted to begin this process by analysing the narrative and thematic uses of sport in selected works of contemporary Irish writing and popular music. As with sport itself, the chosen literary and musical texts reveal the centrality of masculine modes and attitudes to Irish sporting culture, while also showing how sport functions as a rich repository of communal values and aspirations. But rather than condemn sport for its sexism, it may be more productive to examine these textual representations for the light they cast on the lives, interests and passions of Irish men. As Doyle has admitted, it may seem strange that grown men can cry over a soccer match, yet such feelings reveal more than mere emotional enthusiasm for eleven men on a football pitch. As Irish masculinity is refashioned and revisioned, and traditional gender roles transformed by myriad socio-economic forces, sport offers many men a sanctioned space in which to express their emotions without fear of personal ridicule or social stigma. Instead of dismissing or trivialising such public displays of emotion, it is more pertinent to interrogate their deeper significance, and to ask what they may be expressive of.

As I have argued here, representations of sporting adventure and achievement in the works of Doyle, Bolger, O'Connor and The Folk Footballers embody a set of complex meanings about Irish men's attitudes to family and relationships, work and emigration, community and identity. By carefully analysing the varied cast of characters in these narratives, we can better appreciate the multi-layered nature of personal and collective Irish identities, from the intimate localism of the parish or suburb to more diasporic forms of national belonging. The texts discussed here also reveal the continuing force of the urban/ rural, provincial/metropolitan divisions within Irish society, and the ways in which disparate social groupings unite and diverge according to particular sporting contexts, allegiances and affiliations. Above all, they underline the fact that sport is essentially an evanescent or ephemeral pleasure. This is not to suggest that it is historically or culturally unimportant, but rather to argue that it is one component of identity formation, not its very definition, as the fandom thesis claims. While this reading of sports-related texts may represent no more than a basic, and perhaps unsophisticated, beginning, I hope that it nonetheless offers a fresh way of approaching the study of sport within an Irish Studies framework.

NOTES

1. For examples of recent advances in the analysis of sport in Northern Ireland, see Bairner and Shirlow (1998) and Hassan (2002). For recent developments in sports history, see Garnham (2002) and Hunt (2005). For an innovative approach to the study of the Irish diaspora and sport, see Bradley (1999).

2. In recent years this programme has featured the stories of men such as Mick O'Dwyer, Séan Boylan, Jack Lynch and Máirtín Mac Aodha.

3. *Hurl* by Charlie O'Neill was performed at Galway's Black Box Theatre in July 2003. Breandán Mac Gearailt's *Scaoil leis an gCaid/An Saol Eile* was staged at An Taibhdhearc in the same month.

4. See http://www.anfearrua.com

5. It is interesting to note that nearly all of the scholars who have engaged in writing about fandom are themselves football fans.

6. For details of the songs attached to various GAA counties and clubs, see the Dromina GAA club website, http://www.dromina.freeservers. com/songs.html

7. The success of the Irish soccer team spawned a similar phenomenon, so that certain songs such as 'Give it a lash, Jack' and 'Ole, ole, ole, ole' became synonymous with the World Cup soccer campaigns of 1990 and 1994.

8. *Ten Songs About Gaelic* was originally released in 1998 in cassette form, but later added to and released as a CD entitled *The First Fifteen* (Galway: Back Duke Records, 1998). Moran and Stevens have a long collaborative history as a result of their involvement in the Tuam music scene. Moran is a full-time member of The Saw Doctors, while Stevens, an independent musician, also tours regularly with the band. For more information on The Folk Footballers and the shared history between various Tuam bands, see Stevens's website, http://www.padraigstevens.com

9. For a discussion of the functions of Irish music, see Sommers Smith (2001).

10. Llewellyn goes on to argue that The Saw Doctors' music allows 'Irish audiences to invest in the rural and redneck connotations of Country music, and in its determined evocations of a sense of place threatened by the pressures of modernity and dislocation' (Llewellyn, 1998: 12).

11. For a discussion of authenticity in Irish culture, see Graham (1999).

Bibliography

Aalen, F. H. A., Whelan, K. and Stout, M. (eds) (1997) *Atlas of the Irish Rural Landscape* (Toronto: University of Toronto Press)

Adorno, T. and Horkheimer, M. (1979) *Dialectic of Enlightenment*, trans. J. Cumming (London: New Left Books)

Akenson, D. H. (1988) *Small Differences: Irish Catholics and Irish Protestants 1815–1922. An International Perspective* (Kingston: McGill-Queen's University Press)

Akenson, D. H. (1996) *The Irish Diaspora: A Primer* (Belfast: Institute of Irish Studies)

Akenson, D. H. (1999) *The Irish in Ontario: A Study in Rural History* (Montreal: McGill-Queens University Press; 2nd edn)

Aldridge, A. (2000) *Religion in the Contemporary World* (Cambridge: Polity Press)

Allen, K. (1997) *Fianna Fáil and Irish Labour: 1926 to the Present* (London: Pluto Press)

Allen, K. (2000) *The Celtic Tiger: The Myth of Social Partnership in Ireland* (Manchester: Manchester University Press)

An Moltóir (2001) 'On Home Ground – Renamed as D'Unbelievables', *An Fear Rua*, 14 November

Anderson, B. (1983) *Imagined Communities: Reflections on the Origin and Spread of Nationalism* (London: Verso)

Anonymous (1985) 'Disciplinary Reports', *Anglo-Irish Encounter, Conference on Irish Studies in Britain*

Appadurai, A. (1996) *Modernity at Large: Cultural Dimensions of Globalization* (Minneapolis: University of Minnesota Press)

Arensberg, C. (1937) *The Irish Countryman* (London: Macmillan)

Arnold, B. (2002) *Jack Lynch* (Dublin: Merlin)

Aronson, A. (1980) *Music and the Novel: A Study in Twentieth-Century Fiction* (Totowa: Rowman & Littlefield)

Ashcroft, B., Griffiths, G. and Tiffin, H. (2002) [1998] *Key Concepts in Post-Colonial Studies* (London: Routledge)

Ashplant, T. G. and Smyth, G. (eds) (2001) *Explorations in Cultural History* (London: Pluto Press)

Atkinson, A. (1997) *The Europeans in Australia: A History. Volume 1: The Beginning* (Melbourne: Oxford University Press)

Attali, J. (1985) [1977] *Noise: The Political Economy of Music*, trans. B. Massumi (Manchester: Manchester University Press)

Attridge, D. and Howes, M. (eds) (2000) *Semicolonial Joyce* (Cambridge: Cambridge University Press)

Bairner, A. and Shirlow, P. (1998) 'Loyalism, Linfield and the Territorial Politics of Soccer Fandom in Northern Ireland', *Space and Polity*, 2: 2, pp. 163–77

Barker, F., Hulme, P., Iverson, M. and Loxley, D. (eds) (1986) *Literature, Politics and Theory, Papers from the Essex Conference 1976–84* (London: Methuen)

Barker, S. (1982) 'Editorial', *LTP [Literature, Teaching, Politics]*, 1, p. 1

Barkley, J. M. (1966) *The Anti-Christ* (Belfast: Presbyterian College)

Bartlett, T., Curtin, C., O'Dwyer, R. and Ó Tuathaigh, G. (eds) (1988) *Irish Studies: A General Introduction* (Dublin: Gill and Macmillan)

Bartlett, T., Dickson, D., Keogh, D. and Whelan, K. (eds) (2003) *1798. A Bicentenary Perspective* (Dublin: Four Courts)

Barton, R. (2004) *Irish National Cinema* (London: Routledge)

Bauerle, R. H. (ed.) (1993) *Picking up Airs: Hearing the Music in Joyce's Text* (Urbana: University of Illinois Press)

Bauman, Z. (1990) *Modernity and Ambivalence* (Cambridge: Polity Press)

Bell, D. (1988) 'Ireland Without Frontiers? The Challenge of the Communications Revolution', in Kearney, R. (ed.), *Across the Frontiers: Ireland in the 1990s* (Dublin: Wolfhound Press)

Bell, D. (1990) *Acts of Union: Youth Culture and Sectarianism in Northern Ireland* (London: Macmillan)

Bell, D. (2004) 'Telling Tales: Narrative, Evidence, and Memory in Contemporary Documentary Film Practice', in Barton, R. and O'Brien, H. (eds), *Keeping it Real: Irish Film and Television* (London: Wallflower Press), pp. 88–99

Benjamin, W. (2003) [1972] 'On the Concept of History', in Benjamin, W., *Selected Writings*, vol. 4, 1938–1940, trans. E. Jephcott, H. Eiland and M. Jennings (Cambridge, MA: Belknap Press of Harvard University Press), pp. 389–400

Benson, C. (2004) 'The Unthinkable Boundaries of Self: The Role of Negative Emotional Boundaries in the Formation, Maintenance and Transformation of Identities', in Harré, R. and Moghaddam, F. (eds), *The Self and Others: Positioning Individuals and Groups in Personal, Political and Cultural Contexts* (New York: Praeger), pp. 61–84

Bew, P. (1987) *Conflict and Conciliation in Ireland, 1890–1910* (Oxford: Clarendon Press)

Bew, P. (1994) *Ideology and the Irish Question. Ulster Unionism and Irish Nationalism, 1912–1916* (Oxford: Clarendon Press)

Bloomfield, K. (1998) *We Will Remember Them* (Belfast: Stationery Office)

Bolger, D. (1992) 'In High Germany', in Bolger, D., *A Dublin Quartet* (London: Penguin), pp. 71–109

Bolton, G. (1986) 'The Irish in Australian Historiography', in Kiernan, C. (ed.), *Australia and Ireland, 1788–1988: Bicentenary Essays* (Dublin: Gill and Macmillan), pp. 5–19

Booker, M. K. (1997) 'Late Capitalism Comes to Dublin: "American" Popular Culture in the Novels of Roddy Doyle', *Ariel*, 28: 3, pp. 27–45

Booth, D. and Tatz, C. (2000) *One-Eyed: A View of Australian Sport* (Sydney: Allen and Unwin)

Bourdieu, P. (1984) *Distinction* (London: Routledge and Kegan Paul)

Bourdieu, P. (1990a) *In Other Words: Essays Toward a Reflexive Sociology* (Cambridge: Polity Press)

Bourdieu, P. (1990b) *Logic of Practice* (Cambridge: Polity Press)

Bourdieu, P. (1991) *Language and Symbolic Power* (Cambridge: Polity Press)

Bourdieu, P. (2000) 'The Biographical Illusion', in du Gay, P., Evans, J. and Redman, P. (eds), *Identity: a Reader* (London: Sage), pp. 297–303

Bourdieu, P. and Passeron, J.-C. (1977) *Reproduction in Education, Society and Culture* (London: Sage)

Bourdieu, P. and Wacquant, L. (1992) *An Invitation to Reflexive Sociology* (Chicago: Chicago University Press)

Bourke, A., Kilfeather, S., Luddy, M., MacCurtain, M., Meaney, G., Ní Dhonnchadha, M. and O'Dowd, M. (eds) (2002) *The Field Day Anthology of Irish Writing*, vols IV and V (Cork: Cork University Press)

Bourke, J. (1993) *Husbandry to Housewifery: Women, Economic Change and Housework in Ireland 1890–1914* (Oxford: Clarendon Press)

Bowyer Bell, J. (1987) *The Gun in Politics: an Analysis of Irish Political Conflict, 1916–1986* (New Brunswick: Transaction Books)

Boyce, D. G. and O'Day, A. (eds) (1996) *The Making of Modern Irish History: Revisionism and the Revisionist Controversy* (London: Routledge)

Bracken, P. and O'Sullivan, P. (2001) 'The Invisibility of Irish Migrants in British Health Research', *Irish Studies Review*, 9: 1, pp. 41–51

Bradley, J. (1999) 'The Gaelic Athletic Association and the Irish Diaspora in Scotland, 1897–1947', *International Journal of the History of Sport*, 16: 3, pp. 81–96

Bradshaw, B. (1994a) 'The Bardic Response to Conquest and Colonisation', *Bullán*, 1: 1, pp. 119–21

Bradshaw, B. (1994b) 'Nationalism and Historical Scholarship in Modern Ireland', in Brady, C. (ed.), *Interpreting Irish History: The Debate on Historical Revisionism, 1938–1994* (Dublin: Irish Academic Press), pp. 191–216

Bradshaw, B. and Morrill, J. (eds) (1996) *The British Problem, c1534–1707: State Formation in the Atlantic Archipelago* (Basingstoke: Macmillan)

Brady, C. (ed.) (1994) *Interpreting Irish History: The Debate on Historical Revisionism* (Dublin: Irish Academic Press)

Brady, C. and Gillespie, R. (eds) (1986) *Natives and Newcomers: the Making of Irish Colonial Society 1534–1641* (Dublin: Irish Academic Press)

Brady, C. and Ohlmeyer, J. (eds) (2005) *British Interventions in Early Modern Ireland* (Cambridge: Cambridge University Press)

Brewer, J. (1998) *Anti-Catholicism in Northern Ireland 1600–1998* (Basingstoke: Macmillan)

Brewer, J. (2003a) 'Are There any Christians in Northern Ireland?', in Gray, A., Lloyd, K., Devine, P., Robinson, G. and Heenan, D. (eds), *Social Attitudes in Northern Ireland: The Eighth Report* (London: Pluto), pp. 22–8

Brewer, J. (2003b) 'Continuity and Change in Contemporary Ulster Protestantism', Paper presented to Institute for British-Irish Studies, University College Dublin

Brown, A. (ed.) (1998) *Fanatics! Power, Identity and Fandom in Football* (London: Routledge)

Brown, T. (1988) 'Yeats, Joyce and the Irish Critical Debate', in Brown, T., *Ireland's Literature: Selected Essays* (Mullingar: Lilliput Press), pp. 77–90

Brown, T. (2004) *Ireland: A Social and Cultural History 1922–2002* (London: Harper Perennial)

Brubaker, R. (2001) 'Cognitive Perspectives', *Ethnicities*, 1: 1, pp. 15–17

Brubaker, R. and Cooper, F. (2000) 'Beyond "Identity"', *Theory and Society*, 29: 1, pp. 1–47

Bruce, S. (1996) [1986] *God Save Ulster: The Religion and Politics of Paisleyism* (Oxford: Clarendon Press)

Buchanan, R. H., Jones, E. and McCourt, D. (eds) (1971) *Man and His Habitat: Essays Presented to Emryn Estyn Evans* (London: Routledge and Kegan Paul)

Busteed, M. (1998) 'Songs in a Strange Land – Ambiguities of Identity Amongst Irish Migrants in Mid-Victorian Manchester', *Political Geography*, 17: 6, pp. 627–65

Busteed, M. (2005) 'Parading the Green. Procession as Subaltern Resistance in Manchester in 1867', *Political Geography*, 24: 8, pp. 903–33

Cambrensis, G. (1982) [c.1200 AD] *History and Topography of Ireland*, ed. and trans. J. J. O'Meara (London: Penguin)

Campbell, M. (1997) *The Kingdom of the Ryans: the Irish in Southwest New South Wales, 1816–90* (Sydney: UNSW Press)

Campbell Ross, I. 'Fiction to 1800', in Deane, S. (ed.) (1991) *The Field Day Anthology of Irish Writing*, 3 vols (Derry: Field Day), vol. I, pp. 682–7

Canny, N. (ed.) (1994) *Europeans on the Move: Studies in European Migration, 1500–1800* (Oxford: Oxford University Press)

Canny, N. (ed.) (1998) *The Oxford History of the British Empire, 1: The Origins of Empire* (Oxford: Oxford University Press)

Carpenter, A. (1998) *Verse in English from Eighteenth-Century Ireland* (Cork: Cork University Press)

Cathcart, R. (1984) *The Most Contrary Region* (Belfast: Blackstaff Press)

Chandler, J. (2006) 'A Discipline in Shifting Perspective: Why We Need Irish Studies', *Field Day Review*, 2, pp. 19–39

Charbonneau, A. and Sévigny, A. (1997) *1847, Grosse Île: A Record of Daily Events* (Ottawa: Canadian Heritage Parks Canada)

Chartier, R. (1988) *Cultural History: Between Practices and Representations* (Cambridge: Polity Press)

Clancy, P., Drudy, S., Lynch, K. and O'Dowd, L. (eds) (1986) *Ireland: A Sociological Profile* (Dublin: Institute of Public Administration)

Clark, M. (1995) *A Short History of Australia* (Melbourne: Penguin; 4th edn)

Clarke, A. (1988/89) 'Robert Dudley Edwards (1909–1988)', *Irish Historical Studies*, xxvi, pp. 121–7

Clayton-Lea, T. and Taylor, R. (1992) *Irish Rock: Where It's Come From, Where It's At, Where It's Going* (Dublin: Gill and Macmillan)

Clear, C. (2000) *Women of the House: Women's Household Work in Ireland 1921–1961* (Dublin: Irish Academic Press)

Cleary, J. (2002) *Literature, Partition and the Nation State: Culture and Conflict in Ireland, Israel and Palestine* (Cambridge: Cambridge University Press)

Cleary, J. (2003) 'Misplaced Ideas? Colonialism, Location and Dislocation in Irish Studies', in Connolly. C. (ed.), *Theorizing Ireland* (Basingstoke: Palgrave), pp. 91–104

Cleary, J. and Connolly, C. (eds) (2005) *The Cambridge Companion to Modern Irish Culture* (Cambridge: Cambridge University Press)

Cleary, P. S. (1933) *Australia's Debt to Irish Nation Builders* (Sydney: Angus and Robertson)

Cline Kelly, A. (2002) *Jonathan Swift and Popular Culture: Myth, Media and the Man* (Basingstoke: Palgrave)

Coakley, J. (1998) 'Religion, Ethnic Identity and the Protestant Minority in the Republic', in Crotty, W. and Schmitt, D. (eds), *Ireland and the Politics of Change* (Harlow: Addison Wesley Longman), pp. 86–106

Cohen, S. (1991) *Rock Culture in Liverpool: Popular Music in the Making* (Oxford: Clarendon)

Comerford, R. V. (2003) *Ireland: Inventing the Nation* (London: Arnold)

Commission on Emigration and Other Population Problems, 1948–54 (1955) (Dublin: Stationery Office)

Condon, J. (2000) 'The Patriotic Children's Treat: Irish Nationalism and Children's Culture at the Twilight of Empire', *Irish Studies Review*, 8: 2, pp. 167–78

Connolly, C. (ed.) (2003) *Theorizing Ireland* (Basingstoke: Palgrave)

Connolly, L. (2002) *The Irish Women's Movement: From Revolution to Devolution* (Basingstoke: Palgrave)

Connolly, L. (2004) 'The Limits of "Irish Studies": Historicism, Culturalism, Paternalism', *Irish Studies Review*, 12: 2, pp. 139–62

Connolly, S. J. (1992) *Religion, Law and Power: the Making of Protestant Ireland* (Oxford: Clarendon Press)

Connolly, S. J. (ed.) (1999) *Kingdoms United? Great Britain and Ireland since 1500. Integration and Diversity* (Dublin: Four Courts)

Conroy Jackson, P. (1992) 'Outside the Jurisdiction: Irish Women Seeking Abortion', in Smyth, A. (ed.), *The Abortion Papers Ireland* (Dublin: Attic Press), pp. 119–37

Cooney, J. (1999) *John Charles McQuaid: Ruler of Catholic Ireland* (Dublin: O'Brien Press)

Corcoran, F. (2004) *RTÉ and the Globalisation of Irish Television* (Bristol: Intellect Books)

Corkery, D. (1931) *Synge and Anglo-Irish Literature* (Cork: Cork University Press)

Cosgrove, D. E. (1984) *Social Formation and Symbolic Landscape* (London: Croom Helm)

Coulter, C. (1999) *Contemporary Northern Irish Society: an Introduction* (London: Pluto Press)

Coulter, C. and Coleman, S. (eds) (2003) *The End of Irish History? Critical Reflections on the Celtic Tiger* (Manchester: Manchester University Press)

Crawford, R. M. (1975) *'A Bit of a Rebel': the Life and Work of George Arnold Wood* (Sydney: Sydney University Press)

Cronin, M. (1997) *The Blueshirts and Irish Politics* (Dublin: Four Courts)

Cronin, M. (1999) *Sport and Nationalism in Ireland: Gaelic Games, Soccer and Irish National Identity since 1884* (Dublin: Four Courts)

Cronin, M. and Adair, D. (2002) *The Wearing of the Green. A History of St Patrick's Day* (London: Routledge)

Crotty, R. (1986) *Ireland in Crisis: a Study in Capitalist Colonial Undevelopment* (Dingle: Brandon)

Cullen, L. M. (1981) *The Emergence of Modern Ireland 1600–1900* (London: Batsford)

Cullen, L. M. (1988) *The Hidden Ireland: Reassessment of a Concept* (Mullingar: Lilliput Press)

Cullen, L. M. (2000) *The Irish Brandy Houses in Eighteenth-Century France* (Dublin: Lilliput)

Cullen, L. M. and Smout, T. C. (eds) (1977) *Comparative Studies of Scottish and Irish Economic and Social History* (Edinburgh: Donald)

Curran, J. (2002) *Media and Power* (London: Routledge)

Currey, C.H. (1954) *The Irish at Eureka* (Sydney: Angus and Roberston)

Curtis, L. (1984) *Ireland: The Propaganda War* (London: Pluto Press)

Curtis, L. P. (1971) *Apes and Angels: The Irishman in Victorian Caricature* (Newton Abbot: David and Charles)

Dalsimer, A. M. and Kreilkamp, V. (1993) 'Introduction', in Dalsimer, A. M. (ed.), *Visualizing Ireland. National Identity and the Pictorial Tradition* (Boston: Faber), pp. 3–8

Daly, M. E. (1997a) 'Recent Writings on Modern Irish History, the Interaction Between Past and Present', *Journal of Modern History*, 69: 3, pp. 512–33

Daly, M. E. (1997b) *The Buffer State. The Historical Roots of the Department of the Environment* (Dublin: Institute of Public Administration)

Daly, M. E. (2002) 'Revisiting the Great Famine', *Saothar*, 27, pp. 73–6

Daly, M. E. and Dickson, D. (eds) (1990) *The Origins of Popular Literacy in Ireland* (Dublin: Trinity College Dublin and University College Dublin)

Davie, G. (1994) *Religion in Britain since 1945: Believing Without Belonging* (Oxford: Blackwell)

Deane, S. (1986) 'Heroic Styles: The Tradition of an Idea', in Field Day Theatre Company, *Ireland's Field Day* (London: Hutchinson), pp. 45–58

Deane, S. (ed.) (1991) *The Field Day Anthology of Irish Writing*, 3 vols (Derry: Field Day)

Deane, S. (2005) *Foreign Affections: Essays on Edmund Burke* (Cork: Cork University Press)

Debray, R. (1981) *Teachers, Writers, Celebrities: The Intellectuals of Modern France*, trans. D. Macey (London: New Left Books)

Delaney, E. (2000) *Demography, State and Society, Irish Migration to Britain, 1921–1971* (Liverpool: Liverpool University Press)

Derrida, J. (1976) [1967] *Of Grammatology*, trans. G. Spivak (Baltimore: Johns Hopkins University Press)

Dickson, D. (2000) *New Foundations: Ireland 1660–1800* (Dublin: Irish Academic Press, 2nd rev. edn)

Dixson, M. (1999) *The Imaginary Australian: Anglo-Celts and Identity, 1788 to the Present* (Sydney: UNSW Press)

Dolan, A. (2003) *Commemorating the Irish Civil War. History and Memory, 1923–2000* (Cambridge: Cambridge University Press)

Donnelly, B. (2000) 'Roddy Doyle: From Barrytown to the GPO', *Irish University Review*, 30: 1, pp. 17–31

Donoghue, D. (1997) 'Fears for Irish Studies in an Age of Identity Politics', *Chronicle of Higher Education*, 21 November, pp. 4–5

Doolan, L. and Quinn, B. (1969) *Sit Down and Be Counted* (Dublin: Wellington)

Doorley, M. (2002) *Stella Days: 1957–1967. The Life and Times of a Rural Irish Cinema* (Nenagh: Dubhairle Publications)

Doyle, D. N. (1990) 'The Irish as Urban Pioneers in the United States, 1850–1870', *Journal of American Ethnic History*, 10, pp. 36–53

Doyle, R. (1991) *The Van* (London: Martin Secker and Warburg)

Doyle, R. (1992) *The Commitments* (London: Minerva)

Dudley Edwards, R. W. (1988/89) 'T. W. Moody and the Origins of Irish Historical Studies', *Irish Historical Studies*, xxvi, pp. 1–2

Duncan, J. (1990) *The City as Text: the Politics of Landscape Interpretation in the Kandyan Kingdom* (Cambridge: Cambridge University Press)

Dunne, T. (1992) 'New Histories: Beyond "Revisionism"', *The Irish Review*, 12, pp. 1–12

Dunphy, E. (1988) *Unforgettable Fire: The Story of U2* (London: Penguin)

Dunphy, R. (1995) *The Making of Fianna Fáil Power in Ireland, 1923–1948* (Oxford: Clarendon Press)

Durkheim, E. (1976) [1915] *The Elementary Forms of the Religious Life* (London: Allen and Unwin)

Dyreson, M. (1998) *Making the American Team: Sport, Culture and the Olympic Experience* (Chicago: University of Illinois Press)

Eagleton, T. (1976) *Criticism and Ideology: A Study in Marxist Literary Theory* (London: Verso)

Eagleton, T. (1984) *The Function of Criticism: From the Spectator to Post-Structuralism* (London: Verso)

Eagleton, T. (1995) *Heathcliff and the Great Hunger* (London: Verso)

Eagleton, T. (1997a) 'The Ideology of Irish Studies', *Bullán: An Irish Studies Journal*, 3: 1, pp. 5–14

Eagleton, T. (1997b) 'Rewriting Ireland', *Bullán: An Irish Studies Journal*, 3: 2, pp. 129–38

Eagleton, T. (1998) *Crazy John and the Bishop and Other Essays on Irish Culture* (Cork: Cork University Press)

Edge, A. (1999) *Faith of Our Fathers: Football as a Religion* (Edinburgh: Mainstream)

Edkins, J. (2003) *Trauma and the Memory of Politics* (Cambridge: Cambridge University Press)

Elliott, B. S. (1988) *Irish Migrants in the Canadas: A New Approach* (Montreal: McGill-Queens University Press)

Ellis, S. (1994) 'Nationalist Historiography and the English and Gaelic Worlds in the Late Middle Ages', in Brady C. (ed.), *Interpreting Irish History: The Debate on Historical Revisionism* (Dublin: Irish Academic Press), pp. 161–80

Emmons, D. M. (1989) *The Butte Irish: Class and Ethnicity in an American Mining Town, 1875–1925* (Chicago: University of Illinois Press)

English, R. (2003) *Armed Struggle: a History of the IRA* (London: Macmillan)

Fabricant, C. (2003) 'Swift the Irishman', in Fox, C. (ed.), *The Cambridge Companion to Jonathan Swift* (Cambridge: Cambridge University Press), pp. 48–72

Fahey, T. (1992) 'Catholicism and Industrial Society in Ireland', in Goldthorpe, J. H. and Whelan, C. T. (eds), *The Development of Industrial Society in Ireland* (Oxford: Oxford University Press), pp. 241–63

Fallon, B. (1998) *An Age of Innocence: Irish Culture 1930–1960* (Dublin: Gill and Macmillan)

Fanning, R. (1982) 'Irish Neutrality – an Historical Perspective', *Irish Studies in International Affairs*, 1: 3, pp. 27–38

Fanning, R. (1994) '"The Great Enchantment": Uses and Abuses of Modern Irish History', in Brady C. (ed.), *Interpreting Irish History: The Debate on Historical Revisionism* (Dublin: Irish Academic Press), pp. 146–60

Fanning, R. (2001) 'British and Irish Responses to Northern Ireland 1968–9', *Irish Studies in International Affairs*, 12, pp. 57–86

Farred, G. (2002) 'Long Distance Love: Growing Up a Liverpool Football Club Fan', *Journal of Sport and Social Issues*, 26: 1, pp. 6–24

Farrell, B. (ed.) (1984) *Communications and Community in Ireland* (Cork: Mercier Press)

Farrell, B. (ed.) (1988) *De Valera's Constitution and Ours* (Dublin: Gill and Macmillan)

Fauske, C. (2002) *Jonathan Swift and the Church of Ireland, 1710–1724* (Dublin: Irish Academic Press)

Fennell, D. (2003) *Cutting to the Point: Essays and Objections 1994–2003* (Dublin: Liffey Press)

Ferguson, S. (1834) 'Hardiman's Irish Minstrelsy', *Dublin University Magazine*, vols 3–4

Finnegan, R. (1989) *The Hidden Musicians: Music-making in an English Town* (Cambridge: Cambridge University Press)

Fitzgerald, M. (1985) 'Irish Studies and the Anglo-Irish Relationship', *Anglo-Irish Encounter, Conference on Irish Studies in Britain*, p. 14

Fitzpatrick, B. (1951) *The Australian People, 1788–1945* (Melbourne: Melbourne University Press)

Fitzpatrick, D. (1994) *Oceans of Consolation: Personal Accounts of Irish Migration to Australia* (Ithaca: Cornell University Press)

Fitzpatrick, D. (1997) 'Women and the Great Famine', in Kelleher, M. and Murphy, J. H. (eds), *Gender Perspectives in Nineteenth-Century Ireland* (Dublin: Irish Academic Press), pp. 50–69

Fitzpatrick, D. (1998) *The Two Irelands, 1912–1939* (Oxford: Opus)

Flannery, E. (2005) 'External Association: Ireland, Empire and Postcolonial Theory', *Third Text*, 19: 5, pp. 449–59

Fletcher, R. (2000) 'National Crisis, Supranational Opportunity: The Irish Construction of Abortion as a European Service', *Reproductive Health Matters*, 8: 16, pp. 35–44

Flynn, R. (2002) 'Broadcasting and the Celtic Tiger: From Promise to Practice', in Kirby, P., Gibbons, L. and Cronin, M. (eds), *Reinventing Ireland: Culture, Society and the New Economy* (London: Pluto Press), pp. 160–76

Foley, T. and Bateman, F. (eds) (2000) *Irish-Australian Studies: Papers Delivered at the Ninth Irish-Australian Conference, Galway, April 1997* (Sydney: Crossing Press)

Foster, J. W. (1991) *Colonial Consequences* (Mullingar: Lilliput Press)

Foster, R. F. (1994), 'History and the Irish Question', in Brady, C. (ed.), *Interpreting Irish History: The Debate on Historical Revisionism, 1938–1994* (Dublin: Irish Academic Press), pp. 122–45

Foster, R. F. (1997) *W. B. Yeats. A Life I: The Apprentice Mage* (Oxford: Oxford University Press)

Foster, R. F. (2001) *The Irish Story: Telling Tales and Making It Up in Ireland* (London: Allen Lane)

Foster, R. F. (2003) *W. B. Yeats. A Life II: The Arch-Poet* (Oxford: Oxford University Press)

Fraser, L. (ed.) (2000) *A Distant Shore: Irish Migration and New Zealand Settlement* (Dunedin: University of Otago Press)

Fraser, N. (1989) *Unruly Practices: Power, Discourse and Gender in Contemporary Social Theory* (Minneapolis: University of Minnesota Press)

Fraser, T. G. (ed.) (2000) *The Irish Parading Tradition* (Basingstoke: Macmillan)

Frazier, A. (2003) 'Revisiting the Rising', *Irish Times*, 12 July

Frith, S. (1996) 'Popular Music Policy and the Articulation of Regional Identities' in European Music Office (ed.), *Music in Europe* (Brussels: European Union), pp. 98–103

Fuller, L. (2002) *Irish Catholicism since 1950: The Undoing of a Culture* (Dublin: Gill and Macmillan)

Fussell, P. (1975) *The Great War and Modern Memory* (Oxford: Oxford University Press)

Gaffney, G. (1936a) 'The Girl Emigrant', *Irish Independent*, 7 December, p. 6

Gaffney, G. (1936b) 'The Girl Emigrant', *Irish Independent*, 15 December, p. 7

Garnham, N. (2002) 'Professionals and Professionalism in pre-Great War Irish Soccer', *Journal of Sports History*, 29: 1, pp. 77–93

Garrett, P. M. (2000) 'The Hidden History of the PFIs: the Repatriation of Unmarried Mothers and their Children from England to Ireland in the 1950s and 1960s', *Immigrants and Minorities*, 19: 3, pp. 25–44

Garvin, T. (1996) *1922. The Birth of Irish Democracy* (Dublin: Gill and Macmillan)

Geary, L. M. (ed.) (2001) *Rebellion and Remembrance in Modern Ireland* (Dublin: Four Courts)

Geertz, C. (1983) *Local Knowledge. Further Essays in Interpretive Anthropology* (New York: Basic Books)

Gibbons, L. (1988) 'Coming out of Hibernation? The Myth of Modernity in Irish Culture', in Kearney, R. (ed.), *Across the Frontiers: Ireland in the 1990s* (Dublin: Wolfhound Press), pp. 205–18

Gibbons, L. (1996) *Transformations in Irish Culture* (Cork: Cork University Press)

Gibbons, L. (1998) 'Ireland and the Colonization of Theory', *Interventions*, 1: 1, p. 27

Gibbons, L. (2003) *Edmund Burke and Ireland* (Cambridge: Cambridge University Press)

Giddens, A. (1990) *The Consequences of Modernity* (Cambridge: Polity Press)

Gilroy, P. (1997) 'Diaspora and the Detours of Identity', in Woodward, K. (ed.), *Identity and Difference* (London: Sage), pp. 299–343

Giulianotti, R. (1996) 'Back to the Future: an Ethnography of Ireland's Football Fans at the 1994 World Cup Finals in the USA', *International Review for the Sociology of Sport*, 31: 3, pp. 323–47

Glassie, H. (1982) *Passing the Time in Ballymenone* (Philadelphia: University of Pennsylvania Press)

Goffman, E. (1969) *The Presentation of Self in Everyday Life* (Harmondsworth: Penguin)

Goheen, P. (1990), 'Symbols in the Streets: Parades in Victorian Urban Canada', *Urban History Review*, 18, pp. 237–43

Goheen, P. (1993), 'Parading: a Lively Tradition in Early Victorian Toronto', in Baker, A. R. H. and Gideon, B. (eds) *Ideology and Landscape in Historical Perspective* (Cambridge: Cambridge University Press), pp. 330–51

Goldthorpe, J. H. and Whelan, C. T. (eds) (1992) *The Development of Industrial Society in Ireland* (Oxford: Oxford University Press)

Gorham, M. (1967) *Forty Years of Irish Broadcasting* (Dublin: Talbot Press)

Goulding, J. (1998) *A Light in the Window* (Dublin: Poolbeg)

Gouldner, A. (1979) *The Future of Intellectuals and the Rise of the New Class* (New York: Seabury Press)

Grace, R. J. (1993) *The Irish in Quebec: an Introduction to the Historiography Followed by an Annotated Bibliography* (Quebec: Institut Québécois de Recherche sur la Culture)

Graham, B. J. (1994) 'No Place of Mind: Contested Protestant Representations of Ulster', *Ecumene*, 1: 3, pp. 257–81

Graham, B. J. (ed.) (1997) *In Search of Ireland* (London: Routledge)

Graham, B. J. and Proudfoot, L. J. (eds) (1993) *An Historical Geography of Ireland* (London: Academic Press)

Graham, B. J. and Shirlow, P. (2002) 'The Battle of the Somme in Ulster Memory and Identity', *Political Geography*, 21, pp. 881–904

Graham, C. (1996) 'Post-colonial Theory and Kiberd's Ireland', *Irish Review*, 19, pp. 62–7

Graham, C. (1999) '...Maybe That's Just Blarney: Irish Culture and the Persistence of Authenticity', in Graham, C. and Kirkland, R. (eds), *Ireland and Cultural Theory. The Mechanics of Authenticity* (London: Macmillan), pp. 7–28

Graham, C. (2001) *Deconstructing Ireland: Identity, Theory, Culture* (Edinburgh: Edinburgh University Press)

Gramsci, A. (1971) *Selections from the Prison Notebooks*, ed. and trans. Q. Hoare and G. Nowell-Smith (London: Lawrence and Wishart)

Gray, B. (2000) 'Gendering the Irish Diaspora', *Women's Studies International Forum*, 23: 2, pp. 167–85

Gray, B. and Ryan, L. (1998) 'The Politics of Irish Identity and the Interconnections Between Feminism, Nationhood and Colonialism', in Roach Pierson, R. and Chaudhuri, N. (eds), *Nation, Empire, Colony* (Bloomington: Indiana University Press), pp. 121–38

Gray, P. (1995) *Famine, Land and Politics: British Government and Irish Society* (Dublin: Irish Academic Press)

Gregory, A. (1972) *Our Irish Theatre* (Gerrards Cross: Colin Smythe)

Gregory, D. (1994) *Geographical Imaginations* (Oxford: Blackwell)

Greiner, A. L. and Jordan-Bychkov, T. G. (2002) *Anglo-Celtic Australia: Colonial Immigration and Cultural Regionalism* (Sante Fe: Center for American Places), pp. 73–98

Guinnane, T. (1997) *The Vanishing Irish. Households, Migration, and the Rural Economy in Ireland, 1850–1914* (Princeton: Princeton University Press)

Habermas, J. (1989) *The Structural Transformation of the Public Sphere: An Inquiry into a Category of Bourgeois Society*, trans. T. Burger and F. Lawrence (Cambridge: Polity Press)

Hamilton, H. (2003) *The Speckled People* (London: Fourth Estate)

Hart, P. (1998) *The I.R.A. and its Enemies. Violence and Community in Cork 1916–1923* (Oxford: Oxford University Press)

Harte, L. (1997) 'A Kind of Scab: Irish Identity in the Writings of Dermot Bolger and Joseph O'Connor', *Irish Studies Review*, 20, pp. 17–22

Hassan, D. (2002) 'A People Apart: Soccer, Identity and Irish Nationalists in Northern Ireland', *Soccer and Society*, 3: 3, pp. 65–83

Hawes, C. (2004) 'Three Times Round the Globe: Gulliver and Colonial Discourse', in *Gulliver's Travels and Other Writings by Jonathan Swift*, ed. Hawes C. (Boston: Houghton Mifflin), pp. 438–64

Hayes, A., Rossiter, A. and Sexton, M. (2003) *Ireland's Hidden Diaspora: Irish Abortion Seekers in Britain* (London: Action Group for Irish Youth)

Healy, A. and McCaffrey, E. (2001) *St Thérèse in Ireland: Official Diary of the Irish Visit, April–July 2001* (Dublin: Columba)

Heaney, S. (2004) 'Preface', in Flanagan, T. *There You Are: Writings on Irish and American Literature and History* (New York: New York Review Books), pp. ix–xiii

Hederman, M. P. and Kearney, R. (1977) 'Editorial 1/Endodermis', *The Crane Bag*, 1: 1, pp. 3–5

Hewitt, J. (1974) *Rhyming Weavers, and Other Country Poets of Antrim and Down* (Belfast: Blackstaff Press)

Hickey, J. (1984) *Religion and the Northern Ireland Problem* (Dublin: Gill and Macmillan)

Higgins, G. and Brewer, J. (2003) 'The Roots of Sectarianism in Northern Ireland', in Hargie, O. and Dickson, D. (eds), *Researching the Troubles: Social Science Perspectives on the Northern Ireland Conflict* (Edinburgh: Mainstream), pp. 107–21

Hill, J., McLoone, M. and Hainsworth, P. (eds) (1994) *Border Crossing: Film in Ireland, Britain and Europe* (Belfast: Institute of Irish Studies)

Hobsbawm, E. (1994) *Age of Extremes. The Short Twentieth Century, 1914–1991* (London: Michael Joseph)

Hoppen, K. T. (1984) *Elections, Politics and Society in Ireland, 1832–1995* (Oxford: Clarendon Press)

Horgan, J. (2001) *Irish Media: A Critical History Since 1922* (London: Routledge)

Houston, C. J. and Smyth, W. J. (1980) *The Sash Canada Wore: A Historical Geography of the Orange Order in Canada* (Toronto: University of Toronto Press)

Houston, C. J. and Smyth W. J. (1990) *Irish Emigration and Canadian Settlement: Links, Patterns and Letters* (Toronto: University of Toronto Press)

Howe, S. (2000) *Ireland and Empire* (Oxford: Oxford University Press)

Hughes, E. (1987/88) 'The Irish Studies Centre at the Polytechnic of North London: The First Year', *British Association for Irish Studies Newsletter*, 1: 2, p. 21

Hunt, T. (2005) 'The Early Years of Gaelic Football and Cricket in County Westmeath', in Bairner, A. (ed.), *Sport and the Irish: Histories, Identities, Issues* (Dublin: UCD Press), pp. 22–43

Hussey, G. (1985) 'Speech by Mrs Gemma Hussey TD, Minister for Education', in *Anglo-Irish Encounter, Conference on Irish Studies in Britain*

Imhof, R. (2002) *The Modern Irish Novel: Irish Novelists after 1945* (Dublin: Wolfhound)

Inglis, T. (1980) 'Dimensions of Irish Students' Religiosity', *Economic and Social Review*, 11: 4, pp. 837–56

Inglis, T. (1998) *Moral Monopoly: The Rise and Fall of the Catholic Church in Modern Ireland* (Dublin: UCD Press; 2nd edn)

Inglis, T. (2003) 'Catholic Church, Religious Capital and Symbolic Domination', in Böss, M. and Maher, E. (eds), *Engaging Modernity: Readings of Irish Politics, Culture and Literature at the Turn of the Century* (Dublin: Veritas), pp. 43–70

Innes, C. L. (1993) *Woman and Nation in Irish Literature and Society* (London: Harvester Wheatsheaf)

Jackson, A. (1999) *Ireland 1798–1998* (Oxford: Blackwell)

Jackson, J. A. (1963) *The Irish In Britain* (London: Routledge and Kegan Paul)

Jacobsen, J. K. (1994) *Chasing Progress in the Irish Republic* (Cambridge: Cambridge University Press)

Jarman, N. (2001) 'Preface', in Kelly, W., *Murals: the Bogside Artists* (Derry: Guildhall Press), pp. 6–8

Jarman, N. and Bryan, D. (1998) *From Riots to Rights. Nationalist Parades in the North of Ireland* (University of Ulster: Centre for the Study of Conflict)

Jeffery, K. (2000) *Ireland and the Great War* (Cambridge: Cambridge University Press)

Jenkins, R. (1996) *Social Identity* (London: Routledge)

Jenkins, W. (2003) 'Between the Lodge and the Meeting-House: Mapping Irish Protestant Identities and Social Worlds in Late Victorian Toronto', *Social and Cultural Geography*, 4, pp. 75–98

Johnson, N. (2003) *Ireland, the Great War and the Geography of Remembrance* (Cambridge: Cambridge University Press)

Jones, I. (2000) 'A Model of Serious Leisure Identification: the Case of Football Fandom', *Leisure Studies*, 19, pp. 283–98

Jones, I. (2003) *Ned Kelly: A Short Life* (Melbourne: Lothian Books; 2nd edn)

Joyce, P. W. (1909) *Old Irish Folk Music and Songs* (Dublin: Dublin University Press)

Kaizen, W. R. (2001) 'Interview with Brian Tolle', *BOMB* 76, http://www.bombsite.com/tocsum01.html

Keane, J. (ed.) (1988) *Civil Society and the State: New European Perspectives* (London: Verso)

Keane, J. (1998) *Civil Society: Old Images, New Visions* (Cambridge: Cambridge)

Kearney, H. (1989) *The British Isles: A History of Four Nations* (Cambridge: Cambridge University Press)

Kearney, R. (1988) *Transitions: Narratives in Modern Irish Culture* (Manchester: Manchester University Press)

Kearns, G. (2004) 'Mother Ireland and the Revolutionary Sisters', *Cultural Geographies*, 11, pp. 443–67

Keating, A. (2003) 'The Legalisation of Adoption in Ireland', *Studies: Irish Quarterly Review*, 93: 371, pp. 172–82

Keating, M. F. (1954) 'The Marriage Shy Irish', in O'Brien, J. A. (ed.), *The Vanishing Irish* (London: W. H. Allen Press), pp. 164–76

Kelleher, M. (1997) *The Feminization of Famine. Expressions of the Inexpressible?* (Cork: Cork University Press)

Kelleher, M. (2002) 'Hunger and History: Monuments to the Great Irish Famine', *Textual Practice*, 16: 2, pp. 249–76

Kelleher, M. (2003) 'Introduction', *Irish University Review*, 33: 1, pp. viii–xii

Kelly, M. J. and O'Connor, B. (eds) (1997) *Media Audiences in Ireland* (Dublin: UCD Press)

Kelly, P. (2003) 'Swift on Money and Economics', in Fox, C. (ed.), *The Cambridge Companion to Jonathan Swift* (Cambridge: Cambridge University Press), pp. 128–45

Kelly, W. (2001) *Murals: the Bogside Artists* (Derry: Guildhall Press)

Kennedy, B. P. (1993) 'The Traditional Irish Thatched House: Image and Reality, 1793–1993', in Dalsimer, A. M. (ed.), *Visualizing Ireland. National Identity and the Pictorial Tradition* (Boston: Faber), pp. 165–80

Kennedy, L. (1996) *Colonialism, Religion and Nationalism in Ireland* (Belfast: Institute of Irish Studies)

Kennedy, M. (1996) *Ireland and the League of Nations 1919–1926* (Dublin: Irish Academic Press)

Kennedy, M. (2000) *Division and Consensus. The Politics of Cross-Border Relations in Ireland, 1925–1969* (Dublin: Institute of Public Administration)

Kenny, I. (1994) *Talking to Ourselves: Conversations with the Editors of the Irish News Media* (Galway: Kenny's Bookshop)

Kenny, K. (2000) *The American Irish. A History* (London: Longman)

Keogh, D. (1991) 'Mannix, de Valera and Irish Nationalism', in O'Brien, J. and Travers, P. (eds), *The Irish Emigrant Experience in Australia* (Dublin: Poolbeg), pp. 196–225

Keogh, D. (1994) *Twentieth-Century Ireland. Nation and State* (Dublin: Gill and Macmillan)

Keogh, D. and Whelan, K. (eds) (2001) *Acts of Union: The Causes, Contexts and Consequences of the Act of Union* (Dublin: Four Courts)

Keohane, K. (1997) 'Traditionalism and Homelessness in Contemporary Irish Music', in Mac Laughlin, J. (ed.), *Location and Dislocation in Contemporary Irish Society: Emigration and Irish Identities* (Cork: Cork University Press), pp. 274–303

Kerr, D. (1994) *'A Nation of Beggars'? Priests, People and Politics in Ireland 1846–52* (Oxford: Oxford University Press)

Keymer, T. (2002) *Sterne, the Moderns and the Novel* (Oxford: Oxford University Press)

Kiberd, D. (1995) *Inventing Ireland: The Literature of the Modern Nation* (London: Jonathan Cape)

Kiberd, D. (2000) *Irish Classics* (London: Granta)

Kiberd, D. (2005) *The Irish Writer and the World* (Cambridge: Cambridge University Press)

Kiernan, T. J. (1954) *The Irish Exiles in Australia* (Melbourne: Burns and Oates)

Kinealy, C. (1997) *A Death-Dealing Famine: the Great Hunger in Ireland* (London: Pluto Press)

Kinealy, C. (2001) *The Great Irish Famine. Impact, Ideology and Rebellion* (Basingstoke: Palgrave)

King, A. (2000) 'Football Fandom and Post-National Identity in the New Europe', *British Journal of Sociology*, 51: 3, pp. 419–42

Kirby, P. (1997) *Poverty Amid Plenty: World and Irish Development Reconsidered* (Dublin: Trocaire/Gill and Macmillan)

Kirby, P., Gibbons, L. and Cronin, M. (eds) (2002) *Reinventing Ireland: Culture, Society and the New Economy* (London: Pluto Press)

Kong, L. and Yeoh, B. (1997) 'The Construction of National Identity Through the Production of Ritual and Spectacle', *Political Geography*, 16, pp. 213–39

Kreilkamp, V. and Curtin, N. J. (1998) 'Introduction', *Éire-Ireland. Special Issue: The Visual Arts*, 33: 3 & 4, pp. 5–8

Kuper, H. (1972) 'The Language of Sites in the Politics of Space', *American Anthropologist*, 74, pp. 411–25

Lamb, J. (1989) *Sterne's Fiction and the Double Principle* (Cambridge: Cambridge University Press)

Lambert, S. (2003) 'Irish Women's Emigration to England, 1922–60', in Hayes, A. and Urquhart, D. (eds), *Irish Women's History* (Dublin: Irish Academic Press), pp. 152–67

Lee, J. J. (1989) *Ireland 1912–1985: Politics and Society* (Cambridge: Cambridge University Press)

Leerssen, J. (1986) *Mere Irish and Fíor-Ghaeil: Studies in the Idea of Irish Nationality, its Development and Literary Expression Prior to the Nineteenth Century* (Amsterdam: Benjamins)

Leerssen, J. (1996) *Remembrance and Imagination: Patterns in the Historical and Literary Representation of Ireland in the Nineteenth Century* (Cork: Cork University Press)

Leerssen, J. (2001) 'Monument and Trauma: Varieties of Remembrance', in McBride, I. (ed.), *History and Memory in Modern Ireland* (Cambridge: Cambridge University Press), pp. 204–22

Lentin, R. (1998) '"Irishness", the 1937 Constitution and Women: a Gender and Ethnicity View', *Irish Journal of Sociology*, 8, pp. 5–24

Leonard, J. (1996) *The Culture of Commemoration* (Dublin: Cultures of Ireland)

Ley, D. and Olds, K. (1988) 'Landscape as Spectacle: World's Fairs and the Culture of Heroic Consumption', *Environment and Planning D: Society and Space*, 6, pp. 191–212

Litton, H. (1994) *The Irish Famine. An Illustrated History* (Dublin: Wolfhound Press)

Llewellyn, M. (1998) 'Beyond the Transatlantic Model: A Look at Popular Music as if Small Societies Mattered', *Critical Musicology Journal. A Virtual Journal on the Internet* http://www.leeds.ac.uk/music/info/critmus/articles/1998/02/01.html

Lloyd, D. (1993) *Anomalous States: Irish Writing and the Post-colonial Moment* (Dublin: Lilliput Press)

Lloyd, D. (1999) *Ireland After History* (Cork: Cork University Press)

Lloyd, D. (2002) 'Colonial Trauma/Postcolonial Recovery', *Interventions*, 2: 2, pp. 212–28

Longley, E. (1986) *Poetry in the Wars* (Newcastle-upon-Tyne: Bloodaxe)

Luddy, M. (1995) *Women in Ireland 1800–1918: A Documentary History* (Cork: Cork University Press)

Luddy, M., Cox, C., Lane, L. and Urquhart, D. (1999) *A Directory of Sources of Women's History in Ireland* (Dublin: Manuscripts Commission) (Cd-rom)

Lukács, G. (1971) *History and Class Consciousness: Studies in Marxist Dialectics*, trans. R. Livingstone (Cambridge, MA: MIT Press)

Lydenberg, R. (2003) 'From Icon to Index: Some Contemporary Visions of the Irish Stone Cottage', in Kreilkamp, V. (ed.) *Eire/Land* (Chicago: University of Chicago Press), pp. 127–34

MacDonagh, O. (2001) 'The Irish in Victoria in the Nineteenth Century', in Jupp, J. (ed.), *The Australian People: an Encyclopedia of the Nation, its People and their Origins* (Cambridge: Cambridge University Press), pp. 467–71

Macherey, P. (1978) *A Theory of Literary Production* (London: Routledge and Kegan Paul)

Macintyre, S. and Clark, A. (2003) *The History Wars* (Melbourne: Melbourne University Press)

MacLaughlin, J. (1994) *Ireland: The Emigrant Nursery and the World Economy* (Cork: Cork University Press)

MacRaild, D. M. (1998) *Culture, Conflict and Migration: the Irish in Victorian Cumbria* (Liverpool: Liverpool University Press)

Madden, D. (1996) *One by One in the Darkness* (London: Faber and Faber)

Maddox, B (1996) 'A Fine Old Irish Stew', *New Statesman*, 29 November, pp. 21–2

Mahony, C. H. (2003) 'Funds, Faculties, and a Nostalgia Gap', *Irish Times Weekend*, 9 April, p. 9

Mandle, W. F. (1987) *The Gaelic Athletic Association and Irish Nationalist Politics* (London: Croom Helm)

Manne, R. (ed.) (2003) *Whitewash: On Keith Windschuttle's Fabrication of Aboriginal History* (Melbourne: Schwartz)

Mannion, J. (1974) *Irish Settlements in Eastern Canada: A Study of Cultural Transfer and Adaptation* (Toronto: University of Toronto Press)

Martin, A. K. (2000) 'Death of a Nation: Transnationalism, Bodies and Abortion in Late Twentieth Century Ireland', in Mayer, T. (ed.), *Gender Ironies of Nationalism* (London: Routledge), pp. 65–88

Mathews, P. J. (ed.) (2000) *New Voices in Irish Criticism* (Dublin: Four Courts Press)

Maume, P. (1999) *The Long Gestation. Irish Nationalist Life, 1891–1918* (Dublin: Gill and Macmillan)

McBride, I. (1997) *The Siege of Derry in Ulster Protestant Mythology* (Dublin: Four Courts)

McBride, I. (ed.) (2001) *History and Memory in Modern Ireland* (Cambridge: Cambridge University Press)

McCarthy, C. (2000) *Modernisation, Crisis and Culture in Ireland, 1969–1992* (Dublin: Four Courts)

McClaughlin, T. (ed.) (1998) *Irish Women in Colonial Australia* (Sydney: Allen and Unwin)

McConville, C. (1987) *Croppies, Celts and Catholics: the Irish in Australia* (Melbourne: Edward Arnold)

McCormack, W. J. (1984) 'Goldsmith, Biography and the Phenomenology of Anglo-Irish Literature', in Swarbrick, A. (ed.), *The Art of Oliver Goldsmith* (London: Vision Press), pp. 168–94

McCormack, W. J. (1986) *The Battle of the Books: Two Decades of Irish Cultural Debate* (Mullingar: Lilliput Press)

McCormack, W. J. (1994) *From Burke to Beckett: Ascendancy, Tradition and Betrayal in Literary History* (Cork: Cork University Press)

McCourt, F. (1996) *Angela's Ashes. A Memoir of a Childhood* (London: Flamingo)

McCullough, D. (1998) *A Makeshift Majority. The First Inter-Party Government, 1948–51* (Dublin: Institute of Public Administration)

McGarry, F. (1999) *Irish Politics and the Spanish Civil War* (Cork: Cork University Press)

McGarry, J. and O'Leary, B. (1995) *Explaining Northern Ireland* (Oxford: Blackwell)

McGinley, M. E. R. (1991) 'The Irish in Queensland: an Overview', in O'Brien, J. and Travers, P. (eds), *The Irish Emigrant Experience in Australia* (Dublin: Poolbeg), pp. 103–19

McGuigan, J. (1999) *Modernity and Postmodern Culture* (Buckingham: Open University Press)

McIlroy, B. (1998) *Shooting to Kill: Filmmaking and the 'Troubles' in Northern Ireland* (Trowbridge: Flicks Books)

McIlroy, B. (1989) *Ireland, World Cinema 4* (Trowbridge: Flicks Books)

McIntosh, G. (1999) *The Force of Culture: Unionist Identities in Twentieth-Century Ireland* (Cork: Cork University Press)

McKibbin, R. (1998) *Classes and Cultures: England 1918–51* (Oxford: Oxford University Press)

McKillop, J. (ed.) (1999) *Contemporary Irish Cinema* (Syracuse: Syracuse University Press)

McLaughlin, N. and McLoone, M. (2000) 'Hybridity and National Musics: the Case of Irish Rock Music', *Popular Music*, 19: 2, pp. 181–200

McLoone, M. (2000) *Irish Film: The Emergence of a Contemporary Cinema* (London: British Film Institute)

McLoone, M. and MacMahon, J. (eds) (1984) *Irish Television and Society* (Dublin: RTÉ/Irish Film Institute)

McMullin, R. (1991) *The Light on the Hill: the Australian Labor Party, 1891–1991* (Melbourne: Oxford University Press)

Meaney, G. (1991) *Sex and Nation: Women in Irish Culture and Politics* (Dublin: Attic Press)

Megahey, A. (2000) *The Irish Protestant Churches in the Twentieth Century* (Basingstoke: Macmillan)

Mellin, R. (2003) *Tilting* (New York: Princeton Architectural Press)

Mennell, S., Elliot, M., Stokes, P., Rickard, A. and Malley-Dunlop, E. (2000) 'Protestants in a Catholic State – A Silent Minority in Ireland', in Inglis, T., Mach, Z. and Mazanek, R. (eds), *Religion and Politics: East–West Contrasts from Contemporary Europe* (Dublin: UCD Press), pp. 68–92

Merton, R. K. (1957) *Social Theory and Social Structure* (New York: Free Press)

Miller, K. A. (1985) *Emigrants and Exiles: Ireland and the Irish Exodus to North America* (New York: Oxford University Press)

Miller, K. A., Schrier, A., Boling, B. and Doyle, D. N. (2003) *Irish Immigrants in the Land of Canaan. Letters and Memoirs from Colonial and Revolutionary America, 1675–1815* (Oxford: Oxford University Press)

Mitchell, A. (1995) *Revolutionary Government in Ireland. Dáil Éireann 1919–22* (Dublin: Gill and Macmillan)

Mitchell, C. (2003) 'Catholicism in Northern Ireland and the Politics of Conflict', Paper presented to Institute for British-Irish Studies, University College Dublin

Molloy, F. (2001) 'The Celtic Twilight in Australia', *The Australian Journal of Irish Studies*, 1, pp. 99–106

Molloy, F. (2002) '"Affection's Broken Chain": the Irish and Colonial Poetry', *The Australian Journal of Irish Studies*, 2, pp. 122–34

Moore, B. (1988) [1955] *The Lonely Passion of Judith Hearne* (London: Paladin Books)

Morash, C. (1995) *Writing the Irish Famine* (Oxford: Clarendon Press)

Morash, C. and Hayes, R. (eds) (1996) *'Fearful Realities': New Perspectives on the Famine* (Dublin: Irish Academic Press)

Morrissey, J. (2003) *Negotiating Colonialism* (London: Royal Geographical Society)

Morrissey, J. (2005) 'Cultural Geographies of the Contact Zone: Gaels, Galls and Overlapping Territories in Late Medieval Ireland', *Social and Cultural Geography*, 6, pp. 551–66

Moser, P. (1993) 'Rural Economy and Female Emigration in the West of Ireland', *UCG Women's Studies Centre Review*, 2, pp. 41–51

Mouton, M. and Pohlandt-McCormick, H. (1999) 'Boundary Crossing: Oral History of Nazi Germany and Apartheid South Africa', *History Workshop Journal*, 48, pp. 41–63

Mulhern, F. (1998) *The Present Lasts a Long Time: Essays in Cultural Politics* (Cork: Cork University Press)

Mulholland, M. (2000) *Northern Ireland at the Crossroads. Ulster Unionism in the O'Neill Years 1960–9* (Basingstoke: Palgrave)

Mulryan, P. (1988) *Radio Radio* (Dublin: Borderline)

Mulvey, H. F. (1984/85) 'Theodore William Moody (1907–1984): An Appreciation', *Irish Historical Studies*, xxiv, pp. 121–30

Murray, P. (2000) *Oracles of God. The Roman Catholic Church and Irish Politics, 1922–37* (Dublin: UCD Press)

Nairn, T. (1998) *Faces of Nationalism: Janus Revisited* (London: Verso)

Nally, D. (2004) 'Geography in Ireland in Transition – Some Comments', *Irish Geography*, 37: 2, pp. 131–4

Nash, C. (1993) 'Embodying the Nation: the West of Ireland Landscape and Irish Identity', in Cronin, M. and O'Connor, B. (eds), *Tourism in Ireland: A Critical Analysis* (Cork: Cork University Press), pp. 86–114

Nash, C. (1997) 'Embodied Irishness: Gender, Sexuality and Irish Identity', in Graham, B. J. (ed.), *In Search of Ireland* (London: Routledge), pp. 108–27

Neal, F. (1998) *Black '47: Britain and the Famine Irish* (London: Macmillan)

Negt, O. and Kluge, A. (1993) *Public Sphere and Experience: Toward an Analysis of the Bourgeois and Proletarian Public Sphere*, trans. P. Labanyi (Minneapolis: University of Minnesota Press)

Nic Ghiolla Phadraig, M. (1976) 'Religion in Ireland: Preliminary Analysis', *Social Studies*, 5: 2, pp. 113–80

Nolan, B., O'Connell, P. J. and Whelan, C. T. (eds) (2000) *Bust to Boom? The Irish Experience of Growth and Inequality* (Dublin: Institute of Public Administration)

Nolan, E. (2000) 'State of the Art: Joyce and Postcolonialism', in Attridge, D. and Howes, M. (eds), *Semicolonial Joyce* (Cambridge: Cambridge University Press), pp. 78–95

Novick, P. (2000) *The Holocaust and Collective Memory* (London: Bloomsbury)

O'Brien, E. (2003) Review of *Deconstructing Ireland: Identity, Theory, Culture* by C. Graham, *Irish University Review*, 33: 1, pp. 222–4

O'Brien, H. (2004) *The Real Ireland: The Evolution of Ireland in Documentary Film* (Manchester: Manchester University Press)

Ó Buachalla, B. (1996) *Aisling Ghéar: Na Stiobhartaigh agus an t-Aos Léinn, 1603–1788* (Baile Átha Cliath: Clóchomhar)

O Cíosáin, N. (1997) *Print and Popular Culture in Ireland, 1750–1800* (Basingstoke: Macmillan)

O'Connor, C. (1985) *Christy O'Connor: His Autobiography* (Dublin: Gill and Macmillan)

O'Connor, J. (1991) *Cowboys and Indians* (London: Flamingo)

O'Connor, J. (1994) *The Secret World of the Irish Male* (Dublin: New Island Books)

O'Connor, J. (2002) *Star of the Sea* (London: Secker and Warburg)

O'Dowd, L. (1988) 'Neglecting the Material Dimension: Irish Intellectuals and the Problem of Identity', *Irish Review*, 3, pp. 8–17

O'Dowd, L. (1991) 'The States of Ireland: Some Reflections on Research', *Irish Journal of Sociology*, 1, pp. 96–106

O'Driscoll, R. (1987) 'A Greater Renaissance: The Revolt of the Soul Against the Intellect', in Zach, W. and Kosok, H. (eds), *Literary Interrelations, Ireland, England and the World. Volume 3, National Images and Stereotypes* (Tubingen: Gunter Narr Verlag)

O'Farrell, P. (2000) *The Irish in Australia, 1788 to the Present* (Sydney: UNSW Press; 3rd edn)

O'Gallagher, M. (1984) *Grosse Île: Gateway to Canada, 1832–1937* (Quebec: Carraig Books)

O'Gallagher, M. and Masson Dompierre, R. (1995) *Eyewitness Grosse Île 1847* (Quebec, Carraig Books)

Ó Gráda, C. (1994) *An Dhrochshaol: Béaloideas agus Amhráin* (Baile Átha Cliath: Coiscéim)

Ó Gráda, C. (1999) *Black '47 and Beyond: the Great Irish Famine in History, Economy and Memory* (Princeton: Princeton University Press)

O'Halpin, E. (1999) *Defending Ireland. The Irish State and its Enemies Since 1922* (Oxford: Oxford University Press)

Ó hAnnracháin, T. (2002) *Catholic Reformation in Ireland: the Mission of Rinnucini* (Oxford: Oxford University Press)

O'Hearn, D. (1998) *Inside the Celtic Tiger: The Irish Economy and the Asian Model* (London: Pluto Press)

Ohlmeyer, J. (1993) *Civil War and Restoration in Three Stuart Kingdoms* (Cambridge: Cambridge University Press)

O Laoghaire, L. (1945) *Invitation to Film* (Tralee: The Kerryman)

O'Leary, B. (1999) 'The Nature of the British-Irish Agreement', *New Left Review*, 233, pp. 66–96

O'Leary, R. (2000) 'The President's Communion', in Slater, E. and Peillon, M. (eds), *Memories of the Present: A Sociological Chronicle of Ireland 1997–1998* (Dublin: Institute of Public Administration), pp. 145–52

O'Malley, P. (1990) *Northern Ireland: Questions of Nuance* (Belfast: Blackstaff)

Ó Maolfabhail, A. (1973) *Camán: 2,000 Years of Hurling in Ireland* (Dundalk: Dundalgan Press)

O'Neill, K. (2001) 'The Star-Spangled Shamrock: Memory and Meaning in Irish America', in McBride, I. (ed.), *History and Memory in Modern Ireland* (Cambridge: Cambridge Unviersity Press), pp. 118–38

O'Reilly, E. (1988) *Masterminds of the Right* (Dublin: Attic Press)

O'Riordan, M. (1990) *The Gaelic Mind and the Collapse of the Gaelic World* (Cork: Cork University Press)

Orr, D. and Whitaker, K. (1985) 'Foreword', *Anglo-Irish Encounter, Conference on Irish Studies in Britain*, St Peter's College, Oxford, 20–22 September

Ó Súilleabháin, M. (1981) 'Irish Music Defined', *The Crane Bag*, 5: 2, pp. 83–7

Ó Súilleabháin, M. (1998) '"Around the House and Mind the Cosmos": Music, Dance and Identity in Contemporary Ireland', in Pine, R. (ed.), *Music in Ireland 1848–1998* (Cork: Mercier Press), pp. 76–86

O'Sullivan, P. (ed.) (1996) *The Meaning of the Famine* (Leicester: Leicester University Press)

O'Sullivan, P. (1997) 'Irish Studies *vs* Irish Diaspora Studies', http://www.brad. ac.uk/acad/diaspora

O'Toole, F. (1982) 'The Man from God Knows Where. An Interview with Brian Friel', *In Dublin*, 28 October, pp. 20–3

O'Toole, M. (1992) *More Kicks than Pence: A Life in Irish Journalism* (Dublin: Poolbeg Press)

Ó Tuathaigh, G. (1984) 'The Media and Irish Culture', in Farrell, B. (ed.), *Communication and Community in Ireland* (Cork: Mercier Press), pp. 97–110

Palmer, P. A. (2001) *Language and Conquest in Early Modern Ireland* (Cambridge: Cambridge University Press)

Parkhill, T. (2002/03) '"That's Their History": Can a Museum's Historical Programme Inform the Reconciliation Process in a Divided Society?', *Folk Life*, 41, pp. 37–44

Partlon, A. (2000) '"Singers Standing on the Outer Rim": Writing about the Irish in WA', in Reece, B. (ed.), *The Irish in Western Australia: Studies in Western Australian History*, 20, pp. 188–90

Paschel, U. (1998) *No Mean City? The Image of Dublin in the Novels of Dermot Bolger, Roddy Doyle and Val Mulkerns* (Frankfurt: Peter Lang)

Patterson, B. (ed.) (2002) *The Irish in New Zealand: Historical Contexts and Perspectives* (Wellington: Victoria University)

Paulin, T. (1984) *Ireland and the English Crisis* (Newcastle-upon-Tyne: Bloodaxe)

Peillon, M. (2002) 'Culture and State in Ireland's New Economy', in Kirby, P., Gibbons, L. and Cronin, M. (eds), *Reinventing Ireland: Culture, Society and the New Economy* (London: Pluto Press), pp. 38–53

Peillon, M. and Slater, E. (eds) (1998) *Encounters with Modern Ireland: A Sociological Chronicle 1995–96* (Dublin: Institute of Public Administration)

Petrie, G. (2002) [1855] *The Petrie Collection of the Ancient Music of Ireland* (Cork: Cork University Press)

Pettitt, L. (2000) *Screening Ireland: Film and Television Representation* (Manchester: Manchester University Press)

Pettitt, L. (2001) 'Introduction', Special Issue: Cinema and Television, *Irish Studies Review*, 9: 2, pp. 150–3

Pine, R. (2002) *2RN and the Origins of Irish Radio* (Dublin: Four Courts)

Plunkett, J. (1969) *Strumpet City* (London: Panther)

Pocius, G. (1991) *A Place to Belong: Community Order and Everyday Space in Calvert, Newfoundland* (Athens: University of Georgia Press)

Pocock, J. G. A. (1975) 'British History: a Plea for a New Subject', *Journal of Modern History*, 47: 4, pp. 601–21

Pocock, J. G. A. (2005) *The Discovery of Islands: Essays in British History* (Cambridge: Cambridge University Press)

Pope, S. W. (1997) *Patriotic Games: Sporting Traditions in the American Imagination, 1876–1926* (New York: Oxford University Press)

Portéir, C. (1995a) *Glórtha ón Ghorta* (Dublin: Coiscéim)

Portéir, C. (1995b) *Gneithe den Ghorta Eagarthoir* (Dublin: Coiscéim)

Potts, S. (2001) *Paidí Ó Sé* (Dublin: Townhouse)

Powell, J. (1990) *Desert Orchid: Story of a Champion* (London: Hutchinson)

Prendergast, M. J. (1987) *Irish Rock: Roots, Personalities, Directions* (Dublin: O'Brien Press)

Quinn, B. (2001) *Maverick: A Dissident View of Broadcasting Today* (Dingle: Brandon)

Radstone, S. (ed.) (2000) *Memory and Methodology* (Oxford: Berg)

Raftery, M. and O'Sullivan, E. (1999) *Suffer the Little Children. The Inside Story of Ireland's Industrial Schools* (Dublin: New Island)

Ramsay Silver, L. (2002) *Australia's Irish Rebellion: the Battle of Vinegar Hill, 1804* (Sydney: Watermark Press; 2nd edn)

Readings, B. (1996) *The University in Ruins* (Cambridge, MA: Harvard University Press)

Redhead, S. (1997) *Post-Fandom and the Millenial Blues: The Transformation of Soccer Culture* (London: Routledge)

Reece, B. (ed.) (1989) *Irish Convicts: the Origins of Convicts Transported to Australia* (Dublin: Trinity College Dublin)

Reece, B. (ed.) (1993) *Irish Convict Lives* (Sydney: Crossing Press)

Reece, B. (2000a) 'The Irish and the Aborigines', in Foley, T. and Bateman, F. (eds), *Irish-Australian Studies: Papers Delivered at the Ninth Irish-Australian Conference, Galway, April 1997* (Sydney: Crossing Press), pp. 192–204

Reece, B. (ed.) (2000b) The Irish in Western Australia: Studies in Western Australian History 20 (Crawley: University of Western Australia Press)

Regan, J. M. (1999) *The Irish Counter-Revolution, 1921–1936. Treatyite Politics and Settlement in Independent Ireland* (Dublin: Gill and Macmillan)

Retallack, G. B. (1999) 'Razors, Shavers and Gender Construction: An Inquiry into the Material Culture of Shaving', *Material History Review*, 49, pp. 4–19

Retallack, G. B. (2002/03) 'Paddy, the Priest, and the Habitant: Inflecting the Irish Cartoon Stereotype in Canada', *Canadian Journal of Irish Studies*, 28: 2/29: 1, pp. 124–47

Richards, E. (1991) 'Irish Life and Progress in Colonial South Australia', *Irish Historical Studies*, xxvii: 107, pp. 216–36

Richards, E. (1998) 'Irish in Australia', in Davison, G., Hirst J. and Macintyre, S. (eds), *The Oxford Companion to Australian History* (Melbourne: Oxford University Press), pp. 350–1

Richards, S. (1999) 'Foreword', in Brewster, S., Crossman, V., Becket, F. and Alderson, D. (eds), *Ireland in Proximity: History, Gender, Space* (London: Routledge), pp. xi–xv

Richman Kenneally, R. (2003) 'Now You Don't See it, Now You Do: Situating the Irish in the Material Culture of Grosse Île', *Éire-Ireland*, 38: 3/4, pp. 33–53

Richtarik, M. (1994) *Acting Between the Lines: The Field Day Theatre Company and Irish Cultural Politics 1980–1984* (Oxford: Clarendon Press)

Ricoeur, P. (1992) *Oneself as Another* (Chicago: University of Chicago Press)

Robbins, C. (2004) *The Empress of Ireland: Chronicle of an Unusual Friendship* (London: Scribner)

Rolston, B. (2001) '"This Is Not a Rebel Song": the Irish Conflict and Popular Music', *Race and Class*, 42: 3, pp. 49–67

Rolston, B. (2003) 'Changing the Political Landscape: Murals and Transition in Northern Ireland', *Irish Studies Review*, 11: 1, pp. 3–16

Ronayne, J. (2002) *First Fleet to Federation: Irish Supremacy in Colonial Australia* (Dublin: Trinity College Press)

Ronsley, J. (1999) 'The Canadian Association for Irish Studies, 1968–1990: A History', *Canadian Journal of Irish Studies*, 25: 1/2, pp. 1–20

RTÉ Prime Time/TNS MRBI (2003) *Religious Issues Poll: Report of Findings* (Dublin: TNS MRBI)

Rudin, R. (1994) 'One Model, Two Responses: Quebec, Ireland and the Study of Rural Society', *Canadian Papers in Rural History*, 9, pp. 259–89

Rudin, R. (1997) 'Contested Terrain: Commemorative Celebrations and National Identity in Ireland and Quebec', in Bouchard, G. and Lamonde, Y. (eds), *La Nation Dans Tous Ses États: Le Quebec en Comparaison* (Montreal: Harmattan), pp. 183–204

Rule, P. (2000) 'Challenging Conventions: Irish-Chinese Marriages in Colonial Victoria', in Foley, T. and Bateman, F. (eds), *Irish-Australian Studies: Papers Delivered at the Ninth Irish-Australian Conference, Galway, April 1997* (Sydney: Crossing Press), pp. 205–16

Russell, C. (1990) *The Fall of the British Monarchy, 1637–1642* (Oxford: Oxford University Press)

Ryan, L. (1996) 'The Massacre of Innocence: Infanticide in the Irish Free State', *Irish Studies Review*, 14, pp. 17–20

Ryan, L. (2002a) 'Sexualising Emigration: Discourses of Irish Women's Emigration in the 1930s', *Women's Studies International Forum*, 25: 1, pp. 51–65

Ryan, L. (2002b) 'I'm going to England: Women's Narratives of Leaving Ireland in the 1930s', *Oral History*, 30: 1, pp. 42–53

Ryan, L. (2002c) *Gender, Identity and the Irish Press 1922–37: Embodying the Nation* (New York: Edwin Mellen Press)

Ryan, L. (2003) 'The Press, Police and Prosecution: Perspectives on Infanticide in the 1920s', in Hayes, A. and Urquhart, D. (eds), *Irish Women's History* (Dublin: Irish Academic Press), pp. 137–51

Ryan, R. (2002) *Ireland and Scotland: Literature and Culture, State and Nation, 1966–2000* (Oxford: Oxford University Press)

Said, E. (1984) *The World, the Text, and the Critic* (London: Faber)

Said, E. (1993) *Culture and Imperialism* (London: Chatto and Windus)

Salmon, T. (1989) *Unneutral Ireland* (Oxford: Clarendon Press)

Savage, R. (1996) *Irish Television: The Political and Social Origins* (Cork: Cork University Press)

Schrier, A. (1958) *Ireland and the American Emigration 1850–1900* (Minneapolis: University of Minnesota Press)

Scott, E. (1947) *A Short History of Australia* (Melbourne: Oxford University Press)

Schama, S. (2002) 'Pangs: A Patch of Earth', *The New Yorker*, 19 and 26 August, pp. 58, 60

See, S. W. (1993) *Riots in New Brunswick: Orange Nativism and Social Violence in the 1840s* (Toronto: University of Toronto Press)

Sharkey, S. (1993) *Ireland and the Iconography of Rape* (London: UNL Press)

Sharkey, S. (1997a) 'A View of the Present State of Irish Studies', in Bassnett, S. (ed.), *Studying British Cultures: An Introduction* (London: Routledge), pp. 113–34

Sharkey, S. (1997b) 'Irish Cultural Studies and the Politics of Irish Studies', in McGuigan, J. (ed.), *Cultural Methodologies* (London: Sage), pp. 155–77

Simms, A. (2000) 'Perspectives on Irish Settlement Studies', in Barry, T. (ed.), *A History of Settlement in Ireland* (London: Routledge), pp. 228–47

Skelly, J. M. (1997) *Irish Diplomacy at the United Nations, 1945–1965* (Dublin: Irish Academic Press)

Skilbeck, M. (2001) *The University Challenged: A Review of International Trends and Issues with Particular Reference to Ireland* (Dublin: Higher Education Authority)

Slide, A. (1988) *The Cinema and Ireland* (Jefferson, NC: McFarland and Company)

Smith, T. (2000) 'The Fragmentation of Irish Musical Thought and the Marginalisation of Traditional Music', *Studies: Irish Quarterly Review*, 89: 354, pp. 149–58

Smyth, A. (1992) 'A Sadist Farce: Women and Abortion in the Republic of Ireland', in Smyth, A. (ed.), *The Abortion Papers Ireland* (Dublin: Attic Press), pp. 7–24

Smyth, G. (1992) 'Who's the Greenest of Them All? Irishness and Popular Music', *Irish Studies Review*, 2, pp. 3–5

Smyth, G. (1996) '"The natural course of things": Matthew Arnold, Celticism, and the English Poetic Tradition', *The Journal of Victorian Culture*, 1: 1, pp. 35–53

Smyth, G. (1997) *The Novel and the Nation. Studies in the New Irish Fiction* (London: Pluto Press)

Smyth, G. (1998) *Decolonisation and Criticism: The Construction of Irish Literature* (London: Pluto Press)

Smyth, G. (2001) *Space and the Irish Cultural Imagination* (Basingstoke: Palgrave)

Smyth, G. (2004) 'Introduction', *Irish Studies Review*, 12: 1, pp. 3–10

Smyth, G. (2005) *Noisy Island: A Critical History of Irish Rock Music* (Cork: Cork University Press)

Smyth, L. (1998) 'Narratives of Irishness and the Problem of Abortion: The X case 1992', *Feminist Review*, 60, pp. 61–83

Smyth, W. J. (1997) 'A Plurality of Irelands: Regions, Societies, Mentalities', in Graham, B. J. (ed.), *In Search of Ireland* (London: Routledge), pp. 1–15

Soja, E. W. (1989) *Postmodern Geographies* (London: Verso)

Sommers Smith, S. K. (2001) 'Irish Traditional Music in a Modern World', *New Hibernia Review*, 5: 2, pp. 111–25

Southerton, D. (2002) 'Boundaries of "Us" and "Them": Class, Mobility and Identification in a New Town', *Sociology*, 36: 1, pp. 171–93

Stebbins, R. (1997) 'Serious Leisure and Well-being', in Haworth, J. (ed.), *Leisure and Well-being* (London: Routledge), pp. 117–30

Stith Bennett, H. (1980) *On Becoming a Rock Musician* (Amherst: University of Massachusetts Press)

Stokes, M. (ed.) (1994) *Ethnicity, Identity and Music: The Musical Construction of Place* (Oxford: Berg)

Stout, G. (2002) *Newgrange and the Bend of the Boyne* (Cork: Cork University Press)

Sugden, J. and Bairner, A. (1993) *Sport, Sectarianism and Society in Ireland* (Leicester: Leicester University Press)

Swift, R. (ed.) (2002) *Irish Migrants in Britain, 1815–1914. A Documentary History* (Cork: Cork University Press)

Swingewood, A. (1998) *Cultural Theory and the Problem of Modernity* (Basingstoke: Macmillan)

Tanner, M. (2003) *Mick The Miller: Sporting Icon of the Depression* (London: Highdown)

Taylor, C. (1995) *Philosophical Arguments* (Cambridge, MA: Harvard University Press)

Taylor, T. D. (1998) 'Living in a Postcolonial World: Class and Soul in *The Commitments*', *Irish Studies Review*, 6: 3, pp. 291–302

Thompson, J. B. (1995) *The Media and Modernity* (Cambridge: Polity Press)

Townshend, C. (1999) *Ireland: The 20th Century* (London: Arnold)

Ulster Museum (1998) *Up in Arms, The 1798 Rebellion in Ireland. A Bicentenary Exhibition* (Belfast: Ulster Museum)

Valente, J. (2000) 'Neither Fish nor Flesh; or How "Cyclops" Stages the Double-bind of Irish Manhood', in Attridge, D. and Howes, M. (eds), *Semicolonial Joyce* (Cambridge: Cambridge University Press), pp. 96–127

Valiulis, M. (1995) 'Gender, Power and Identity in the Irish Free State', in Hoff, J. and Coulter, M. (eds), *Irish Women's Voices* (Bloomington: Indiana University Press), pp. 117–36

Valone, D. A. and Kinealy, C. (eds) (2002) *Ireland's Great Hunger: Silence, Memory and Commemoration* (Lanham, MD: University Press of America)

Waldersee, J. (1974) *Catholic Society in New South Wales, 1788–1860* (Sydney: Sydney University Press)

Walter, B. (2001) *Outsiders Inside: Whiteness, Place and Irish Women* (London: Routledge)

Walter, B. (2005) 'Exploring Diaspora Space: Entangled Irish/English Genealogies', in Harte, L., Whelan, Y. and Crotty, P. (eds), *Ireland: Space, Text, Time* (Dublin: Liffey Press), pp. 157–76

Ward, R. (1966) *The Australian Legend* (Melbourne: Oxford University Press; 2nd edn)

Waters, J. (1994) *Race of Angels: Ireland and the Genesis of U2* (Belfast: Blackstaff Press)

Watson, A. (2003) *Broadcasting in Irish* (Dublin: Four Courts)

Watson, G. J. (1979) *Irish Identity and the Literary Revival* (London: Croom Helm)

Weaver, J. W. (1998) *Joyce's Music and Noise: Theme and Variation in his Writings* (Tallahassee: University Press of Florida)

Weber, M. (1978) *Economy and Society*, 2 vols (ed.), Roth, G. and Wittich, C. (Berkeley: University of California Press)

Whelan, K. (1996) *The Tree of Liberty: Radicalism, Catholicism and the Construction of Irish Identity, 1760–1830* (Cork: Cork University Press)

Whelan, K. (1998) *Fellowship of Freedom: The United Irishmen and the 1798 Rebellion* (Cork: Cork University Press)

Whelan K. (2001) 'The Colossus of Clonegal: Interview with Kevin Whelan', in *History Ireland*, 9: 4, pp. 42–5

Whelan, Y. (2003) *Reinventing Modern Dublin: Streetscape, Iconography and the Politics of Identity* (Dublin: UCD Press)

White, C. (2001) *Reading Roddy Doyle* (Syracuse: Syracuse University Press)

White, H. (1998) *The Keeper's Recital: Music and Cultural History in Ireland, 1770–1970* (Cork: Cork University Press)

White, J. (2000) 'Pat Murphy's *Maeve* and Michael Brault's *Les Ordres*', *Canadian Journal of Irish Studies*, 26: 2, pp. 89–103

Whyte, J. H. (1980) *Church and State in Modern Ireland 1923–1979* (Dublin: Gill and Macmillan)

Wilson, C. A. (1994) *A New Lease on Life: Landlords, Tenants and Immigrants in Ireland and Canada* (Montreal: McGill-Queens University Press)

Windsor, G. (1983) 'Grafting Ireland onto Australia: Some Literary Attempts', in MacDonagh, O., Mandle, W. F. and Travers, P. (eds), *Irish Culture and Nationalism, 1750–1950* (London: Macmillan), pp. 194–211

Young, J. E. (1993) *The Texture of Memory. Holocaust Memorials and Meaning* (New Haven: Yale University Press)

Young, R. (1994) 'Reviews', *Wasafiri*, 20, pp. 77–8

Yuval-Davis, N. (1993) 'Gender and Nation', *Ethnic and Racial Studies*, 16: 4, pp. 621–32

Yuval-Davis, N. (1997) *Gender and Nation* (London: Sage)

Notes on Contributors

Michael Brown is Lecturer in Irish and Scottish History at the University of Aberdeen. He is the author of *Francis Hutcheson in Dublin, 1719–1730: The Crucible of his Thought* (2002) and co-editor, with Patrick M. Geoghegan and James Kelly, of *The Irish Act of Union: Bicentennial Essays* (2003). He has also co-edited *Converts and Conversion in Ireland, 1650–1850* (2005) with Charles Ivar McGrath and Thomas P. Power, and is currently writing a study of the Irish Enlightenment.

Mike Cronin is Professor and Academic Director of Irish Studies at Boston College, Dublin. His publications include *The Blueshirts and Irish Politics* (1997), *Sport and Nationalism in Ireland: Gaelic Games, Soccer and Identity since 1884* (1999) and *Wearing the Green: A History of St. Patrick's Day* (2002), co-authored with Daryl Adair. He is currently researching the history of Irish state formation and the national image during the period 1922–66.

Mary E. Daly is Professor of History and Principal of the College of Arts and Celtic Studies at University College Dublin. Her many publications include *The Famine in Ireland* (1986), *Industrial Development and Irish National Identity* (1992), *The First Department: A History of the Department of Agriculture* (2002) and *Roger Casement in Irish and World History* (2005).

Liam Harte is Lecturer in Irish and Modern Literature at the University of Manchester. He is co-editor with Michael Parker of *Contemporary Irish Fiction: Themes, Tropes, Theories* (2000) and joint editor with Patrick Crotty and Yvonne Whelan of *Ireland: Space, Text, Time* (2005). His edited volume, *Modern Irish Autobiography: Self, Nation and Society*, is forthcoming from Palgrave Macmillan.

Tom Inglis is Associate Professor of Sociology at University College Dublin. He is the author of *Moral Monopoly: The Rise and Fall of the Catholic Church in Ireland* (1998) and *Lessons in Irish Sexuality* (1998). His most recent book is *Truth, Power and Lies: Irish Society and the Case of the Kerry Babies* (2003). He is a research director of the Identity, Diversity and Citizenship project at UCD, a qualitative study of the transformations in identities in the island of Ireland.

Michael Kenneally is Chair in Canadian Irish Studies at the Centre for Canadian Irish Studies, Concordia University, Montreal. He is the author of *Portraying the Self: Sean O'Casey and the Art of Autobiography* (1987) and editor of three essay collections on Irish writing: *Cultural Contexts and Literary Idioms in Contemporary Irish Literature* (1988), *Irish Literature and Culture* (1992) and *Poetry in Contemporary Irish Literature* (1995).

Christina Hunt Mahony is Associate Director of the Centre for Irish Studies at the Catholic University of America in Washington, DC. She is the author of *Contemporary Irish Literature: Transforming Tradition* (1999) and editor of *Out of History: Essays on the Writings of Sebastian Barry* (2006).

Elizabeth Malcolm holds the Gerry Higgins Chair in Irish Studies at the University of Melbourne. She is author of numerous books and articles including *'Ireland Sober, Ireland Free': Drink and Temperance in Nineteenth-Century Ireland* (1986), *Medicine, Disease and the State in Ireland 1650–1940* (1999), co-authored with Greta Jones, and *The Irish Policeman, 1822–1922: A Life* (2005). She is currently working on a large-scale study of gender and violence in Ireland.

Conor McCarthy is Lecturer in Irish Studies and English at the Mater Dei Institute of Education, Dublin City University. He is the author of *Modernisation, Crisis and Culture in Ireland 1969–1992* (2000) and essays on contemporary Irish literature, popular culture and intellectual politics. He recently established the Twentieth-Century Irish Studies Society, which aims to promote new research on all aspects of modern Irish culture and society.

Lance Pettitt is Principal Lecturer in Media Studies at Leeds Metropolitan University. He has written extensively on Irish media and popular culture and is the author of *December Bride* (2001) and *Screening Ireland: Film and Television Representation* (2000). He is currently completing a monograph, *Irish Media and Popular Culture*, for Routledge.

Shaun Richards is Professor of Irish Studies at Staffordshire University. A founder member of the British Association for Irish Studies, he has published widely in the field of Irish drama and cultural politics. He is the co-author with David Cairns of *Writing Ireland: Colonialism, Nationalism and Culture* (1988) and editor of *The Cambridge Companion to Twentieth-Century Irish Drama* (2004).

Louise Ryan is Deputy Head of the Social Policy Research Centre at Middlesex University, where her current research focuses on motherhood, migration and work. Her publications include *Gender, Identity and the Irish Press, 1922–37: Embodying the Nation* (2002) and *Irish Women and Nationalism: Soldiers, New Women and Wicked Hags* (2004), co-edited with Margaret Ward.

Gerry Smyth is Reader in Cultural History at Liverpool John Moores University. He is the author of *The Novel and the Nation: Studies in the New Irish Fiction* (1997), *Decolonisation and Criticism* (1998) and *Space and the Irish Cultural Imagination* (2001). His most recent publications are *Beautiful Day: 40 Years of Irish Rock*, co-written with Sean Campbell, and *Noisy Island: A Critical History of Irish Rock Music*, both published in 2005.

Yvonne Whelan is Lecturer in Human Geography at the University of Bristol, where her research focuses on the relationships between landscape, memory and identity in contested cultural contexts. She is the author of *Reinventing Modern Dublin* (2003) and joint editor with Patrick Crotty and Liam Harte of *Ireland: Space, Text, Time* (2005).

Index